THE AMERICAN WESTERN

For John Hunter and Ernest Austin McVeigh

The American Western

Stephen McVeigh

Edinburgh University Press

Edinburgh University Press Ltd
22 George Square, Edinburgh

Typeset in Goudy Old Style by
Iolaire Typesetting, Newtonmore, and
printed and bound in Great Britain by
Cromwell Press, Trowbridge, Wilts

A CIP record for this book is available from the British Library

ISBN 978 0 7486 2140 8 (hardback)
ISBN 978 0 7486 2141 5 (paperback)

Contents

Preface   vii

1. The American West in the 1890s – a Pivotal Decade   1
2. Founding Western History: Theodore Roosevelt and
       Frederick Jackson Turner   13
3. Buffalo Bill's Wild West and the Codification of the Western   27
4. Western Literature from *The Virginian* to *Shane*   38
5. Western Film from Silent to Noir   58
6. The Western and the Cold War: the Gunfighter, Heroic
       Leadership and Political Culture   76
7. New Western Perspectives: History and Literature   140
8. The Western and Political Culture, 1960–1992: Revisions of *Shane*   155
9. Wanted Dead or Alive: 9/11 and the American Western   213

Bibliography   221
Web References   233
Index   235

Preface

The American Western

On 17 September 2001, less than a week after the terrorist attacks on the World Trade Center and the Pentagon, President Bush was responding to questions from the press about America's mobilization for the so-called War on Terrorism. One reporter asked, "Do you want bin Laden dead?" Bush replied, "I want justice. There's an old poster out West, as I recall, that said, 'Wanted: Dead or Alive.'"

Q: Are you saying you want him dead or alive, sir? Can I interpret . . .

BUSH: I just remember, all I'm doing is remembering when I was a kid I remember that they used to put out there in the old West, a wanted poster. It said: "Wanted, Dead or Alive." All I want and America wants him brought to justice. That's what we want.

That the president and former governor of Texas should articulate himself in this way was surprising only to the extent that, as one of the world's most senior statesmen, such language and allusion seemed to convey a lack of seriousness. However, if his turn of phrase was not a surprise, America's reaction to it was. A vast number of Americans at the beginning of the twenty-first century (and Bush's approval ratings in the months immediately following 9/11 bear this out) willingly accepted his rhetorical style and Western imagery. In this way, the Western was evoked as a means of, firstly, understanding what had happened, and, secondly, shaping the American response. Whether or not this use of imagery was deliberate, Bush linked past and present in a very sophisticated manner. The repeated use of the word "remember," the reference to childhood and the explicit naming of the "old West" in the same space suggests nostalgia, innocence, tradition, progress, and the previous American triumph of civilization over savagery. In the same press conference, Bush offers a portrait of an enemy who "likes to hide and burrow in," who have "no rules," who are "barbaric," who "slit throats," and who "like to hit, and then they like to hide out." If these characteristics sounded familiar to Americans acquainted with a century of Westerns, Bush's response was similarly resonant: "But we're going to smoke them out."

With the allusion to the wanted poster as a symbol of frontier justice from his, and in a sense America's, childhood in relation to the horror of the contemporary situation, Bush evokes the myth of the West to both provide contemporary events with a sense of familiarity, and hence security, and as a way of legitimizing a military response through the suggestion of a past where violence was righteous and redemptive. This will be explored in more detail later. However, it is enough to note as a starting point for the book that with Bush's appeal to the West of the popular imagination (and it is a pop culture reference: even though wanted posters were a feature in the West, the vast majority of Americans would only have seen them in movies) as a way of framing the contemporary political crisis, the Western took on a relevance that it had not known since the era of the Cold War.

And this return to prominence is surprising too. The myth of the West had come under attack from a number of directions in the latter decades of the twentieth century. The values that underpinned the mythology of the West, values such as individualism, democracy, equality, were eroded in the 1960s in the wake of the struggle for civil rights and the Vietnam War, at home and abroad. The New Western History, formalized in the 1980s, revisited the West and returned with unheard tales from a landscape, not of heroic endeavor, progress and civilization, but racism, oppression and violent conquest. In the postmodern 1990s, President Clinton campaigned and won elections, not by celebrating the past as Reagan had, but by "building bridges to the future." Even in purely popular culture terms, the Western had ebbed far away from the centre of the American imagination.

The question emerges, then, of how the Western, seemingly exhausted at the end of the twentieth century was so readily rehabilitated at the beginning of the twenty-first. The attempt to answer that question forms part of the purpose of this book.

The book's broader aim is to track and interrogate the Western as a narrative that has been fundamentally connected to the evolving political culture of the United States from the turbulent 1890s, through the Cold War, up to the repercussions of 9/11 and the War on Terror. Indeed, the book argues that the myth of the West was a deliberate creation, one that was specifically constructed in response to political anxiety. The American Western was, then, from its inception at the end of the nineteenth century, a form that reflected, shaped and challenged the American political landscape. And that is where the book begins.

CHAPTER ONE

The American West in the 1890s – a Pivotal Decade

To begin to assess the influence of Western mythology on the political culture of the United States in the twentieth century, one must account for the processes by which the West of history transformed into the West of mythology. In this context, the decade of the 1890s represents a pivotal moment in time. It is in this decade that many of the elements that constituted the experience of the West as a historical reality seemingly "closed" or ended, a decade in which patterns, peoples, the very culture of the West, was irrevocably altered. Yet simultaneously, the decade offers the prospect of continuity between old and new Wests. Among these changes, many defining features in the landscape of the evolving mythological West had their origin.

When the American Historical Association met in Chicago in 1893 as part of the World Columbian Exposition celebrating the discovery of the New World, there was no expectation that a lecture to be presented to the small gathering of historians present would have the profound effect it did, would indeed inaugurate a new vantage point from which to frame American history and explain American identity. Frederick Jackson Turner, a young history professor from the University of Wisconsin, delivered on the evening of 12 July 1893 his epochal essay *The Significance of the Frontier in American History*. The huge impact it would have was not immediately apparent: his audience in Chicago were not shaken into a new way of thinking, nor was the wider historical profession forced there and then to re-evaluate the foundations of their discipline. Yet within a short space of time it did dramatically alter the way historians looked at both the American West specifically, and the broader sweep of American history. On that evening in Chicago in 1893 Turner had presented perhaps the most significant and certainly the most influential interpretation yet advanced concerning American history and culture.

The "frontier thesis," as it became known, represented nothing short of a direct challenge to firmly established notions that the structures and institutions of American civilization had their origins in Europe, that the legacy of the Old World represented the most significant formative influence in American history. In the paper, Turner asserted that values such as democracy, individualism and nationalism, the values which he believed underpinned American society, were generated not by European traditions but rather by the American Frontier. In perhaps the strongest assertion in the essay as it was published, Turner stated that "the existence of an area of free land, its continuous recession and the advance of American settlement Westward explain American development" (Turner 1996: 1). However, he ended his address on a pessimistic note, stating that this frontier sweep across the continent had now come to an end. The occasion for this conclusion was the census of 1890 which clearly indicated that the frontier was no more. By 1890, there existed a line of albeit scattered settlements across much of the previously open spaces of the Western interior, such inhabitation rendering the concept of a frontier redundant. The final sentence of Turner's lecture stated the importance he accorded this ending of the frontier: "And now, four centuries from the discovery of America, at the end of a hundred years of life under the Constitution, the frontier has gone, and with its going has closed the first period in American history" (Turner 1996: 38).

For Turner, and the many historians who followed in his footsteps, the 1890s thus seemed a true watershed in time, the end of the great frontier and the beginning of a new era in which the US would face an unknown future without the vast resources and beneficial influences of its pioneer past. Looking back nostalgically, they identified a number of the decade's trends, all of which seemed to signify the closing of an era.

The Indians of the West, for example, had by this moment found their cultures irrevocably transformed. Before 1850, Indians had existed within a system of subsistence, raising crops and livestock, hunting buffalo and fishing, gathering and raiding. There were interactions between Indians and Europeans in this period: pueblo dwelling tribes such as the Hopis and the Zunis of the Southwest had come to arrangements with Spanish-speaking ranchers; the traditional agricultural practices meant that Indians traded mutton and produce for metal hoes, glass beads, knives and guns. However, beyond these generally positive encounters and exchanges, European contact did more to disrupt Indian life and culture. Most devastating was the introduction of diseases such as measles and diphtheria, carried by traders and settlers, and which ravaged tribes across the region.

After 1850 the whites who were moving Westward to exploit the resources of the region increasingly perceived Indians as a hindrance to their manifest destiny and moved toward eliminating them from their path. The Americans who headed for the plains had little understanding of or respect for the culture of the "savage." A key illustration of this lack of care and understanding and an important aspect of this project to eliminate the Indian was the extermination of the buffalo, an integral element of their ecosystem. The number of these impressive animals roaming wild on the plains numbered as many as 13 million in the early part of the nineteenth century, but by the century's latter years, they had been hunted nearly to extinction. Native Americans were largely dependent on these animals for food, clothing, shelter, and tools, which, as Alan Trachtenberg notes in *The Incorporation of America*, explains why white men were encouraged to kill as many buffalo as they could: because "every buffalo dead is an Indian gone" (Trachtenberg 1982: 30). In addition to the racial implications involved in the hunting of the buffalo as a means of destabilizing Indian society, the loss of the great herds graphically illustrates the enormous ecological toll Westward expansion took on the Western landscape.

The policies of the American government reinforced the private efforts of settlers to remove Indians from their path. The United States' attempts to deal with Indians had from the outset been problematic. In keeping with the lack of comprehension, from the very beginning, Washington had based its approach to Indian affairs on some careless assumptions. The federal government, for example, had overestimated the notion of tribal organization. The reality was that Native Americans were organized into hundreds of confederacies, comprising some two hundred languages and dialects. American officials however considered Indians in terms that equated the tribe as an individual nation with which treaties could be negotiated. Necessarily, given their actual confederate nature, even if a chief or chiefs agreed to a treaty, they were unable to guarantee all bands within the group abide by it. Combine this with the fact that whites, believing that they had a right to settle wherever they wished, seldom acknowledged treaties anyway and the flaws in the system designed to protect Native American land rights become apparent. Even though some Indians did give up their land claims, other groups took revenge, attacking white settlements and their herds. This in turn prompted military reprisals, murder and massacre.

By the 1870s federal officials and reformers were promoting more peaceful means of dealing with Indians. Instead of being considered as separate nations, the new belief was that they should be "civilized" through education. White missionaries and teachers sought to impress upon the Indian such American values as the work ethic, which embodied such concepts as ambition, materialism and self-interest. However, the adoption of such values meant nothing less than the abandonment of their own native cultures and traditions. The essential feature of this plan was the reservation, a place where the process of "civilization" could be facilitated. Yet reservation policy ultimately made Indians more vulnerable than they had been previously and it did so for a number of reasons. Firstly, the Indians were afforded no agency over their own affairs on the reservation. This, combined with Supreme Court decisions in

1884 and 1886 which denied Indians the ability to become American citizens, meant they were left unprotected by the Fourteenth and Fifteenth Amendments. Secondly, whites continued to hold to the belief that they had a god-given right to land for their own purposes. Thirdly, the officials responsible for relocating the Indians took no consideration of native history, culture or practice which meant, for example, that warring factions could be located on the same reservation. In the face of this policy, there was some resistance; there were efforts among some groups to protect their native culture by co-operating and working with whites. There were also violent actions, uprisings intended to defend Indian homelands. These conflicts climaxed in June 1876 when 2500 Lakota led by the chiefs Rain-in-the-Face, Sitting Bull and Crazy Horse annihilated 256 Fifth Cavalrymen, under the leadership of George Armstrong Custer, near the Little Big Horn River in southern Montana. Despite such victories, which demonstrated a distinct proficiency for military strategy, the Indians were eventually overwhelmed through a combination of unending and well-equipped pursuit and their own insufficient resources.

In 1887, Congress reversed its reservation policy and passed the Dawes Severalty Act. The act ended communal ownership of Indian lands and specified land allotments to Native American families, with the intention of further facilitating their assimilation, as farmers, into the mainstream of American society. The act, sponsored by Henry Laurens Dawes of Massachusetts, proposed to introduce the Indians to individual land ownership and agriculture while at the same time opening up Indian reservations for encroaching white settlers. The act permitted the President discretionary powers to survey and to divide the lands of any tribe, giving 160 acres to the head of families, plots of 80 acres to single males over 18 years of age and 40 acre plots to boys (in keeping with the times, there was no provision in the act for women). Indians not located on a reservation could choose to settle on any unappropriated government land. After the land allotment to Indians, the remaining lands were opened for sale to whites. In its initial conception, the act clearly intended humanitarian objectives. While Indians generally opposed it, breaking up as it did tribal lands, whites uniformly supported it: Western congressmen supported it because it allowed their constituents to acquire Indian land, and Eastern congressmen backed the act because of their belief in the evidence of Indian activists who claimed that the reservation system prevented the civilization of the Indian. Yet in spite of the act's best intentions, it did very little but further damage the Indians in a number of ways: undistributed land was sold which reduced the reservation; white squatters refused to acknowledge the act and retained their land on reservations; land agents prevented Indians claiming allotments on the best land; and despite supposed federal safeguards, land sharks played upon the Indian's inexperience of private ownership and duped them out of their claim. The result was that by the 1890s, the Indians had lost much of their land, their resistance had collapsed and they were spiraling into poverty. As Trachtenberg suggests, by 1893 America had witnessed "the end not only of 'frontier' but of independent native societies" (Trachtenberg 1982: 12).

Like the Indian, another key figure in the landscape of the West, the cowboy, was in decline by the 1890s. The open-range stockman was being similarly embattled by encroaching forces of progress. Since the Homestead Act of 1862, which allowed anyone over twenty-one or the head of a family, who was a US citizen or in the process of becoming one, and who had not fought against the United States in a war to claim 160 acres of land, the open spaces that had characterized the West had been shrinking. Cattlemen of this type needed vast tracts of land upon which to graze their herds. Access to such "free" space was considered to be a right. As the numbers of homesteaders increased, this necessary access to public lands was increasingly restricted. Anxious and indignant about this intrusion by unwanted settlers the ranchers' ire led to conflict. The loss of control over grazing pasture compelled some ranchers to fence land to which they had no legal entitlement. The most telling symbol of the changing face of the West was barbed wire. As David Dary writes in *Cowboy Culture*, barbed wire "brought an end to the frontier and the era of the open range" (Dary 1989: 308). Previously crews of cowboys would round up cattle on the open ranges twice a year: to brand new calves in the spring and subsequently to drive mature animals to market in the autumn. The drive was one of the chief generators of the romantic notion of the cowboy. Treks of up to 1500 miles, days on horseback, evenings around the campfire would suggest adventure and romance to Easterners. In reality the drive was an extremely inefficient means of bringing produce to the marketplace and had the capacity to adversely affect both the cattle and the cowboy; the quality of the meat was often damaged by the arduous and stressful trip while herds moving through lands belonging to Indians or farmers were sometimes shot at. Accordingly, the drive was a relatively short-lived phenomenon and ranchers raised herds near to railroad routes as a more effective means of distribution. The fencing of the frontier was a cultural change that many cattlemen and cowboys had great difficulty accepting. One Texas trail driver, writing in 1884, offers a reflection upon the changes brought about by barbed wire:

In 1874 there was no fencing along the trails in the North, and we had lots of range to graze on. Now there is so much land taken up and fenced in that the trail for most of the way is little better than a crooked lane, and we have hard times to find enough range to feed on. Those fellows from Ohio, Indiana and other northern and Western states – the "bone and sinew of the country," as the politicians call them – have made farms, enclosed pastures and fenced in water-holes until you can't rest; and I say, Damn such bone and sinew! They are the ruin of the country, and have everlastingly, eternally, now and forever, destroyed the best grazing land in the world. The range country, sir, was never intended for raising farm-truck. It was intended for cattle and horses, and was the best stock-raising land on earth until they got to turning over the sod – improving the country, as they call it. Lord forgive them such improvements! I am sick . . . when I think of onions and Irish potatoes growing where mustang ponies should be exercising, and where four-year-old steers should be getting ripe for market. Fences, sir, are the curse of this country! (Dary 1989: 319)

For the most part, land that was fenced was owned or leased by the ranchers. However, some ranchers did enclose pieces of public land which could block roads and interfere with deliveries, and cut off schools or churches. Some ranchers placed fences around other farms and small ranches in an attempt to lay claim to every possible acre of grazing land. In either case, conflict inevitably ensued. The cutting of fences began, and it was not long before ranchers hired men to do the job. In Texas, in the summer and autumn of 1883, where ranchers had endured a tough period of drought, fence cutting led to striking levels of violence. Fence cutting was undertaken at night and usually by groups of armed men. After cutting the fences and perhaps pulling the fence posts out of the ground, they would leave warnings and threats against rebuilding the fence. In some cases though, the owner of the fence would be waiting when the cutters arrived, and in those instances, gunfights usually followed. Dary reports that perhaps six men were killed in this 1883 altercation. The Texas state legislature tried to tackle the problem by making fence cutting a felony punishable by up to five years in prison, while knowingly fencing off public lands without permission was made a misdemeanor, with the order to the builders to remove them within six months. Though such attempts to legislate did bring about the end of large-scale fence cutting, the practice continued.

In 1885 President Grover Cleveland ordered the removal of illegal fencing on public lands as well as reservations. Enforcement was slow but the true importance of the ruling was a clear signal that unrestricted access to public lands was coming to an end. Indeed by 1890, the reality of the cowboy was over as big business began to take over the cattle industry. The effects of corporatization combined with new scientific developments in breeding and feeding removed any sense of the romance once and for all. Now, most ranchers owned the land they used or leased the right to use other tracts.

The huge increase in homesteaders spoke to the conviction that the West was rich and bountiful, almost unlimited in its resources. However, the farmers too faced hard times in the depressed 1890s, a decade marked by severe droughts and low prices caused by global overproduction. In the 1870s and 1880s, the settlement of the West saw the largest period of migration in American history. Hundreds of thousands of people streamed into states like Kansas, Nebraska, Texas and California. More acres were cultivated during these two decades than in the previous two hundred and fifty years. The lure for these waves of migration came from advertisements, originated by states looking to bring settlers West. Railroads, which were invariably rich in land, were particularly aggressive in such claims. They promised cheap land, ready credit arrangements, reduced fares and even instant success. However, these heady claims and promises were not necessarily borne out by the reality. To be a farmer was to experience hardship. Timber, which was essential for building as well as heat, was often scarce. Consequently pioneer families were forced to build homes from sod and to burn manure to heat them. In some places in the West, water was as hard to come by as timber. If the land in the West could be less than hospitable to the farmer, the weather, in its unpredictability as well as its changeability, could be equally unfriendly. Each season created its own difficulties. Summer could see weeks of scorching heat and dry winds that suddenly give way to violent storms capable of washing away crops and property alike. In the winter, blizzards could halt outdoor movement altogether. In the spring, the thaw swelled streams and the floods threatened millions of acres of farmland. In the autumn, any period without rain would dry the grasslands to tinder meaning prairie fires were common. Even if the weather was good, hardship could still befall the farmer. For example, good weather breeds insects and the 1870s and 1880s were marked by swarms of grasshoppers capable of consuming entire crops. New developments in agricultural technology did offer some respite: it increased productivity, cut costs and reduced labor at harvest time. However, such benefits came at a cost, the most significant that technologies which made farming more economical also led to over production, and hence prices and profits fell.

For others groups extracting the bounties offered by the West, the 1890s also seemed a time of transition. The oldest of the Western industries, metal mining, experienced profound changes. Mining had been the dominant form of Western industry since the initial fever of the 1849 gold rush, (a fever which had passed by 1851), with further big strikes in Colorado and Nevada in the late 1850s and into the 1860s. Except for a couple of later strikes, such as those at Homestake, South Dakota (1874–5) or Cripple Creek, Colorado (1891–4), few high-grade gold seams now remained. In addition the value of the other key precious metal of the region, silver, had collapsed with the termination of federal silver purchases, an action taken in an attempt to offset the effects of the devastating panic of 1893. This panic and subsequent depression would have a far-reaching impact for the West.

The panic began with the failure, in February of that year, of the Philadelphia and Reading Railroad on Wall Street. Shortly before Grover Cleveland's inauguration, the railroad company, once a thriving and profitable line, went bankrupt. Like other railroads the Philadelphia and Reading line had borrowed heavily to invest in infrastructure, track, stations, bridges, and so forth. However, such ambitious overexpansion cut into profits, and ultimately the company was unable to meet its debts. The collapse of the railroad company came at a time when confidence in the economy was already weakening over a concern about the government's ability to redeem paper money for gold on demand. Economic problems in London in 1890 had led to British investors unloading millions of dollars of American holdings for gold: some $68 million in American gold had flowed across the Atlantic to Britain. As the depression deepened the currency problem reached crisis point. The Sherman Silver Purchase Act of 1890 had committed the government to buying 4.5 million ounces of silver each month. Payment was to be in gold at the ratio of 1oz of gold for every 16oz of silver. But a Western mining boom made silver more plentiful causing its value relative to gold to drop. Thus every month the government was exchanging gold, with a value that remained fairly constant, for cheaper silver. Fearing a decrease in the value of the dollar, its value being based on federal treasury holdings in these two precious metals, merchants at home and abroad began cashing in paper money and securities for gold. Consequently, the nation's gold reserve began to dwindle, and in early 1893, fell below the psychologically significant level of $100 million. Vowing to protect the gold reserve, President Cleveland called a special session of Congress to repeal the Sherman Silver Purchase Act. The repeal was passed in late 1893 but the run on the treasury continued. In early 1895 gold reserves fell to $41 million. In desperation, Cleveland accepted an offer of 3.5 million ounces of gold in return for $62 million worth of government bonds from a banking syndicate led by financier J. P. Morgan. When the bankers resold the bonds to the public they netted substantial profits, and all at America's expense. Cleveland claimed he had saved the gold reserves, but many saw the President's deal with big business men as sordid and humiliating.

Like previous hard times, the depression ultimately ran its course, but the recession of the 1890s quickened the collapse of the old economic system and the emergence of a new one. The central features of the new business system – consolidation and a trend toward bigness – had just begun to solidify when the depression hit. The economy of the US had now become national rather than sectional, meaning in essence that the success or otherwise of big business in one part of the country was felt elsewhere. This connectedness would be amply demonstrated. By the 1890s many companies had expanded too rapidly. When contraction occurred their overreaching dragged them down, and as one industry fell, other industries were pulled down with them. In 1893 more than 16,000 businesses filed for bankruptcy. European economies also slumped and more than ever before the fortunes of one country affected the fortunes of other countries. The downward spiral ended in late 1897 but the depression exposed problems that demanded reform and set the agenda for years to come. As a result, precious-metal mining drastically declined as a primary regional industry during the 1890s. From this point on, the fortunes of the industry would derive mainly from the harvesting of what was now the key Western metal, copper, with mines in Arizona, Utah, Nevada, and Montana out-producing those in Michigan which had been the center of copper extraction. This displacement of industry was replicated in other resources. The lumber industry moved Westward from the Great Lakes region in the upper Midwest to the Pacific Coast, and in so doing altered the economy of the Northwest. Oil's migration, moving West to Texas, California and Oklahoma from the Mid-Atlantic States represented another shift in America's industrial demography. By the end of the decade then, the industrial landscape was substantially different.

As economically turbulent as the 1890s were, in political terms the 1890s was a decade of genuine upheaval. The Panic of 1893 that changed the economic face of the United States also brought an abrupt end to the political calm that had characterized the 1880s. More specifically, it generated deep interregional conflict between the industrial East and the underdeveloped South and West. The depth of feeling is best illustrated by the formation of the "People's Party" or more commonly, the Populists. In both the South and the West, the Populist Party emerged as a genuinely radical vehicle of protest against the capitalist exploitation of these regions by corporations (primarily railroad, banking and mining interests) located in the East. Those who came to make up the constituency of the Populists sprang largely from the agricultural and mining industries. The Western Populists were characterized by a series of demands and issues: in the first place they demanded inflationary coinage of silver dollars, and they pushed for substantial democratic reforms like the initiative, the referendum and the popular election of US senators. In addition, they advocated more general federal regulation of industry, and even the nationalization of the railroads. As a political entity, however, they failed, beginning with the defeat of the Populist-Democratic presidential candidacy of Nebraska's William Jennings Bryan in 1896 at the hands of the conservative Republican William McKinley; by 1901 the party was coming to the end.

The origins of the Populist Party lie in the agricultural alliance movement of the 1870s. Granges, formed by farmers in the Midwest and the Great Plains, and the Alliance movement made up of farmers from the West and the South, were attempts to ameliorate the economic plight of those working in these regions. They advocated co-operative buying and selling, as well as proposing a scheme to relieve the most serious rural problems: lack of cash and lack of credit. Called the Subtreasury Plan it had two parts. The first called for the federal government to construct warehouses where farmers could store non-perishable crops while awaiting higher prices. The government would then loan farmers treasury notes amounting to 80 per cent of the market price that the stored grain or cotton would bring. Farmers could use these notes as legal tender to pay debts and make purchases. Once the stored crops were sold, farmers would repay the loans plus a small amount of interest and storage fees. The second part of the plan called for the government to provide low-interest loans to farmers who wanted to buy land. The Subtreasury Plan was introduced at the St. Louis conference of 1889, a conference notable for two further reasons. First, it brought the various organizations together in terms of political demands; and second, it made clear the impracticality of bringing all such organizations together in one large alliance. That is to say that the conference demonstrated that there was a platform common to these groups, a platform that could form the basis of a political party. And although the notion of forming a third party was disdained by nearly all of the alliance leaders early on, the farmers came to act collectively. Growing membership and rising confidence drew the alliances more deeply into politics. By 1890, farmers had elected several officeholders sympathetic to their programs, especially in the South. In the Midwest, alliance candidates often ran third-party tickets and achieved some success, notably in Kansas, Nebraska and the Dakotas. During the summer of 1890, the Kansas alliance held a "convention of the people" and nominated candidates who swept the state's autumn elections. The formation of this "People's Party" (whose members were called "Populists") gave a name to alliance political activism. Two years later, after overcoming regional differences, the People's Party held a national convention in Omaha where they drafted a platform and nominated a presidential candidate.

The new party's Omaha platform was one of the most comprehensive reform documents in American history. It addressed three central sources of rural unrest: transportation, land and money. Frustrated with weak state and federal regulation, Populists demanded government ownership of railroad and telegraph lines. They urged the federal government to reclaim all land owned for speculative purposes by railroads and foreigners. The monetary plank called for the government to inflate the currency system by printing money to be made available for farm loans and by basing the money on free and unlimited coinage of silver. Other planks advocated a graduated income tax, postal savings bank, direct election of US senators and a shorter workday. As its presidential candidate, the People's Party nominated James B. Weaver of Iowa, a former Union general. Weaver garnered 8 per cent of the total popular vote in 1892, took majorities in four states and twenty-two electoral votes. Not since 1856 had a third party won so many votes on its first national electoral outing. Despite such early successes, a number of problematic issues had emerged. The central dilemma faced by the party was whether it should hold to its principles whatever the cost or to compromise in order to gain power. The election had been successful for Populists only in the West. The Northeast had practically ignored Weaver, and Alabama was the only Southern state that gave the populists as much as one third of its votes. The Populists encountered several problems at the moment when their political goals seemed attainable. As late as 1894, Populist candidates made strong showings in elections in the West and South. Unfortunately, like earlier third parties, the Populists were under-financed and under-organized. They did have a number of strong and colorful candidates, but not nearly enough of them to effectively challenge the major parties.

In the national arena the Populist crusade against big Eastern corporations focused on the issue of silver. Many in the party saw silver as a ready solution to the nation's complex problems. To the Populists, free coinage of silver meant the end of special privileges for the rich and the return of government to the people, and as such they made free coinage their central platform. But as the election of 1896 approached they needed to decide how to best translate their limited previous victories into something larger. The choice they faced was to work together with sympathetic factions of the major parties, but risk a loss of identity, or to remain an independent third party but settle for further limited successes at best. The presidential election of 1896 brought all of this political turbulence to a climax. Each party was divided. The Republicans' campaign manager, Mark Hanna, a prosperous Ohio industrialist, had few problems to deal with. For over a year Hanna had been maneuvering to win the nomination for Ohio's governor, William McKinley. By the time the party convened at St. Louis, Hanna had convinced enough delegates to succeed. The Republicans' only distress occurred when the party adopted a moderate platform supporting gold, rejecting a pro-silver stance proposed by Senator Henry Teller of Colorado. Teller, who had been among the party's founders forty years earlier, walked out of the convention in tears, taking with him a small group of silver representatives.

At the Democrat convention William Jennings Bryan, a 36-year-old Nebraskan, former congressman and silverite, emerged as a candidate. Bryan was hugely distressed by the depression's impact upon Midwestern farmers and he called for the free coinage of silver. His speech outlining this plank to his platform was well received (although some pro-gold democrats shifted allegiance). Bryan's nomination presented the Populists with a dilemma. Should they join the Democrats in support of Bryan or should they nominate their own candidate? Some argued against fusion with Democrats, fearing a loss of identity, while others reasoned that supporting a different candidate would split the anti-McKinley vote and guarantee a Republican victory. In the end a compromise was found in naming former representative Thomas E. Watson of Georgia as the vice-presidential candidate, in an effort to preserve party identity, and then nominating Bryan for president.

Despite Bryan's eloquence in speeches delivered across the country, Hanna's portrayal of him as a radical whose communistic bent would ruin the capitalist system, helped raise a huge campaign chest for McKinley. In the end, the Democrat-Populist-Silverite candidates were completely overwhelmed by the better-organized and better-financed Republican campaign. In the most lopsided presidential election since 1872 McKinley, symbolizing Republican pragmatism and corporate power, beat Bryan. Bryan had worked hard to rally the nation but his obsession with silver undermined his effort and prevented the Populists from building the urban-rural coalition that would have broadened their political appeal. More importantly, labor leaders and socialists did not consider their own interests as being in alignment with America's farmers. In the midst of such insoluble problems, the Populist crusade for democratic reform, equality and an end to corporate power collapsed.

There were still other shifts in Western socio-cultural patterns which identify the 1890s as a period of transformation. The rise of the urban center and the growth of new cities was a highly visible indicator. The demographics of the West were changing, with an ever-increasing number of women and families demonstrating that the West was becoming a safe place of civilization and culture. The writing about the region developed too at the close of the nineteenth century. Where representations of the West had come from local-color writing by the likes of Bret Harte, Joaquin Miller, Mark Twain, and Mary Hallock Foote, or dime fiction featuring romanticized versions of historical figures, increasingly such writing took on a realism as demonstrated in the work of Hamlin Garland, Jack London, and Frank Norris.

It is worth noting here, as a prelude to later chapters, that there are clearly connections between the West of the nineteenth and twentieth centuries, an idea which forms a significant element of the New Western History. Just as the nineteenth-century West had been a landscape of ethnicities, of Indians, Hispanics, Orientals, and Anglos, the twentieth-century West would continue to be. It is also possible to suggest, for example, that far from disappearing from the political map entirely, the spirit and ideas of Populism, as well as some of the adherents, returned in the twentieth century in various political reform movements such as the New Deal.

The 1890s then can be seen to represent both a break with the pioneer past and a bridge of continuity between old and new Wests. And it is from this vantage point that the first histories of the American West would be written.

CHAPTER TWO

Founding Western History: Theodore Roosevelt and Frederick Jackson Turner

The mythology of the West which emerged at the beginning of the twentieth century did not appear organically or naturally. Rather the mythology was deliberately constructed to serve a purpose, and it was constructed by a small group of interconnected men, among them Theodore Roosevelt, Frederick Jackson Turner, William F. Cody, Frederick Remington and Owen Wister. The origin of the myth is bound up in the upheaval of the 1890s, a decade, as we have seen, that saw America's self-concept, as a place of equality, opportunity, virtue and idealism, corrupted by unregulated big business, exploitation of markets, labor disputes, and political protest. On witnessing such rapid and traumatic change, Americans became nostalgic, nostalgic for a simpler version of America. And where previously the West had been the safety-valve, by 1890 the frontier had closed and the resources and bounties of the West no longer seemed limitless. It is in this nostalgic longing that the urge toward mythology can be found. A number of men took the frontier as the embodiment of all that was good about America, presenting it as a place of tradition, inspiration, and heroism, the arena in which the American character was forged in the past, and the repository of these values which could heal America's ills in the present. Dime fiction, Wild West re-enactments, literary fiction and film have all played their part in propagating this fantasy West, but it was the legitimizing histories produced by Roosevelt and Turner that gave a fundamental substance to the myth.

THEODORE ROOSEVELT AND *THE WINNING OF THE WEST* (1889–96)

Although Frederick Jackson Turner's seminal paper *The Significance of the Frontier in American History* is justly considered the founding text of American Western History, work done a number of years prior, by an influential amateur historian, is an important stepping stone toward placing Turner's work in its full and proper context. Theodore Roosevelt's four-volume history of Westward expansion, *The Winning of the West*, predates Turner's more famous essay by a couple of years and is essential in the formation not only of the concept of American Western History, but specifically of Turner's own ideas. That it is Roosevelt who produces this formative history is crucial: he was a figure who held a special and resonant place within the mythology, history and iconography of the West. No American figure had exercised such a profound influence on the history and culture of the American West, an influence he manifested first as a popular writer, and later as president of the United States.

American history of course remembers Roosevelt primarily as president, from 1901 to 1909, rather than as a historian. However, his presidential persona was constructed from his connection to a full assortment of frontier characteristics, allusions, imagery and history. John Milton Cooper Jr suggests that no American president before Roosevelt was more strongly associated with the West of history than he was: "Of all his physical characteristics, only his teeth and eyeglasses identified him better than his broad-brimmed rancher's hat" (Roosevelt 1995: vii). If the frontiersman would come to be recognized as a quintessential American figure of action and heroism, embodying notions of masculinity, strength and individualism, Roosevelt's time in the Dakota Territory, and, perhaps most especially, his experience in Cuba during the Spanish-American War of 1898 established these as qualities he possessed for the American people. The Spanish-American War, among the shortest conflicts the United States has been engaged in, in its way offers another notion of a pivotal moment in the 1890s. This conflict witnessed America seeking to further its economic interests beyond its own borders, by opening up new frontiers abroad, and in this way, the war marks the beginning of the imperialistic drive that would power the coming "American century."

Roosevelt's persona would come to be characterized by an aggressiveness and an activism that stemmed, certainly in his own eyes, from his childhood. That he should come to be characterized thus was by no means obvious. Roosevelt was born physically weak; he suffered from asthma, had weak muscles and was near-sighted. In his *Autobiography* (1913) he notes how these impairments affected him:

> Having been a sickly boy, with no natural bodily prowess . . . I was at first quite unable to hold my own . . . with other boys of rougher antecedents. I was nervous and timid. Yet from reading of the people I admired . . . I felt a great admiration for men who were fearless and who could hold their own in the world and I had a great desire to be like them. (Roosevelt 1913: 32)

He goes on to note how his father challenged him to overcome these physical problems: "You have the mind but not the body. You must make your body. It is hard drudgery, but I know you will do it" (Roosevelt 1913: 32).

To overcome this physical inferiority he began to train his body, he built a gymnasium and learned how to box. That he became, over time, a good fighter, was something he would remain proud of. This physicality, the need to test himself, also remained with him. Such tests manifested themselves in the form of outdoor pursuits, and specifically hunting and riding. In all things he pursued what he termed "a life of strenuous endeavor." His biographer Carleton Putnam, connecting these endeavors with his sense of inferiority, suggested a different perspective however, seeing this drive to demonstrate his physical prowess as "unnecessarily heroic" (quoted in Padover 1960: 289). At the other end of the scale from the displays of physical prowess, the complimentary element of his persona was one which privileged intellectualism. Roosevelt was a voracious reader of books and poetry, in the original language when required. In 1876, he entered Harvard where natural history was his primary interest, though there was little opportunity there to train in the subject at this time, and this ambition was ended. As he would say in his *Autobiography*, his time at university was useful "in the general effect" even if his actual studies did not provide him with much to help "in afterlife" (Roosevelt 1913: 27). Harvard, then, did not prepare him for a career in politics, a career he entered soon after graduating in 1880. In 1881, at the age of twenty three, he was elected to the New York assembly and it was to be the lower house of the New York State Legislature which would supply him with his political education. It was here he learned, for example, that those with economic power also controlled the American political machinery. In his *Autobiography*, he said of this revelation, "it was the first glimpse I had of that combination between business and politics which I was in years after so often to oppose" (Roosevelt 1913: 86).

He spent three years in the New York assembly. After his time in the legislature he left New York and headed West, to North Dakota, to recover from asthma. He was drawn, in 1883, to the Dakota Territory by reports that three years of systematic hunting had all but destroyed the once massive buffalo herd of the northern plains. Roosevelt was determined to add this symbol of the American West to his trophy collection before it became extinct, and despite punishing weather, he remained until he accomplished his goal. At the same time, Roosevelt became enamored of the Western landscape and the strenuous outdoor life of the plains, and purchased two ranches in the Dakota Badlands before heading back East. The next year, 1884, Roosevelt returned to his ranch as a refuge from personal tragedy and professional disappointment. His young wife and his mother had both died on Valentine's Day that year, and in the summer his reformist faction had been defeated at the Republican national convention. The isolation and immensity of the Badlands helped him escape these misfortunes, and offered a retreat where he could pursue his interest in writing. As he would say of the region's recuperative effect, "Black care rarely sits behind a rider whose pace is fast enough." He ran a cattle ranch for three years and enjoyed the outdoor life of the frontiersman, riding and hunting, all endeavors that would fuel his writing. Roosevelt had already published one book, *The Naval War of 1812* (1882), a project he had begun at Harvard. Now his writing took on a pronounced Western bent, publishing such works as *Hunting Trips of a Ranchman* (1885), *Thomas Hart Benton* (1886), and a four-volume history of the early frontier, *The Winning of the West* (1889–96).

In 1886, Roosevelt left his ranch to marry his childhood sweetheart, Edith Kermit Carow, and continued his literary career at their home, Sagamore Hill, near Oyster Bay on Long Island, New York. Among his writings at this time was a series of articles on Western life published by the *Century Magazine* and later collected as *Ranch Life and the Hunting Trail* (1899). If Roosevelt is one of those who deliberately created the mythology of the West, these writings represent a significant element of that process. Drawing on his experience as a rancher and sportsman, Roosevelt constructed a version of the West that prompted a great number of rich Eastern readers to head onto the plains as tourists. In Dakota, the terrible winter of 1886–7, which the cattlemen named the "Great Die-Up," had decimated cattle ranching and brought an end to open-range ranching. In such a dire economic time tourism represented a much needed boost of income to the region. Roosevelt's old neighbors welcomed these visitors eagerly, converting their operations into what would soon be called "dude ranches." As he makes clear in his *Autobiography*, in a chapter entitled "In Cowboy Land," Roosevelt processed the frontier in mythological-literary, if anachronistic terms. Introducing his time in the West in 1883, he writes: "It was still the Wild West in those days, the Far West, the West of Owen Wister's stories and Frederic Remington's drawings" (Roosevelt 1913: 103). This provides an interesting insight into the myth-making process. Wister would not publish *The Virginian* until 1902 and even his short stories did not appear until the early 1890s. And it is significant that Remington was the illustrator of Roosevelt's *Ranch Life and the Hunting Trail*. Remington, like Roosevelt, was an Easterner who went West and translated what he found there into the most famous visual representations of the frontier. Such lines of connection reflect the complex process of mythification in the work of these three men. Such sentiments suggest that beyond simply contributing to the growth of this new tourist industry, Roosevelt's articles significantly contributed to the perception of Western life as imbued with special virtues, qualities such as self-reliance, honor, loyalty, and determination, qualities that made the West a proving ground of the American character. This has no better illustration than his comment, "I never would have become President if it had not been for my experience in North Dakota." In *Ranch Life and the Hunting Trail*, Roosevelt presented the West as a place of stark contrast to the East. He described it as place of "endless breadth" where a man could "steer his course for days and weeks and see neither man to speak to nor hill to break the level" (Roosevelt 1899: 100). He described the men that inhabit the region as strong and vital, necessary qualities to survive in their "stern and unending struggles" of their surroundings and the "grim harshness of their existence," men who "run risks to life and limb that are unknown to the dwellers of cities" (Roosevelt 1899: 79). He praised specifically the cowboy, "as hardy and self-reliant as any men who ever breathed – with bronzed, set faces and keen eyes that look all the world straight in the face without flinching" (Roosevelt 1899: 9). Roosevelt's articles then were an essential element in the construction of the cowboy figure, not as a violent, drunken farm laborer, but as a heroic, iconic American figure. In these articles, Roosevelt held up the West as a model for the nation, but he was also charting its passing. This version of the West, he wrote in 1888,

> must pass away from the onward march of our people; and we who have felt the charm of life, and have exulted in its abounding vigor and its bold restless freedom, will not only regret its passing for our sakes only, but must also feel real sorrow that those who come after us are not to see, as we have seen, what is perhaps the pleasantest, healthiest, and most exciting phase of American existence. (Roosevelt 1899: 24)

Roosevelt's celebration of these qualities and characteristics carried the weight of authenticity because he was writing from his own experience which simultaneously connected him to the values he was celebrating.

Roosevelt described this time as an invigorating period in his life, and so energized, he returned to New York, and ran, unsuccessfully, for mayor. In 1889, at the age of thirty one, he was appointed member of the United States Civil Service commission, a post he would hold for six years in the service of Presidents Benjamin Harrison and Grover Cleveland. In 1895 he became president of the New York City Police Board. His work in this position, his clear-out of corrupt policemen and cleansing the slums of New York, established him as a substantial media presence. Two years later he became Assistant Secretary of the Navy under President McKinley. However, it was to be his role in what John Hay called the "splendid little war" of 1898 that secured his status as a national hero embodying the values of the frontiersman. He served during the Spanish-American War as a colonel, leading a cavalry regiment which was constituted from a significant number of men from the Great Plains and Rocky Mountain regions of the West. This demographic led to the nickname, "the Rough Riders," a reference to a renowned segment in Buffalo Bill's Wild West, and a name that was worn with pride. Their exploits during the war, which were widely reported, perhaps most famously by Stephen Crane in *Stephen Crane at the Front for the World* and *Stephen Crane's Vivid Story of the Battle of San Juan*, would be another factor in his public association with the character and persona of the West, and between such characteristics and the office of president of the United States. Crane's reports were incredibly evocative and, while not shying from the horrors, offered sketches of the war that showed it and the men fighting as heroic. As one commentator put it, Roosevelt "charged up San Juan hill and straight into the White House." His actions, his leadership in the taking of Kettle Hill, one of a series of strategic hills making up San Juan Ridge which ringed Santiago, was the feat that came to embody what the war was about, and, crucially, articulated a very specific conception of the American character, one imbued with the values of the frontiersman: optimism, pro-action, energy, determination.

Home from the war a hero, Roosevelt was elected governor of New York in the autumn of 1898, but his enthusiasm for reform so provoked the state's Republican leadership that, in an effort to sideline him, they arranged for him to run as the party's vice presidential candidate in 1900; when the Republicans won, Roosevelt was no longer a nuisance. However, as is common for frontier heroes, fate stepped in. Less than a year later, on 14 September 1901, the assassination of President William McKinley in Buffalo, New York, brought Roosevelt to the executive office, leading Mark Hanna to label him "that damned cowboy in the White House." Over the next seven years, he worked vigorously to promote social and governmental reform, often using his executive authority to further programs that would have been thrown out by the conservative forces that controlled Congress. He revived the Sherman Anti-Trust Act of 1890 to break up some of the country's biggest corporations and restore competition to the business world. Later, he secured passage of federal regulations to control railroad rates and to set quality standards for foods and drugs. In foreign affairs, he extended the Monroe Doctrine, adding a corollary that asserted the United States' exclusive right to police international relations in the Western Hemisphere. He also precipitated a revolution that separated Panama from Columbia and cleared the way for construction of the Panama Canal.

Even in the office of Chief Executive, the West continued to occupy a good deal of his thoughts. Roosevelt's most important actions in the office of president with regards to the West came in the areas of environmental and conservation policy. Gifford Pinchot, a forester who believed that the natural resources of the West required protection and management to prevent their eradication by developers, urged Roosevelt to use the 1891 Forest Reserves Act. The Act empowered the president to set aside public lands as national forests, and he employed it to increase exponentially federal land reserves, from approximately 40 million acres when he took office to nearly 200 million acres by the end of his second term. In 1905, Roosevelt gave Pinchot responsibility for administering these lands, as head of the newly organized US Forest Service, and in so doing heralded the modern era of Western land management, which seeks to sustain through efficient use the West's natural resources rather than let them be exploited and developed.

Roosevelt initiated similar far-reaching changes in the West with his support of the National Reclamation Act (or Newlands Act) of 1902, which gave the federal government primary responsibility for dam construction and irrigation projects. The creation of a new federal agency, the Reclamation Service, brought scientific expertise as well as bureaucracy to this task, and by 1906 there were water projects underway in all the Western states, establishing federal control of the use of this vital resource as well. Roosevelt also extended federal control over the scenic wonders of the West, using the 1906 Antiquities Act, which had been intended to preserve historic landmarks, to set aside 800,000 acres in Arizona as the Grand Canyon National Monument. All told, he created sixteen national monuments, fifty-one wildlife refuges and five new National Parks, including Crater Lake in Oregon and the Anasazi ruins at Mesa Verde, Colorado, helping to pave the way for eventual recognition of such "national treasures" as natural resources requiring federal management to sustain them for the West's developing tourist industry.

Roosevelt enjoyed, then, a multifaceted association with the frontier and the Western, an association that exists most obviously in elements of his biography and his subsequent public image. However, it is the books that Roosevelt produced about the West that demonstrate his affinity with the region, the character and the ideals of the West, and so provide a part of the foundation of Western historical inquiry.

Away from his more journalistic pieces about the Western outdoor life, he produced, in 1886, a brief and hastily written but significantly positive biography of Thomas Hart Benton, a Missouri politician and advocate of Westward expansion. That it is such a positive portrait is an important indicator of his feelings towards the West. Benton had been an active supporter of Westward expansion; he favored the annexation of Texas, continually agitated for a settlement of the Canadian-US border on the most favorable terms possible to the United States, and was the first to introduce in the Senate a bill demanding exclusive American control of the Oregon country. At a time when most Americans could see little value or future promise in this region, Benton passionately championed its potential. Roosevelt's positive portrait endorses Benton's aims and is suggestive of his affinity with the West.

The West was also the subject of his most important project, thematically, and the most substantial and scholarly writing that he ever produced. Between

1889 and 1896, Roosevelt published four volumes analyzing the Westward expansion of the British colonies and subsequently the United States, from 1763 to 1807. The work was entitled *The Winning of the West* and, despite its many flaws, it stands as a crucial jumping off point for the study of the importance of the West in American history. From his first plans for the work, Roosevelt intended to trace the course of European exploration, emigration and settlement across the entire North American continent. As the brief sketch of his biography suggests, politics, war, and other ambitions interrupted his writing, and he failed to produce the epic history of his initial conception. Nevertheless, the four volumes he did manage to publish indicate clearly the tone and texture of his vision. The first volume focuses on the period between French penetration of the Ohio Valley in 1763 and the organization of Kentucky in 1776. Volume 2 explores the machinations of the European powers in the interior between 1777 and 1783, years dominated by the Revolutionary War.

The third volume explores developments related to accelerated migration and settlement between 1784 and 1790, including Indian wars, Western separatist movements, and the organization of the Northwest and Southwest Territories in 1787 and 1788. Volume 4 deals with the Louisiana Purchase, the explorations of Meriwether Lewis, William Clark and Zebulon Montgomery Pike, and how territorial expansion, the extension of democratic politics and further Indian conflict set the pattern for subsequent Westward exploration in the early years of the nineteenth century. In all, *The Winning of the West* covers about a century-and-a-half of turbulent American history.

The Winning of the West is not conventional history. It is by no means an objective, balanced, historical account of the American expansion across the continent. Rather, the work explores this period in American history from a very specific perspective, a perspective that has its origins in the notion that, for Roosevelt, Westward expansion was an epic of racial conflict. In the books he describes "the spread of the English-speaking peoples over the world's waste space" as the "most striking feature of the world's history" (Roosevelt 1995, vol. 1: 1). Immediately, the racial context is established. In the first instance, the Indians would certainly disagree with the concept of the continent as a "waste space," while, secondly, the suggestion that this process was the most striking in world's history is a clear articulation of American exceptionalism. He continues in this vein, to argue that only "a warped, perverse and silly morality" would condemn the American conquest of the West. He says, "most fortunately, the hard energetic practical men who do the rough pioneer work of civilization in barbarous lands are not prone to false sentimentality" (Roosevelt 1995, vol. 3: 44).

Even though it may not be history as conceived in the walls of academe, this perspective establishes several strong connections and resonances between Roosevelt's work and that of Frederick Jackson Turner, among them, the negation of the Native-American, the focus on the formation of the American character, the priority of the individual who through his own efforts and labor confronts the frontier and tames it, and the centrality of the masculine hero.

Unquestionably the clearest articulation of this connection between the two men comes in a chapter in the third volume, which was published in 1894, a chapter entitled "Kentucky's Struggle for Statehood, 1784–1790":

> As the frontiersmen conquered and transformed the wilderness, so the wilderness in its turn created and preserved the type of man who overcame it. Nowhere else on the continent has so sharply defined and distinctively American a type been produced as on the frontier, and a single generation has always been more than enough for its production. The influence of the wild country upon the man is almost as great as the effect of the man upon the country. The frontiersman destroys the wilderness, and yet its destruction means his own. He passes away before the coming of civilization whose advance guard he has been. Nevertheless, much of his blood remains, and his striking characteristics have great weight in shaping the development of the land. The varying peculiarities of the different groups of men who have pushed the frontier Westward at different times and places remains stamped with greater or less clearness on the people of the communities that grow up in the frontier's stead. (Roosevelt 1995, vol. 3: 207–8)

These sentences have a distinctly familiar resonance to readers familiar with Turner. And well they should. This passage has a footnote: "Frederick Jackson Turner: 'The Significance of the Frontier in American History.' A suggestive pamphlet by the State Historical society of Wisconsin."

FREDERICK JACKSON TURNER AND *THE SIGNIFICANCE OF THE FRONTIER IN AMERICAN HISTORY* (1893)

"The existence of an area of free land, its continuous recession, and the advance of American settlement Westward explain American development" (Turner 1996: 1). In this one sentence from his seminal paper and essay, Frederick Jackson Turner established the basis for Western history as a discrete discipline. The effects of his "frontier thesis" continue to be felt to the present day, even if the thesis itself has been effectively deconstructed by successive waves of historians.

Turner was born in Portage, Wisconsin, in 1861. As a boy growing up, he was a witness to elements of the frontier in action. In his biography of the historian, Ray Allen Billington describes the influence of the "quasi-frontier environment" of Portage on the young Turner:

Portage was just emerging from its pioneer past during his impressionable years . . . All about were reminders of frontier days certain to make their imprint on a small boy. Through the dusty streets each summer lumbered prairie schooners loaded with "emigrants" bound for the free government lands of Northern Wisconsin or the Dakotas. Almost every issue of the local newspaper told of Indian outbreaks in the West, flavored with the editor's damnation of the "savages" who began the Modoc War or wiped out Custer's command on the Little Big Horn. Occasionally, events at home reminded him that civilization was in its swaddling clothes: a hunting party was formed to track down a wolf pack, vigilantes were recruited to help the sheriff capture an over-ambitious horse thief. The wilderness was not quite subdued, and young Turner felt its influence. (Billington 1973: 15)

The other influence from his formative years was his father, Jack Turner, a journalist by trade, "a politician by instinct" (Billington 1973: 12) and local historian on his own time. From his father, and specifically from his years spent in the office of his father's newspaper, the *Register*, he learned to appreciate the importance of local history and the machinations of electoral politics. After his graduation from the University of Wisconsin in 1884, Turner made the decision to become a professional historian, and to that end undertook a Ph.D. at Johns Hopkins University, which he received in 1890. He served as a teacher and scholar at the University of Wisconsin from 1889 to 1910, when he joined the history faculty at Harvard. He retired in 1924 but continued his research until his death in 1932. For generations of historians, Turner's work has shaped the field of Western history, a field of which he is rightly considered to be the founder.

The essence of Turner's contribution to American history was his suggestion that America's frontier past explained the distinctive arc of the nation's history. This thesis was explicated in *The Significance of the Frontier in American History*, which he first delivered to a gathering of historians in 1893, in Chicago, then the site of the World's Columbian Exposition, an enormous fair to mark the four-hundredth anniversary of Columbus' voyage to the New World. It would take some time before the implications of his lecture were felt, but once it had taken hold, it was recognized as the most important contribution to the history of the United States' progress and development yet advanced.

Only three years before Turner's delivery of his frontier thesis, the United States Bureau of the Census had announced that settlement right across the continent was so pervasive that America no longer had a frontier. Turner used the announcement as a vantage point from which to look back at the influence the frontier had exerted on the passage of American history. He proffered a historical interpretation of the frontier which suggested that the abundance of cheap or free land allowed individuals the material basis to construct a wealthy and democratic nation. This frontier process involved successive waves of individuals moving through a series of evolutionary stages in the social formation of the United States. This development, in Turner's description,

> begins with the Indian and the hunter; it goes on with the disintegration of savagery by the entrance of the trader . . . the pastoral stage in ranch life; the exploitation of the soil by the raising of unrotated crops of corn and wheat in sparsely settled farm communities; the intensive culture of the denser farm settlement; and finally the manufacturing organization with the city and the factory system. (Turner 1996: 11)

In this conception, the frontier is truly American because at some time, all of America has been the West. Crucially for Turner, the further significance of the frontier lay in the creation of the American character facilitated by the repeated return to "the meeting point between savagery and civilization." Or to put it another way, Turner is suggesting that interaction with the conditions of the frontier made Americans American. Given the immigrant nature of the population, this provides an answer to the question of what makes such an ethnically diverse group, with different languages, cultures and customs, into Americans in such a short space of time. His answer is to suggest that these interactions with the frontier "Americanize" the individual:

> The wilderness masters the colonist. It finds him a European in dress, industries, tools, modes of travel and thought. It takes him from the railroad car and puts him in the birch canoe. It strips off the garments of civilization and arrays him in the hunting shirt and the moccasin. It puts him in the log cabin of the Cherokee and Iroquois and runs an Indian palisade around him. Before long he has gone to planting Indian corn and plowing with a sharp stick; he shouts the war cry and takes the scalp in orthodox Indian fashion. In short at the frontier the environment is at first too strong for the man. He must accept the conditions which it furnishes, or perish, and so he fits himself into the Indian clearings and follows the Indian trails. Little by little he transforms the wilderness, but the outcome is not the old Europe . . . The fact is that here is a new product that is American. (Turner 1996: 4)

This "new product" was independent of European experience. Turner demonstrated an idealism about the contribution of the frontier. The West he believed, generated democracy and disregarded such Eastern, and by implication European or Old World concepts such as deference to authority and the focus and reliance on social organization. In Turner's conception, because the struggle to survive requires a full and active participation in public affairs, the frontier produced the world's first genuinely free man. In another essay, entitled *Contributions of the West to American Democracy*, Turner makes clear some of these ideas. He writes:

> The paths of the pioneers have widened into broad highways. The forest clearing has expanded into affluent commonwealths. Let us see to it that the ideals of the pioneer in his log cabin shall enlarge into the spiritual life of a democracy where civic power shall dominate and utilize individual achievement for the common good. (Turner 1996: 268)

Quintessential American values and institutions, such as democracy and individualism, were created and propagated through interaction with the frontier. As he claimed, "the frontier is the line of most rapid Americanization." The ongoing engagement with the frontier gives to Americans "that coarseness and strength combined with acuteness and acquisitiveness; that practical inventive turn of mind, quick to find expedients; that masterful grasp of material things . . . that restless, nervous energy; that dominant individualism" (Turner 1996: 37). In this way, the characteristics of the frontier become American characteristics.

Turner's frontier thesis contrasted sharply with a historical orthodoxy that he had encountered at Johns Hopkins University, where Herbert B. Adams taught that American institutions could best be understood in terms of their European origins and where the notion of there being any influences, whether political, geographic or economic, peculiar to America were barely mentioned. This consensus viewed America's European heritage as definitive; America was Europe transplanted. Turner's thesis challenged head on this received version of American history, and explains why, in the immediate aftermath of the delivery of his paper, his ideas were not readily taken up.

Having outlined the central contribution of the frontier to American history and character, Turner suggested that the closing of the frontier marks the end of the first chapter of American history. From this perspective, he offered his frontier thesis as both an analysis of the past and a warning for the future. The tacit question he poses is this: if the frontier, so fundamental to the development of American culture and democracy, is now gone, how then would the nation progress? "And now, four centuries from the discovery of America, at the end of a hundred years of life under the Constitution, the frontier has gone, and with its going has closed the first period of American history" (Turner 1996: 38). Trachtenberg, suggestive of the ways in which Turner's history generates and authenticates myth, writes,

To be sure, [Turner] argued, the story of the frontier had reached its end, but the product of that experience remains. It remains in the predominant character, the traits of selfhood, with which the frontier experience has endowed Americans, that "dominant individualism" which now must learn to cope with novel demands. The thesis projects a national character, a type of person fit for the struggles and strategies of an urban future. (Trachtenberg 1982: 15–16)

How that national type carries forward and the ways in which the frontier continued to be at the forefront of America's conception of itself, its culture and its political landscape is the subject of subsequent chapters.

ROOSEVELT AND TURNER: A QUESTION OF INFLUENCE

Roosevelt was among the first to grasp the significance of Turner's frontier thesis. Given that Turner had only delivered his paper a year earlier, that its published form was a limited run pamphlet and that the reviews he had received were discouraging, it is important to note Roosevelt's speedy recognition of its importance. He wrote to Turner on 10 February 1894:

I have been greatly interested in your pamphlet on the frontier. It comes at the right time for me, for I intend to make use of it in writing the third volume of my Winning of the West, of course making full acknowledgement. I think you have struck some first class ideas and you have put definite shape to a good deal of thought that has been floating around rather loosely.

Roosevelt's reference to this loose thought is without doubt about his own, earlier expressions of such ideas. Yet the issue of influence is an interesting one, and not as simple as the amateur historian taking his cues from the professional academic. Although Turner's interest in the West and speculations about the frontier began in his youth, it was the chance to review the first two volumes of *The Winning of the West* in 1889 that presented him with an early opportunity to organize and express some of his own ideas. In the review, Turner made some early observations of the influence of the West on the nation's development. He asserted that in the West, not in New England, lay the nation's "center of gravity," for it was beyond the Appalachians that "a new composite nationality is being produced, a distinct American people, speaking the English language, but not English." This is clearly a version of Roosevelt's observation that "the backwoodsmen, whatever their blood, had become Americans, one in speech, thought, and character . . . they had lost all remembrances of Europe, and all sympathy with things European . . . they resembled one another, and differed from the rest of the world – even the world of America, and infinitely more the world of Europe – in dress, in customs and in mode of life." The preparation of the review was an early challenge to the Eastern academic establishment and it was also a waypoint in the development of his thesis. As he wrote in a letter, reading Roosevelt's history impressed upon him "the need of a history of the continuous progress of civilization across the continent" (Billington 1973: 83–4). Roosevelt's volumes then demonstrably provided Turner with an opportunity to organize his thoughts, just as Turner's essay lent a certain respectability to Roosevelt's earlier writing.

By 1893, the frontier was clearly no longer a geographical place for Turner, no longer a historical entity demanding objective analysis. Through the agency of writers like Turner and Roosevelt, the West was becoming a set of symbols that constituted, not history, but an explanation of history, and in that sense a myth. Its significance as a mythic space began to outweigh its importance as a real place with its own peculiar geography, politics and cultures. After 1893, for a vast number of Americans, the West became a landscape known through and completely identified with the fictions created about it.

Among the early examples of such fictions, one man featured prominently, a figure whose life spanned both the West of history and the evolving mythic West. It was precisely his authenticity as a bona fide frontiersman which allowed him to do more than any other to codify the Western's narrative and generic structures. William F. "Buffalo Bill" Cody is a vital piece in the movement of history into myth.

CHAPTER THREE

Buffalo Bill's Wild West and the Codification of the Western

At Theodore Roosevelt's 1905 inauguration celebration, the star attraction, other than the President himself, was Geronimo. In a pageant made up from traditional military and civilian elements, there were representations of Western life. The Rough Riders and General Custer's old Seventh Cavalry passed for presidential review. Geronimo was one of six "wild" Indians whose presence was intended to illustrate the "before and after" of Indian civilization by the federal government. The six, in full tribal dress, rode abreast and passed "the Great White Chief." Angie Debo in her biography of Geronimo suggests that "Geronimo stole the show." She describes how "white men threw their hats into the air and shouted 'hooray for Geronimo!'" She also records the question of Woodworth Clum, a member of the inaugural committee and the son of an Apache agent, who hated Geronimo with a similar intensity as his father: "Why did you select Geronimo to march in your parade, Mr. President? He is the greatest single-handed murderer in American history." Roosevelt's reply is telling: "I wanted to give the people a good show" (Debo 1993: 419).

There are two important aspects to this depiction of the sights and sounds of the frontier on such an occasion and at this moment in history. In the first instance, the images and characters that were being displayed were already reconstructed versions of Western history, mythic elements that were familiar to and consumed by the onlookers. Secondly, the appeal of such elements demonstrates not only Roosevelt's own affinity with the culture of the West, an affinity rooted in nostalgia, but that the crowds too were nostalgic for the recently passed frontier. These twin elements can be connected to the life and work of Buffalo Bill, in all of its mythical, biographical and legendary glory, a figure who embodies perhaps better than any other the myth of the frontier, the man who did more to construct the West in cultural and mythic terms, and the model, the archetype for Western heroism and frontier values which endured and resonated throughout the twentieth century. That Geronimo was received as a star and not a murderer emerges in no small part from his appearance in the ultimate Western show, Buffalo Bill's Wild West.

William F. Cody was born in a log cabin in 1846 in Scott County, Iowa. His childhood was spent on the prairies, a formative period resonant with the Turnerian conception of the frontier as a "meeting point between savagery and civilization." When Cody's father died in 1857, his childhood was effectively ended. Even the briefest sketch of his activities and experiences between the ages of eleven and fourteen makes clear his pedigree and credentials as a frontiersman. After his father's death, he and his mother moved to Kansas where Cody found work for a wagon-freight company as a mounted messenger and wrangler. In 1859, Cody became a prospector in the Pikes Peak gold rush. A year later, in 1860, he joined the Pony Express, after answering an advertisement that asked for "skinny, expert riders willing to risk death daily," a requirement that was no mere exaggeration. Cody would later claim to have made an incredible 322-mile ride in twenty-two hours. At the age of fourteen then, Cody had already proven himself a capable and experienced frontiersman. In fact Cody was present for and, usually, involved in every key moment in the process of Westward expansion. His involvement in the gold rush, and the Pony Express were only the beginnings of his frontier career. Cody's career as a scout during the Civil War brought him to public prominence; it was this work as reported in the newspapers that established his persona as an exemplary frontiersman in the public eye. At the beginning of the war, keeping a promise he had made to his mother not to enlist in the regular army, Cody joined an informal militia responsible for the defense of Kansas against guerillas such as those led by the infamous Colonel William C. Quantrill. The operations in which he was involved were little more than horse-theft, though they had the gloss of having military objectives. However, government officials, upon hearing of these operations, set detectives to investigate and some of those involved were arrested. Learning of her son's involvement, Cody's mother demanded he abandon this business which "was neither honorable nor right" (Carter 2000: 64). In the winter of 1862, Cody joined another informal militia, the Red Legged Scouts (so-called because they wore red leggings made from sheepskin), and even though Cody would defend the paramilitary objectives of the outfit, as Robert A. Carter notes, a Red Leg was "more purely an indiscriminate thief and murderer than a jayhawker" (Carter 2000: 67). In 1863, the death of Cody's mother meant he was free to enlist in the regular Union army, though he did not do so straight away. Indeed, the manner in which he found himself enlisted suggests he did not yearn to see battle.

I met quite a number of my old comrades and neighbors, who tried to induce me to enlist and go south with them. I had no idea of doing anything of the kind; but one day, after having been under the influence of bad whiskey, I awoke to find myself a soldier in the Seventh Kansas. I did not remember how or when I had enlisted, but I saw I was in for it, and that it would not do for me to endeavor to back out. (Cody 1994: 135)

With the Seventh Cavalry, he saw action in Missouri and Tennessee. Of his involvement in the Civil War, Carter writes, "despite the dubious beginnings of his military service and the peculiar circumstances of his enlistment, William Cody had served his country if not with distinction, then with diligence" (Carter 2000: 78). After the war, he married, and continued to work for the Army as a scout and a dispatch rider, based in Fort Ellsworth, Kansas. In 1867, Cody took up the job that would give him his nickname, hunting buffalo to feed the construction crews of the Kansas Pacific Railroad. The legendary nickname was earned, according to his autobiography, after an eight-hour hunting match with another hunter, William Comstock, where he killed sixty nine to Comstock's forty six. By the end of his eighteen-month tenure with the railroad company, Cody would estimate he had killed 4280 head of buffalo.

Beginning in 1868, Cody returned to work for the army. He was chief of scouts for the Fifth Cavalry and took part in sixteen battles, including the Cheyenne defeat at Summit Springs, Colorado in 1869. For his service in these years, he was awarded the Congressional Medal of Honor in 1872, although it was revoked in 1916 on the grounds that Cody was not a regular member of the armed forces at the time (the award was restored posthumously in 1989).

Crucially, while Cody was earning a reputation as a skilled frontiersman and a brave scout in reality, he was to begin the process of becoming a national folk hero, in the first instance through the exploits of Buffalo Bill, the literary persona, in the dime novels of Ned Buntline (the pen name of the author Edward Z. C. Judson). Buntline had made a career writing "blood-and-thunder romancers . . . an endless stream of sea stories, articles about field sports, tales of Mexican War, temperance tracts and Know-Nothing attacks on foreigners" (Smith 2000: 103). Henry Nash Smith estimates that by his death, in 1886, he had written over two hundred dime novels of various subjects. In 1869, Buntline signed a contract that would see him write exclusively for the *New York Weekly*. Although he was best known for sea stories, he was aware that "the nation at large had discovered the West" (Smith 2000: 104). To this end, Buntline needed to find a figure he could turn into a dime-novel hero. The candidate he had in mind was Major Frank North, commander of three companies of Pawnee scouts who had been enlisted in the regular army to fight the Sioux. Upon meeting with North, at Fort McPherson, Nebraska, the Commander declined Buntline's offer. However, he told Buntline, "If you want a man to fit that bill, he's over there under that wagon." Under the wagon,

Buntline found a sleeping Cody, at the time a scout attached to North's command. They talked, and Buntline subsequently observed Cody on a Pawnee scouting expedition. On his return to New York, he wrote the first of the Buffalo Bill stories, *Buffalo Bill, the King of the Border Men*. In the stories, Buntline repeatedly stressed the authenticity of his writing, that he was offering the biography of a living legend, although the stories had only the most fleeting basis in fact. Perhaps of greater importance was Cody's willingness to live up to, and ultimately become, the character Buntline was detailing. As Smith states, "the persona created by the writers of popular fiction was so accurate an expression of the demands of the popular imagination that it proved powerful enough to shape an actual man in its own image" (Smith 2000: 103). The dime novel incarnation was the first version of Cody to have an impact upon audiences, and is the first element of his powerful legacy. The Buffalo Bill dime novels of Ned Buntline and, subsequently, Prentiss Ingraham, "who had become virtually a staff writer for Cody by 1878" (Smith 2000: 107) and produced more than two hundred Buffalo Bill stories himself, in addition to his likely authorship of those attributed to Cody, were enormously successful in the late nineteenth and early twentieth centuries. Indeed, the first story, in its dime novel form, was still in print in 1928.

The wide-ranging appeal of the character of Buffalo Bill continued to grow. In 1872 a play written by Fred G. Maeder and which shared the name of Bill's literary debut in the *New York Weekly*, Buntline's serial acting as a basis for the play's action, appeared in New York. Buntline took Cody to see it. At the end, Cody was introduced to the audience and the manager of the theatre offered him $500 a week to play himself on stage. Cody declined, his brief moment in the spotlight had left him with stage fright, but he would come to be a theatrical performer soon enough. In December of that year, Buntline finally persuaded Cody to come to Chicago and assume the role of Buffalo Bill on stage, starring in his hastily written and largely unrehearsed play. As it is described in his autobiography, it took Buntline four hours to compose the piece and opened within four days of its composition. The play was entitled, *The Scouts of the Prairie*. Cody recorded the reviews it received in the press the following morning:

> The papers gave us a better send off than I expected, for they did not criticize us as actors. The Chicago Times said that if Buntline had actually spent four hours in writing that play, it was difficult for anyone to see what he had been doing all that time. (Cody 1994: 327)

Given that from the moment Cody appeared on stage, the script was almost entirely adlibbed, with Buntline feeding him questions and cues, the focus on the quality of the writing misses the point. The play "proved a decided success financially, if not artistically" (Cody 1994: 328) and drew full houses everywhere it played. It also made Cody a star and the archetype of Western heroism. The performances blurred the line between his actual experiences as a frontiersman and make-believe; it was impossible to discern what was fact and what was fiction amongst the stories depicted on the stage. The real importance of this play can be seen in the imitations that appeared, dramas created to the template, the formula that Buntline and Cody had created. As Sell and Weybright put it,

> the show was copied by enterprising producers in the stock companies of all the large cities. All these shows involved Indians, cowboys, scouts, frontiersmen, a lost maiden to be rescued, and some kind of comic relief. The more violent, more absurd, the more shooting, the more coincidences and predicaments, the better audiences like them. The pattern of latter-day Western movies was emerging . . . [Buffalo Bill] was the original; his imitators were stereotypes. (quoted in Carter 2000: 179)

However, not even celebrity could keep Cody from returning to the West. Between theatre seasons, he regularly escorted rich Easterners and European nobility on Western hunting expeditions. Late in the summer of 1876, history and mythology converged and Cody evolved from a national hero to living legend. The defeat of George Armstrong Custer and his Fifth Cavalry at Little Big Horn on 25 June 1876 saw Cody called back into service as an army scout in the campaign that followed. On this occasion Cody added a pivotal new chapter to his legend. At the Battle of War Bonnet Creek, he dueled with the Cheyenne Chief, Yellow Hair, whom he supposedly shot first with a rifle, then stabbed in the heart and finally scalped "in about five seconds" according to his own account (Cody 1994: 344). Others described the combat differently. Some described the encounter as hand to hand combat, some misreported the Chief's name as Yellow Hand, and the location of the duel was not War Bonnet but Hat Creek. Others suggested that Cody did not kill Yellow Hair at all, he merely lifted the Chief's scalp after he had already fallen in battle. Regardless of the actuality of the fight, Cody characteristically embroidered the event into drama, lifting the gruesome war trophy as "the first scalp for Custer," the name of Buffalo Bill's autumn production back East. Increasingly, even his experiences in the West between theatre seasons were becoming mere materials for the show he would put on when he returned East. An indication of his theatrical awareness can be discerned in his choice of attire at the Battle of War Bonnet Creek. On this occasion, he forewent his usual tasseled buckskins, in favor of a Mexican vaquero outfit, which allowed him to parade the very clothes he wore the day he killed Yellow Hair before Eastern audiences.

Buffalo Bill, the character, was first a fiction constructed to cash in on the nation's fascination with the wild west but subsequently came to symbolize it. William Cody, the man, became so caught up in the role that it came to dominate his life. On 19 May 1883, Cody organized the first proper Wild West in Omaha (Cody had organized an event the year earlier, "Old Glory Blowout" in North Platte, Nebraska, as part of 4 July celebrations which acted as a prototype for the show). From the very first performance, it was a huge success. Although he understood the importance of spectacle and entertainment, Cody was determined to make his version of the West as realistic as possible. The show had a clear mission to educate audiences in the ways of the West. To this end, the Wild West epically reenacted some of the most famous and evocative elements of life on the frontier. Over the course of its run, the show dramatized a buffalo hunt, with real buffalo; an Indian attack on the real Deadwood Stage with real Indians; a pony express ride; and a tableau presentation of Custer's last stand, in which some Lakota who had actually fought in the battle recreated their parts. Once more such recreations further blurred the lines between fact and fiction. The Wild West then was a spectacular outdoor circus but it was also a living history lesson, and Cody took this aspect of the show very seriously.

The contents of the programs that were sold around the showground are the best illustration of this sense of didactic purpose. The Wild West's program was not simply a keepsake, a memento of an exciting day out. Rather, through the program, Cody sought to provide all manner of historical details and fascinating facts to audiences eager for a taste of the West. The programs would contain facts about Indian origins of state names, articles on Western history, biographies of great Civil War scouts and frontiersmen, and throughout it was illustrated with evocative action scenes and portraits. The program presented itself, as the Wild West did, as an authentic, authoritative source of knowledge and information about the West. And yet the Wild West was not history, but rather, like Cody himself, an exaggeration of history. The Wild West codified many of the conventions of the Western. Indeed, the elements of the Western that come to be so troubling to the nation as the twentieth century progresses, for example the representation of the Indian, emerge from some of the most celebrated tableaus. From the very first program, Major John Burke, the show's general manager, provided what he termed a "salutatory." In it can be seen the ways in which Cody's show connects with the histories of Turner and Roosevelt. In the first place it locates the stars of the show as "a part of the development of the great West." It describes these men as "keen of eye, sturdy in build, inured to hardship, experienced in the knowledge of Indian habits and language, familiar with the hunt, and trustworthy in the hour of extremest danger, they belong to a class that is rapidly disappearing from our country." Many of these sentiments foreshadow Turner's conception of the frontiersman.

Burke also notes in the salutatory that, "the pressure of the white man, the movement of the emigrant train, the extension of our railways, together with the military power of the General Government, have, in a measure, broken down the barriers behind which the Indian fought and defied the advance of civilization." This conflict was a major part of the show's dramatic impetus. Segments involving Indians racing around the arena on horseback were central to spreading the perception of the Native American as a whooping savage, a race of wild men. The presence of real Native American actors in the show performing this role served to confirm these notions of "the red-skinned danger" that Burke speaks of at the beginning of the program, and to crystallize the stereotypes of the Indian that Hollywood will come to specialize in. The problematic relations with the Native Americans and Mexicans in his show, while valid concerns, did not trouble Cody. He genuinely believed that he was providing these displaced people with a rewarding and exciting career, and for his time, Cody's treatment of these groups was remarkably liberal. In most of the Wild West's programs, the Indian is referred to as "the Former Foe, Present Friend, the American."

In support of this, Vine Deloria makes two points regarding Cody's relationship with the Indians in his show. In the first instance, he points out that Buffalo Bill's status enabled him to employ individuals considered dangerous by the Bureau of Indian Affairs, individuals the Bureau would rather have in prison. By removing them from the reservations to tour with the Wild West, Cody "probably saved some of the chiefs from undue pressure and persecution by the government at home." Secondly is the status Cody accorded the Sioux, as part of the "Congress of Rough Riders," a gathering of the finest horsemen in the world. As Deloria notes, "Instead of degrading the Indians and classifying them as primitive savages Cody elevated them to a status of equality with contingents from other nations." So even though the show originated and reinforced many of the West's stereotypes, the status Cody afforded the Indian suggested a more sophisticated view. It is worth noting, however, that African-Americans, given the historical reality of their significant numbers in the West, were barely represented in the show. In terms of the creation of stereotypes, Buffalo Bill's Wild West was the point of origin for the premier Western character, the cowboy. Cody's version of the cowboy was not based on the real cowboy of the range or ranch. As evidenced in Roosevelt's need to provide a defense of the cowboy in *Ranch Life and the Hunting Trail*, cowboys were generally considered less than wholesome figures, at best foul-mouthed, drunken delinquents, at worst, criminals capable of any amount of violent excess. This was in keeping with the East's conception of the West as a dangerous, untamed landscape as depicted in sensational newspaper stories and dime novels. Cody was able to remake the cowboy by focusing on the spirit of the West as it was evinced by his lifestyle, an existence marked by an independence from society, impressive skill, an affinity with nature, and an attractive self-confidence. As Cody traveled, first across America and then the world, the image of the cowboy took hold as *the* symbol of the character of the American West, a symbol that would resonate through the twentieth century. The cowboy emerged from the lifestyle of the young men who drove cattle from the range to market and the program notes that if not for the cowboy "the great grazing Pampas of the West would be valueless, and the Eastern necessities of the table, the tan-yard, and the factory would be meager." The romanticized version of the cowboy in the Wild West is a hybrid of these rangers, hired ranch-hands of the post-Civil War West, and the indigenous Vaqueros of the Southwest. Again, the program informs the reader that "between the 'cow-boy' and the 'vaquero' there is only a slight line of demarcation. The one is usually an American, inured from boyhood to the excitements and hardships of his life, and the other represents in his blood the stock of the Mexican, or it may be of the half-breed." Both were a part of the Wild West Show, with Buck Taylor, "the King of the Cowboys," the first cowboy star, receiving top billing. Indeed, the version of the cowboy that emerges from the Wild West and into film would combine the former's "careless and impetuous" spirit with something of the dandy, intricate dress of the latter.

The historical worth of the Wild West was augmented by the fact that many of the acts that comprised the spectacle were reenactments of a world already gone. The buffalo had been hunted practically to extinction, the Mexicans had been repelled, the Indians had been defeated in a series of bloody battles and confined to reservations, and the savage landscape of the frontier was already well on the way to "civilization." In this sense then, Buffalo Bill's Wild West propagated popular myths of an old West suffused with exaggeration and distortion at a time when the real West was rapidly changing. The success of the show suggests a national craving for times past when things were simpler, a nostalgia for a largely imagined territory rich in space, resources and opportunity. Even in its heyday, the Wild West show was celebrating something already lost and replacing it with myth.

The program changed, new stars came and went, but the success of the Wild West continued. In 1893 at the Colombian World Fair, Cody connected his vision of the West with those of Roosevelt and Turner. Not far from where the Wisconsin professor would deliver his epochal paper, Buffalo Bill's Wild West show was the star attraction at the exposition, with an attendance estimated at a total of over six million visitors. The 1893 Wild West saw the show at the height of its popularity. It was also the season that saw the introduction of the section "The Congress of Rough Riders of the World" to the program of Western reenactments. This military feature paraded a group of expert marksmen and riders of all nations before the captivated audience. Thanks to his friend, Theodore Roosevelt, Cody's theatrical act found historical significance when Roosevelt organized his team of Rough Riders to fight in the Spanish-American War. Cody reciprocated by adding to his show, and thereby further associating the war with the West, a reenactment of the charge on San Juan Hill once Roosevelt became president. The act included a number of veterans from Roosevelt's squad. Roosevelt's appropriation of the cowboy myth and its subsequent association with the President was an early indication of the easy relationship between the values of the frontier and American political culture.

From the outset the show was an enormous success and toured the United States for three decades, as well as playing to enthusiastic crowds in Europe. By the end of the 1880s, Cody was almost entirely absorbed in his celebrity persona. If the Wild West show reduced the vast lands of the West, a region with a complex mix of racial, cultural, economic, geographic and ecological issues, to a common archetypal myth, Cody's life as a showman reduced him to the legendary character of Buffalo Bill. Fact and fiction merged so seamlessly in the Wild West that the two elements became indistinguishable. This same blending marked Cody's existence, his real identity becoming confused with the literary and stage character. One reason for this was that Cody was an aggressive promoter of the show and this meant that he was perpetually performing. Cody understood the need for good publicity and that this required him to stay in character anywhere and everywhere he went. In this way, Cody was able to project himself as a national hero and a living legend, a role model, for children certainly, but for all Americans, embodying all that was great about the frontier. Buffalo Bill represented the quintessential American through his embodiment of frontier values. As waves of new immigrants arrived on American soil, Buffalo Bill became the symbol of the American spirit. Crucially, Cody was aware of the responsibility he carried, and he carried it with respect.

However, there was another side of Buffalo Bill, one that was ambitious and fallible. Although Cody will forever be remembered for the Wild West, he had interests and projects outside of the showground and these projects offer further insights into the role Cody played in the interplay of the West of history and the West of mythology. The Wild West was in many ways a means of funding the other ventures he engaged in. Outside of the entertainment industry, Cody's most significant project was that of developing the town of Cody in Wyoming. In his scouting days he had developed a love for the land of the Big Horn Basin. In 1895, Cody began to establish his town there. The way he approached its development was similar to his approach to the show; this was not simply another town, just as the Wild West was not simply another circus. Cody had a great vision of what his town should represent. He imagined nothing less than a utopian metropolis where the values of the old West and modern America could coexist. The scale of his vision was matched by his energy. He used all of his influence and connection to achieve his goal. He had organized finance to dig three irrigation canals using water from the Shoshone River. When his efforts to raise the $2 million necessary for its completion failed to materialize, he turned to his friend, Theodore Roosevelt for support. By 1904, the department of the interior had initiated the Shoshone Reclamation Act and by 1910, two dams were in operation and 16,200 acres were under irrigation.

The year 1907 marked a turning point for the Wild West, and Cody. Financially, the venture began to fail, notably as a result of the death of James Bailey, with whom he had a financial arrangement. Upon Bailey's death, his estate would no longer honor it. As such, Cody was increasingly unable to mount shows up to his exacting standards. On a more personal level, the long tours, moving around the world, began to take their inevitable toll on Cody and in line with the effort he had expended on the project, he displayed signs of homesickness for his ranch in the Big Horn Basin. Although he managed to avoid the most pressing financial problems, such problems would follow him until his death. In 1910, he began a series of farewell tours, after which he intended to retire to Wyoming. Cody's empire crumbled in the last years of his life. The farewell tours took three years to complete and problems followed all the way. He had overextended himself financially and the need to keep the show running and manage activities in Cody proved too much. Although his health and morale suffered, he kept such woes private and continued to try to find new ways of paying his debts. He merged the Wild West with the Sells-Floto Circus, a desperate measure which further removed Cody from control of the show. In September 1913, with the support of the owners of the Sells-Floto circus and in association with the Essanay Company, Cody formed the Colonel W. F. Cody (Buffalo Bill) Historical Pictures Company. Cody had actually been involved in film from the moment of its appearance in America. In 1894, the Wild West had been photographed for the Edison Kinetoscope, an early peepshow machine. In 1905, there had been a much heralded announcement of the formation of the Buffalo Bill and Pawnee Bill Film Company, which intended to produce spectacular Westerns. No spectacular Westerns emerged, though other film-makers took his name which compelled the already finan-cially crippled Cody to sue. Now, Cody saw the opportunity of using film to solve his financial problems. Cody proposed a series of films that would recreate the Battle of Summit Springs, his duel with Yellow Hair, even the massacre at

Wounded Knee. As he had in developing his town, Cody used his status to approach the Secretary of War and the Secretary of the Interior. He explained that he wanted to make historically accurate films that would educate the American public, which would represent not only Indian wars but also Indian progress. On these terms, and after consulting with the Indian agent at Pine Ridge, the government agreed to send Cody three troops of cavalry and materiel and the Pine Ridge reservation and agency Indians. The film was described by the newspapers of the time as "the greatest film ever made, a lasting pictorial history of the early campaigns to hand down to posterity" (Carter 2000: 433). Unfortunately, none of the films Cody made have survived beyond still photographs.

The brief excursion into film did little to relieve Cody's situation and, by 1916, Cody's health was in sharp decline, the medical factors inevitably exacerbated by various legal and financial disputes. Cody made a fortune from his show business success but had lost it to mismanagement. In the end, even the Wild West itself was lost to creditors.

When news of Cody's ill health became public, the Cody family was inundated with letters and telegrams from a concerned nation. The news of his death on 10 January 1917 generated an outpouring of sympathy that was shared by millions of people all over the world. In the course of a life that had spanned careers as a frontiersman, soldier, scout, horse thief, actor, showman, businessman and icon, Cody was responsible for establishing patterns, structures, symbols and narratives that would underpin American cultural production and political rhetoric for the whole of the twentieth century. His legacy is perhaps best summed up in an official resolution in memoriam from the state legislature of California, dated 18 January 1917:

Whereas, the state of California desires to express its appreciation of the courage and fearlessness of this, our last frontiersman, whose life stands forth in the establishment and foundation of our Western country; and whereas in his death that romantic and stirring chapter in our national history that began with Daniel Boone is forever closed.

CHAPTER FOUR

Western Literature from The Virginian *to* Shane

The act of defining what exactly "Western literature" might be is not a straightforward one. This may seem counter-intuitive. The Western is perhaps the most recognizable of American cultural forms. However, as a literary category, it can encompass an enormous range of styles, subjects, locations and characters. As a starting point, a geographical approach would seem logical: Western literature is literature produced in or about the West. The issue then is to locate the West. Is all literature written in or about the lands West of the Mississippi automatically Western? Surely this is unhelpful. And what of the many critics who identify James Fennimore Cooper's *Leatherstocking Tales* as formative Westerns? Four of Cooper's stories take place in significantly Eastern New York State. The problem is, given the progress of Westward expansion, practically the whole of the continent was frontier at some time. Such an observation underlies Leslie Fiedler's analysis, in *The Return of the Vanishing American*, of the Pocahontas story as containing an early Western thematic. Geography then is obviously important, but does not in and of itself identify Western literature. The passage of history, the way the frontier has changed over time, is another important consideration. California in the nineteenth century is the location for many Western stories, a landscape that is rich in the resonances of Turner's frontier process, but what of California in the twentieth century? Can we consider the Los Angeles-based detective novels of Raymond Chandler or Ross MacDonald as Western literature? Some critics would argue that even the presence of the city prevents a given novel's consideration as Western literature, on the basis of the connection between the West and the concept of space, a situation which suggests primitive natural conditions and the struggle to survive. Other scholars argue that Western literature is fundamentally connected to climate. Regions with low rainfall and aridity signify narratives that must be Western. These physical characteristics all have a part to play in Western literature but none of them categorically define the genre.

From a different perspective, one might consider the use of what might be termed frontier themes, literature that explores American history and society, consciously or otherwise, through an interrogation of the myths, symbols and values of the frontier. Such literature might deal with notions of American individualism or democracy, or offer a nostalgic look back at a perceived better time in the past.

Western literature, then, is as slippery a term as it is elastic. However, there are ways of dividing the literary category that facilitate analysis. One approach is to apply an axis from popular to serious. The popular Westerns, like those of Owen Wister, Zane Grey and Max Brand, are essentially romantic and, while worthy of analysis, are intended for mass consumption. The more seriously intended Westerns, like those of Willa Cather, or Walter Van Tilburg Clark, use the context of the frontier to explore wider, sometimes non-Western themes and contexts such as gender, sacrifice, law and order, or morality. In this sense they represent what Thomas J. Lyon labels mature-phase Westerns. Yet even these categories are by no means exhaustive. Jack Schaefer's first novel, *Shane*, which will be extensively discussed later, has a foot in both camps, and, as we shall see, is as pivotal a novel as Wister's *The Virginian*. One thing connects all of these Westerns. Whether popular or serious, romantic or mature, all of them have an element of political purpose, of conveying values and institutions even if, as in the case of the mature-phase fiction, they are deliberately using the popularity of the form to challenge those values and institutions.

If establishing what Western literature might be is difficult, establishing precisely a point of origin for the form is equally problematic. For some critics, the genesis of this type of American fiction emerges from the reports of the Western lands that were sent back East, most famously in the journals of Lewis and Clark. For others, James Fennimore Cooper's *Leatherstocking Tales* represent the first appearance of frontier narratives, which are significant precursors to the Western. Cooper certainly provided the starting point for stories about frontiersmen, creating in Natty Bumpo a character type that Ned Buntline and Buffalo Bill were later to elaborate on with great success. Indeed, it is possible to trace the effects of Cooper's narratives, produced between 1823 and 1841, on the mass-produced dime novels that had their heyday between 1860 and 1900 and led ultimately to the novel considered to represent the birth of the modern Western, Owen Wister's *The Virginian: a Horseman of the Plains* (1902). It is Wister's formularization of the cowboy character, in terms of speech, manner, dress and skills, that lie at the heart of what the Western would become in the twentieth century.

Regardless of earlier types of writing about the frontier and the lands of the West, for the present purposes, the history of the literary Western begins with the pivotal publication of Owen Wister's *The Virginian*, which appeared in

April 1902. The novel was an instant and massive success, going through six printings in six weeks and a further sixteen printings in its first year. It was easily the bestselling fiction in 1902, and such was its enduring popularity that it was recorded as the fifth top seller the following year. As noted, there had been, before *The Virginian*, other novels of the West, even other novels about cowboys (Buck Taylor, Buffalo Bill's "King of the Cowboys," had a series of dime novels centered on him in the late 1880s and 1890s), though mostly they had featured the figure of the frontiersman. However, none of them had the impact or the lasting legacy of Wister's novel. Apart from the model of Western heroism that the book established, it is worth pointing out that in so captivating the nation's imagination, *The Virginian* altered the American publishing industry by creating a substantial market among adults for quality Western fiction, a market that was amply supplied by the vast number of imitations that followed reworking the basic elements of Wister's novel.

THE VIRGINIAN (1902)

Ben Merchant Vorpahl describes Owen Wister as

> a myth-maker of considerable skill and determination who set, in a calcu-lated way, to fashion the cowpuncher into a hero on the model of Gawain, a Tristan or – to use one of his favorite analogies – a prodigal son. How well he succeeded may be judged partly on the basis of the hundreds of horse operas in print, film, and television that have sprung up more or less directly from his vision of what happened when people are transplanted from eastern cities, where they could not help being "all varnished over with Europe," to the wide open spaces of the Western plains, where they became real Americans. (Lyon 1987: 288–9)

Wister was one of the small group of men, alongside Roosevelt and Remington, who consciously created the Western mythology that emerged at the beginning of the twentieth century and which would so resonate with and characterize American culture and politics over its course. Indeed, Wister's background and experience of the frontier was extremely similar to his fellow mythologizers. Wister was born in 1860 to an aristocratic Philadelphia family with southern lineage and connections to the world of American arts and letters. Such luminaries as Henry James and Robert Browning were personal friends of the family and, after performing one of his own compositions before Franz Liszt, the composer described him as a "un talent prononcé" and suggested he should study music at the Conservatoire in Paris. Indeed, music seemed to be the career direction he was heading in. Wister graduated from Harvard, where he majored in music, in 1882, and had hopes of becoming a composer of operas. It is of profound significance that his time at Harvard coincided roughly with Roosevelt's. Roosevelt was to have a great influence on Wister, so great in fact, that he would dedicate *The Virginian* to him and publish a memoir entitled *Theodore Roosevelt: The Story of a Friendship, 1880–1919* (1930).

Wister's intention to be a composer did not find favor with his family. When his physician father pressed him toward a more conventional career, Wister entered the world of banking, which he found dull and depressing. Never in robust health, the stresses of working in such an environment began to take physical form. He suffered paralysis down one side of his face, developed serious eye problems and began to show an array of nervous symptoms including vertigo, hallucinations and recurring nightmares. Suffering from a total nervous collapse, a specialist in the area of nervous disorders and family friend, S. Weir Mitchell (himself a writer of Revolutionary War tales), recommended to him the invigorating effects of the West. As Roosevelt and Remington had before him, Wister went West, to Wyoming for the first time in 1885. He spent that summer at Major Frank Walcott's Deer Creek ranch and it was to have an epipahanal quality. He found the air in Wyoming "better than all other air" and his maladies, which had been so oppressive only weeks before, were relieved. It became Wister's belief that, just as he had been cured by the West, the West held the answers to curing America's current malaise. This was to be one of the main themes in *The Virginian*. His health restored, Wister returned East to study law at Harvard but would nearly every year for the next fifteen years visit the West. As he made these trips, he kept a journal, recording the sights, sounds and characters of the West, material that would form the basis of his Western writing, initially in a number of short stories and eventually in *The Virginian*.

The kind of writing that *The Virginian* would represent sat in the middle ground between two styles of Western writing while setting a precedent all of its own. Dime fiction continued to be popular, but in terms of the Western's development, *The Virginian* borrowed something of the form and function of color writing, whose main exponents were writers like Mark Twain and Bret Harte. This type of writing was undertaken by men who had experience, as Wister had, of the area they describe and was usually presented in a series of humorous or satirical sketches, although there was room for sentiment also. In terms of the political and social outlook of *The Virginian* perhaps the most important aspect of this style of writing was the way in which it viewed the frontier as a social entity, not a natural one. That is to say they highlighted the differences between the West and East, between the values and institutions of the regions, through the articulation of the wilderness-civilization dialectic. Twain's *Roughing It* (1880) does this by describing a greenhorn narrator being initiated into the distinctive society of the West. The narrative tells of how a fictionalized Twain and his brother, Orion, made their way to Nevada in the early 1860s to work in the mining camps. There is very little romantic about Twain's West. To be sure, the narrator marvels at aspects of the Western experience, but also finds it a source of personal corruption, as his lust for wealth demonstrates. For Twain, as it would be for Wister, an important element of the West was the new social hierarchy he discerned there, one which did not adhere to the traditional Eastern conditions, but where the hierarchy changed daily as a strike was made or a claim dried up. Bret Harte was drawn more to the sentimental in his representations of the West, although his perspective of a society distinct from the East, where its rules and institutions held no sway, was similar. In another element that Wister would incorporate in his novel, Harte offered a series of characters who, in the process of interacting with the frontier, rediscovered and reaffirmed life's most important values, even if, in keeping with the lack of romance, their redemption came too late.

The other tradition with which *The Virginian* shares something in common is the realism of writers like Hamlin Garland, Frank Norris and Stephen Crane, writers who brought range and depth to writing about the West. It is generally accepted that Garland began this mode of Western writing, in 1891, in *Main-Traveled Roads*. In it he presents a version of the West that was not the land of opportunities for anyone with the will to work hard, but rather a place where those opportunities are regulated within a capitalist system. In Garland's writing, stereotypes are not as prominent, cowboys do the work of cowboys, Native Americans receive an unusual level of historical realism and the frontier is presented in tangible, less sentimental terms. Crane, not a writer usually associated with the Western, produced several stories which had an influence on the genre's realism. The best known is *The Bride Comes to Yellow Sky* (1897) which takes the familiar romantic views of the West and subverts them to present a portrait that is altogether more realistic. Taking the stock convention of a gunfighter-wannabe aiming to shoot up a town, he finds he has been made irrelevant because the marshal has just been married. In this set up, Crane moves beyond the stereotypical, and offers a version of these men as vulnerable, caught in a process of transformation where their values and skills, their way of life is becoming increasingly anachronistic. Frank Norris was among the first writer to set a serious novel in the city, San Francisco, with *McTeague* (1899) but it is for *The Octopus* (1901) that he is best known. The story concerns the efforts of ranchers to confront the aggressive capitalism of the railroad, the octopus of the title. While this sounds like any number of more conventional Western set ups, Norris imbues his characters with a psychological realism that gives the novel a weight and a purpose beyond any generic limitation.

The Virginian contains elements of both of these styles and perhaps this synthesis, one popular, one more serious, but both seeking to present the West in a more realistic light, goes some way to explaining the novel's phenomenal success. *The Virginian* was, in the first place, a very personal book growing out of Wister's experience of and identification with the values of the West. Wister, as Roosevelt had before him, experienced these values in relation to his East-coast perspective and they subsequently informed his belief that the West has lessons for the East's concept of society and culture. This means that *The Virginian* is not the simple Western narrative that its focus on the romance between the Virginian and Molly Wood, its humor and, in the conflict between the Virginian and Trampas, its escalating action, may suggest. Rather Wister's novel is also a discursive and dense novel engaging in the political, social and cultural debates abroad in turn-of-the-century America.

The Virginian begins with the Eastern narrator arriving in Medicine Bow, tired and disorientated and his trunk missing. Immediately the novel's and Wister's concerns with the contrast between East and West are apparent. It is the narrator's first time in the West, and he is to stay at the ranch of his friend, Judge Henry, which involves a long overland journey. The Virginian, a cowboy on Henry's ranch, has been sent to meet the "tenderfoot" and transport him to his lodging place. The qualities of the Virginian are established early on. As the narrator watches the train pulling away, like "a sort of ship [leaving] me marooned in a foreign ocean," he catches sight of the Virginian:

> Lounging there at ease against the wall was a slim young giant, more beautiful than pictures. His broad, soft hat was pushed back; a loose-knotted, dull-scarlet handkerchief sagged from his throat, and one casual thumb was hooked in the cartridge belt that slanted across his hips. He had plainly come many miles from somewhere across the vast horizon, as the dust upon him showed. His boots were white with it. His overalls were gray with it. The weather beaten bloom of his face shone through it duskily, as the ripe peaches look upon their trees in a dry season. But no dinginess of travel or shabbiness of attire could tarnish the splendor that radiated from his youth and strength. (Wister [1902] 1998: 12–13)

In their first exchange, a good deal of Wister's thesis is established. The narrator, referring to an incident on the station platform, enquires, "find many oddities out here like Uncle Hughey?" The Virginian's response is quick and cutting: "yes, seh, there is a right smart oddities around. They come in on every train." The narrator reflects upon the conversation, why he had elicited "that veiled and skillful sarcasm" and comes to an important realization. Had the Virginian been as familiar with him, the narrator would have resented it, so why shouldn't the Virginian react similarly:

It smacked of patronizing: on this occasion he had come off the better gentleman of the two. Here in flesh and blood was a truth which I had long believed in words, but never met before. The creature we call a gentleman lies deep in the hearts of thousands that are born without the chance to master the outward grace of the type. (Wister 1998: 17)

The narrator subsequently alters his view of the West. Despite the appearance of wildness there was a humanity and an energy that the East had lost sight of and he begins to see the squalor and disorder of the town in quite different terms:

I have seen and slept in many like it since. Scattered wide, they littered the frontier from the Columbia to the Rio Grande, from Missouri to the Sierras. They lay stark, dotted over a planet of treeless dust, like soiled packs of cards. Each was similar to the next, as one five-spot of clubs resembles another. Houses, empty bottles, and garbage, they were forever the same shapeless pattern. More forlorn they were than stale bones. They seemed to have been strewn there by the wind and to be waiting till the wind should come again and blow them away. Yet serene above their foulness swam a pure and quiet light, such as the east never sees; they might be bathing in the air of creation's first morning. Beneath sun and stars their days and nights were immaculate and wonderful. (Wister 1998: 18)

This element of redemption is crucial. Just as the landscape redeems the "stark," "forlorn," "soiled" towns, so a similar purity within the cowboy tempers their outward coarseness:

Even where baseness was visible, baseness was not uppermost. Daring, laughter, endurance, these were what I saw upon the countenance of the cowboys. And this very first day of my knowledge marks a date with me. For something about them, the idea of them, smote my American heart, and I have never forgotten it, nor ever shall, as long as I live. In their flesh our natural passions run tumultuous; but often in their spirit sat hidden a true nobility, and often beneath its unexpected shining their figures took a heroic stature. (Wister 1998: 31)

This description matches Roosevelt's description of the cowboy in *Ranch Life and the Hunting Trail*: "brave, hospitable, hardy and adventurous, he is the grim pioneer of our race" (Roosevelt 1899: 100). This duality is represented in the very name of his central character. Outwardly a cowboy, the link to the aristocratic South suggests something nobler. Although he focuses on the

Virginian, Wister is equally concerned with the nature of Western communities. He discerns a "code of the West," a set of values and practices which have little to do with institutional law and government but rather have grown out of the social and cultural circumstances of the West. The best illustration of this is the depiction of the community's methods of peacekeeping and justice. Molly Wood, the heroine of the novel, a school teacher from Vermont, is horrified by the concept of vigilante justice. Judge Henry defends the practice:

> In Wyoming the law has been letting our cattle-thieves go for two years. We are in a very bad way, and we are trying to make that way a little better until civilization can reach us. At present we lie beyond its pale. The courts, or rather the juries, into whose hands we have put the law, are not dealing the law. They are withered hands, or rather they are imitation hands made for show, with no life in them, no grip. They cannot hold a cattle-thief. And so when your ordinary citizen sees this, and sees that he has placed justice in a dead hand, he must take justice back into his own hands where it was once at the beginning of all things. Call this primitive, if you will. But so far from being a defiance of the law, it is an assertion of it – the fundamental assertion of self-governing men, upon whom our whole social fabric is based. (Wister 1998: 284)

For Wister, the code embodies the moral will of the community while simultaneously supporting the importance of individual honor. In this way, when the Virginian finds himself involved in a lynching and a shootout, both illegal actions according to civilization's laws, they are here recognized as obligations. If anything presents the Virginian with a problem it is the arrival of Molly Wood. Women pose a threat to the code insofar as they are symbolic of civilization, and everything that goes with it: law and order, police, justice systems, schools, children, domesticity. Indeed, his love for Molly leads him to break the code and reveal the villainy of Trampas:

> Having read his sweetheart's mind very plainly, the lover now broke his dearest custom. It was his code never to speak ill of any man to any woman. Men's quarrels were not for women's ears. In his scheme, good women were to know only a fragment of men's lives. He had lived many outlaw years, and his wide knowledge of evil made innocence doubly precious to him. But today he must depart from his code, having read her mind well. He would speak evil of one man to one woman, because his reticence had hurt her. (Wister 1998: 295)

If Molly represents a threat to the code, the Virginian's conflict with Trampas demonstrates his resolute adherence to it. From the famous first exchange between the two, when Trampas provokes the Virginian during a card game, and is met with the line, "when you call me that, smile!" the code is enacted; the Virginian is not afraid of violent confrontation, but neither will he bring it on by his own actions. True heroism operates within moral limits. Wister then sees in the West, in the figure of the cowboy and in the values and processes of community, a set of qualities that so-called civilized society needs. In this sense, as Cawelti puts it, "Wister resolved the old ambiguity between nature and civilization by presenting the West not as a set of natural values basically antithetical to civilization, but as a social environment in which the American dream could be born again" (Cawelti 1976: 225).

The Virginian embodied Wister's beliefs that the code of the West should be the code of America. Again John Cawelti provides insight into Wister's purpose, "the kind of individual moral courage and community responsibility embodied in the code is a vital part of the American tradition and need to be reawakened in modern American society" (Cawelti 1976: 222). The idea that this code could revitalize the staid society and institutions of the East is illustrated at the end of the novel, by which point the Virginian has transformed from cowboy to foreman to rancher and is on his way to becoming a leading citizen in Wyoming. The Virginian represents for Wister a new American aristocrat, one whose position is not based on anything as intangible as a family name, but rather based on the demonstration of individual worth in competition with other men.

It was on this terrain that the cowboy became a national symbol. *The Virginian* crystallized the values of the frontier for twentieth century audiences and the character was repeated endlessly thereafter.

THE WESTERN NOVEL IN THE WAKE OF *THE VIRGINIAN*

Following the phenomenal success of *The Virginian*, hundreds, if not thousands, of imitations appeared, a flood of romantic Western potboilers fashioned after the basic model of Wister's novel. B. M. Bower, a Westerner living and writing in Montana, was perhaps the first to stake a claim to this post-Virginian literary territory. Bower's Westerns tended toward the melodramatic, but they have an interest in the fact that Bower was a woman. Bertha Muzzy Bower, hiding her gender behind the initials, began writing stories in magazines in 1904, with the story *Chip of the Flying U*. She expanded this story into her most famous novel in 1906. Bower went some way to bringing a woman's perspective to the Western: for example her most serious novel, *Lonesome Land* (1912) focuses specifically on the role of women in the West.

Unlike Bower, who drew inspiration from the real West in which she lived, Clarence Edward Mulford wrote Westerns from Brooklyn. In 1906, he published his first novel, *Bar 20*, a novel that emerged entirely from reading about the West and his imagination. Mulford was responsible for creating Hopalong Cassidy, a darker hero with a limp and a violent tendency who was a cowboy model that emphasized violence and action super-heroics. As well as establishing a more violent nature for the cowboy, Mulford presented a version of the West that would resonate in the evolving cinematic representation of the West. Writing in *Hopalong Cassidy* (1910), he describes "the raw and mighty West, the greatest stage in all the history of the world for so many deeds of daring which verge on the insane . . . seared and cross-barred with grave-lined trails and dotted with presumptuous, mushroom towns of brief stay whose inhabitants flung their primal passions in the face of humanity" (Mulford 1910: 51). It is apparent then that the Western in the wake of *The Virginian* was accessible to writers with very different intentions and perspectives.

Two writers loom larger that any other in the post-*Virginian* literary scene: Zane Grey and Max Brand. Grey, like Wister, was a well-off Easterner, who was bored with his career as a dentist and had become evangelical about the West after spending his honeymoon in Arizona in 1907. Although he had written three novels between 1903 and 1909, they did not have much of an impact. These early stories concerned the Ohio frontier and held clear distinctions between wilderness and civilization; for example, he made his heroes Eastern military or political figures. However, his experience of the Southwest transformed his perspective and he began to produce stories celebrating the openness of the landscape, and the redemptive qualities of the region. His first novel in this style was *The Heritage of the Desert* (1910), a romance in which an ailing Easterner falls in love with a part-Indian woman in Arizona. The story recounts the physical and spiritual rejuvenation of the man from the East. This theme was to recur in Grey's fiction. As Gary Topping writes, "the basic Zane Grey plot is a drama in which a jaded, disillusioned, and perhaps physically frail or ill member of Eastern society comes West to find a complete reorientation of values" (quoted in Milner et al. 1994: 714). This passage from the novel illustrates his theme: "The desert regeneration had not stopped at turning weak lungs, vitiated blood and flaccid muscles into a powerful man; it was at work on his mind, his heart, his soul."

Between 1910 and 1915, Grey continued to produce variations of this narrative, in the novels *Riders of the Purple Sage*, *Desert Gold* (1913), *The Light of the Western Stars*, *The Lone Star Ranger* (1914) and *The Rainbow Trail* (1915). Thereafter he wrote novels about almost every conceivable Western event. To this end he conducted research, interviews, and visited sites across America, all in pursuit of accuracy. By the 1920s many of Grey's novels were being adapted into movies, which in his drive for authenticity, he specified, by contractual obligation, had to be made on location. Grey then not only popularized the form in the wake of Wister's prototype, but imbued the West with a romantic significance that was of his own creation. He continued to write into the mid-1930s becoming one of the best known, and one of the richest of American writers.

As prolific as Grey was, he does not come close to matching the productivity of his contemporary, Max Brand, the pen name of author Frederick Faust. Between 1918 and 1938, Faust published over 300 book-length Western stories, the most famous of which, *Destry Rides Again*, was published in 1930, and hundreds more for pulp magazines in other genres. Unlike the other writers, he did not have a strong sense of historical realism or place and was not concerned with the West as a restorative or redemptive landscape. He wrote most of his Westerns from his Italian villa in the 1920s and 1930s. And even though he was brought up in California, he considered the West "disgusting." Max Brand's Westerns then privileged the mythology, avoiding specific historical or geographical settings for narratives that make use of generic conventions of the West and in that sense offered a truly imaginative, fantastical version of the West, one which would influence early Hollywood.

Other novelists took the opportunity to use the frontier to explore serious themes and to question the values of the West that Roosevelt, Wister, Turner, and Grey so admired. Willa Cather's novels are very far removed from romance and nostalgia. She was born in 1873 in Virginia and moved to Nebraska with her family when she was nine. She spent her first months there on a ranch in Webster County, and then moved to the village of Red Cloud which would be a source of inspiration for much of her writing. It was here that she observed immigrant life among the Scandinavian pioneers and specifically the work of women in this environment. In an interview she explains their influence:

> I grew fond of these immigrants – particularly the old women, who used to tell me of their home country. I used to think them underrated, and want to explain them to their neighbors. Their stories used to go round and round in my head at night. This was, with me, the initial impulse. I didn't know any writing people. I had an enthusiasm for a kind of country and a kind of people. (Cather 2003: 289)

In her second novel, *O Pioneers!* (although she preferred to think of it as her first, the first in her own voice), Cather used directly these experiences and memories of those pioneers, their struggle to tame the land, the unforgiving climate and the exhilaration of the harvest. Cather channeled these women into the character of Alexandra Bergson, a second generation Scandinavian pioneer, who becomes the leader of the farming community of which her family is a part. The story sees Alexandra determining to make the land suitable for farming, something her father had been unable to do, the wild land resisting his every effort. In her success, Cather presents Alexandra as a founding mother who unlocks the mystery of the land that had eluded her father's generation. The basis for her success is a genuine and pure love for the country. In an evocative passage Cather describes the nature of Alexandra's relationship with the land:

> When the road began to climb the first long swells of the Divide, Alexandra hummed an old Swedish hymn, and Emil wondered why his sister looked so happy. Her face was so radiant that he felt shy about asking her. For the first time, perhaps, since that land emerged from the waters of the geologic ages, a human face was set toward it with love and yearning. It seemed beautiful to her, rich and strong and glorious. Her eyes drank in the breadth of it, until her tears blinded her. Then the Genius of the Divide, the great free sprit which breathes across it, must have bent lower than it ever bent to a human will before. The history of every country begins in the heart of a man or a woman. (Cather 2003: 63–4)

To this extent, *O Pioneers!* resembles previous incarnations of the West and the spiritual relationship between the land and the people. However, though this relationship has generated success, there is a price. Cather presents Alexandra as an uncomplicated woman: "her mind was slow, truthful and steadfast. She had not the least spark of cleverness" (Cather 2003: 61). She is also a woman who has had to sacrifice elements of herself, most importantly, her sexuality. This repression has devastating repercussions when, because the only relationship she has had time for has been with the land, she does not recognize the love that is developing between her brother and Marie, who is married to a local farmer. Cather notes that Alexandra's sexual inexperience meant that though Marie "was beautiful, impulsive and barely two years older than Emil, these facts had had no weight with Alexandra" (Cather 2003: 253) so consequently, and innocently, she "omitted no opportunity of throwing Marie and Emil together" (Cather 2003: 252). In the novel's climactic scenes, the jealous husband of Marie kills the lovers and leaves the community reeling. Cather's novel is a counter voice to Wister's insofar as she suggests that while there are bounties and benefits to life out West, it is not necessarily an ideal one.

SHANE (1949)

Jack Schaefer's first novel, *Shane*, represents the first major evolution of the cowboy character after *The Virginian*. *Shane* was published in 1949, the character emerging, again, at an important historical and cultural moment:

the beginning of the Cold War. Although treated as pulp even today, on close inspection *Shane* is a literary Western every bit as important and influential as Wister's. Schaefer is a serious writer, well read in history and almost academic, and as such *Shane* is a serious literary Western. In the novel, Schaefer pared the popular Western story down to its essential mythology, in a way that appealed to post-war America, and recast the cowboy as a hero for the Cold War era. In so doing he produced a novel that effectively combined popular entertainment with serious literature. In *Shane*, Schaefer created the ultimate Western morality tale, rich in meanings associated with community, sexuality, and family. Of perhaps greater importance for the onset of the 1950s, the Cold War, and the Atomic Age is the way the novel offered a means of thinking about violence and leadership that would resonate in American political culture in the coming decades.

Schaefer wrote *Shane* "primarily as a means of relaxation" while he was working as a newspaper editor, "as a relief from constant editorials on mine strikes, local politics, court decisions, the United Nations and such." It began as a short story "about the basic legend of the West" (Nuwer 1973: 279) but grew and grew, ultimately into the length of a novella. But, when *Shane* was finished in 1945, Schaefer had little knowledge of literary markets and did not know what to do with the manuscript. In an interview, he tells how the manuscript came to be almost accidentally published by *Argosy* where it eventually appeared in three parts, in the July, September and October issues of 1946. Schaefer's approach to writing fiction is revealing:

> I write fiction for money, yes, but also because I firmly believe that the best approach to truth about people and their doings as well as about any period in history is through fiction. *Shane* was my first real attempt in the field and began primarily as a relaxation. I wrote it during the last months of the Second World War when I was acting editor of the *Norfolk Virginia-Pilot* working long hours with a much depleted staff. Every night, on coming home, just to ease the tension, I put in an hour or two on the story. I was not and am not a reader of Western stories. They plain bore me. Probably, if I had been really aware of the constant flood of Westerns drugging the market, I would have shied away from that field. But I had for years been collecting and reading all authentic material of Western history I could find. *Shane* began as a study of the basic legend of the West, the man with a gun using it to right wrongs, in a sense the American version of a knight on horseback. I deliberately presented the story through the eyes of a boy so that the man himself, seen thus, could be thrown up larger than life, more heroic, without the tale degenerating into outright overblown melodrama. (letter to Gene Gressley, 30/12/57)

Several issues emerge here. Schaefer from the outset believed that fiction was an indicator of contemporary situations and was capable of representations of people and events. This reflection of societal influences is as important for the writer as is the writing of the novella itself. Schaefer wrote *Shane* whilst still in the midst of writing his vast number of editorials; *Shane* is not an enterprise that can be disconnected from his journalism. In his description of the origins of *Shane*, in the Western history and construction of mythology, he presents himself as much more an academic than a novelist. Schaefer considers his work above the "constant flood" of traditional Western fiction. Indeed, throughout interviews and lectures, he is at pains to stress his difference from such material. In one such interview, he answers the question of whether he has ever regretted writing Westerns in these terms:

> No. In fact, I developed a question that I always ask . . . I started going to a lot of those literary affairs. Inevitably someone would come up and ask me what it was I did for a living . . . I would shout out, "*I write Westerns!*" Then, in self defense, I would ask the listener a question of my own. I would ask, "Can you give me one good reason why a writer cannot 'write' good literature about the West the same as he could about the east or anywhere else?" And do you know, no-one has yet been able to answer me. (Nuwer 1973: 282)

Although he will admit to writing Westerns, Schaefer does not consider himself a Western writer. This sense of separation from the horde is mirrored strongly in the contemporary critical assessments of *Shane* on its publication in 1949.

The reviews of *Shane* that appeared in a vast number of local newspapers and journals provide substance to Schaefer's demand to be set apart from mass-produced generic Western fictions. In almost every instance, the reviewer sees *Shane* as new, different, with a longevity likened to Owen Wister's 1902 classic, *The Virginian*. W. J. Mahoney articulates these feelings in his review for the *Montgomery Advertiser* in October 1949. He describes *Shane* in these terms:

> Occasionally, out of the welter of fiction comes a book that defies cataloging . . . The publishers see in this book one reminiscent of *The Virginian* both in the fact doubtless that the locale is the West, and that it is a story that will live.

Al Chase's review for the *Chicago Sunday Tribune* in November 1949 is perhaps more precise:

> Altho' *Shane* is not another *Virginian* it has the same quality, dignity and appeal which made Owen Wister's famous novel of years ago read by people who scoffed at "Westerns."

This recognition in *Shane* of something more vital, something more literary, is echoed in pieces with headlines like, "Western novel rings bell for quality" (*Desert News*, 11 December 1949) or "*Shane* makes you think of *The Virginian*" (*Omaha World Herald*, 10 October 1949) or "A tragic Western of same dignity as *Virginian*"(*Chicago Tribune*, 13 November 1949) The stress on *Shane*'s connection to *The Virginian* is important not necessarily in any structural or narrative sense, but in the way that both novels act as starting points for new developments in the genre, and offer models of Western heroes who become enormously influential.

The opening lines of *Shane* establish two central concerns:

> He rode into our valley in the summer of '89. I was a kid then, barely topping the backboard of father's old chuck wagon. I was on the upper rail of our small corral, soaking in the late afternoon sun, when I saw him far down the road where it swung into the valley from the open plain beyond . . . In that clear Wyoming air I could see him plainly, though he was still several miles away. (Schaefer 1984: 61)

The paramount importance of the arrival of Shane, the "he" that begins the narrative, may seem an obvious point to mark as having significance, given that Shane is the explicit subject of the novel. But the importance lies in the notion of arrival, the onset of a new narrative, of new relationships. This idea of beginning is also articulated in the narrator's voice. On the surface, the voice is a simple one, that of a young boy. And certainly some reviewers of Schaefer's novel understood and subsequently criticized this narrative voice in these terms. A review in the *Sunday Herald Traveler* in 1967, upon the publication of Schaefer's collected short novels is illustrative:

> Shane's dismounting "in a single flowing tilt". The reporter of that action is supposed to be a small boy, a small Western boy. Any time a Western boy is impressed by the way a man gets off his horse – unless he falls off – I'll eat my Stetson.

It is surprising that as late as the 1960s, a critic could misunderstand the complexity of Schaefer's narrator to such a degree. The fascinated description of Shane's movement is not supposed to be the description of "a small Western boy." This is the description by the older Bob Starrett remembering the summer of 1889. It is a child-like wonder articulated in adult language. Within this adult voice reliving a series of events from his childhood is a narrative voice deliberately capable of innocent awe and mature respect. This dual voice gives his testimony a peculiar quality, an unusual tone. If the character of Shane seems exaggerated because of the interpretation of a child, the portrait is equally skewed by an adult longing for that character still to be part of his experience. Consequently, Bob Starrett's voice is a mix of the childishly innocent and the achingly nostalgic. This doubled narrative voice means that Schaefer is able to discuss the beginning of the community in both the present and the past, through the eyes of a boy almost as it happens, and from the reminiscences of that time by the boy now grown up.

As Fred Erisman notes, Schaefer throughout his fiction is concerned with the notion of maturation. It is certainly an important aspect of Bob's dual perspective narration. But there is another level to this notion of growing up:

> Schaefer's repeated treatments of the topic . . . take on additional signifi-
> cance when one relates them to the fuller scope of the novels in which they
> appear. He sets his tales of growing up squarely within the context of the
> "classical" Western story . . . limited to the period in United States history
> from 1865 to 1910. This period is a turbulent one, embracing years in which
> the United States itself was growing up, changing from an idealistic
> experiment in popular government to a sophisticated, if unwilling, world
> power. (Work 1984: 290–1)

This passage is provocative. Firstly, as Erisman goes on, Schaefer's novels parallel these historic currents. But Erisman does not go far enough. The way in which he describes the period 1865 to 1910 sounds extremely similar to the post-war period in which Schaefer is writing, both as a journalist and, crucially, as a novelist. By extending Erisman's contention to consider the historical climate of the late 1940s and early 1950s, *Shane*'s acclaim is brought into relief. And given the political climate of the 1950s, it is easy to see how a character like Shane would be seen as different, unusual. Shane in this mode is something of a father figure, certainly to Bob, but also to the community, *deus ex machina*. It is because of Shane that the group of characters can forge a new beginning.

Shane's arrival in the valley is not a clear cut, pre-meditated event. Whilst he is the focus of the novel, the narrative trail is not immediately set. Although he is approaching Bob, he is not specifically heading for the Starrett place. At the outset, Shane is a blank canvas of a character, devoid of the usual generic conventions. He is, at least at the beginning, capable of anything:

> He came steadily on, straight through the town without slackening pace,
> until he reached the fork a half-mile below our place. One branch turned left
> across the river ford and on to Luke Fletcher's big spread. The other bore

ahead along the right bank where we homesteaders had pegged our claims in a row up the valley. He hesitated briefly, studying the choice, and moved again steadily on our side. (Schaefer 1984: 62)

Shane is clearly not on a mission then, he is not a deliberate savior, somehow sent to protect the valley from the threats and oppression of the cattle baron, Luke Fletcher. Shane has no pre-conceived objective; the choice he makes could have easily been to move toward Fletcher's place. This is the essence of Shane's existentialism. From the very first, Shane is a character who can define himself. Shane can decide which side he joins and he is not doing it out of some notion of civic responsibility. Consequently, those who witness his arrival into the valley, like Bob, are unable to place him, in much the same way as some of the novel's critics:

> There seemed nothing remarkable about him, just another stray horseman . . . I saw a pair of cowhands, loping past him, stop and stare after him with a curious intentness. (Schaefer 1984: 61)

Although Bob (and some of the critics) try to fit him into a category, he is immediately made aware of something odd, a tacit recognition of Shane's difference. This difference is further articulated in Bob's vivid description of Shane's unusual garb:

> He wore dark trousers of some serge material tucked into tall boots and held at the waist by a wide belt, both of a soft black leather, tooled in intricate designs. A coat of the same dark material as the trousers was neatly folded and strapped to his saddle-roll. His shirt was finespun linen, rich brown in color. The handkerchief knotted loosely around his throat was black silk. His hat was not the familiar Stetson, not the familiar gray or tan. It was plain black, soft in texture, unlike any hat I had ever seen . . . All trace of newness was long since gone from these things. The dust of difference was beaten into them . . . Yet a kind of magnificence remained and with it a hint of men and manners. (Schaefer 1984: 62)

Although Bob places much import upon the clothes, Shane's difference is demonstrably wrapped up in something else. The description of Stark Wilson, the gunfighter Fletcher hires to persuade the homesteaders to sell up their claims, provides a useful counterpoint:

> This stranger was something of a dude about his clothes. Still that did not mean anything. When he turned, the coat he wore matching his pants

flapped open . . . He was carrying two guns, big capable forty-fives, in holsters hung fairly low and forward. (Schaefer 1984: 228)

This description is significant because Wilson is immediately recognized as a type. Although his clothes may signal something different, as Shane's do, the guns and the holsters categorize him as gunfighter. Shane, at least initially, does not wear a gun, and thus in combination, the unusual clothing and the lack of the expected revolver, Schaefer articulates and encapsulates his difference. Unable to categorize Shane, Bob can only offer impressions: "then I forgot the clothes in the impact of the man himself" (Schaefer 1984: 63).

Much is made throughout the novel of Shane's power as a character in these impressionistic terms. Shortly after the Staretts take Shane in, Marion articulates her sense of him:

"But there's something about him. Something underneath the gentleness . . . Something . . ." Her voice trailed away.

"Mysterious?" suggested father.

"Yes, of course. Mysterious. But more than that. Dangerous."

"He's dangerous all right." Father said it in a musing way. Then he chuckled. "But not to us, my dear . . . in fact, I don't think you ever had a safer man in your house." (Schaefer 1984: 75)

This contradictory mix of characteristics is a succinct evocation of the expected qualities of Cold War heroic leadership, the danger/safety paradigm being an especially useful way of thinking about the man with a finger on the atomic button. This kind of analysis can be extended by thinking of Shane in terms of the technology of violence, and the control thereof. At the conclusion of the novel, after Shane has defeated Fletcher, Bob, now with a distinctly adult reminiscence recalls: "I would see the man and the weapon welded in the one indivisible deadliness. I would see the man and the tool, a good man and a good tool, doing what had to be done" (Schaefer 1984: 273).

Throughout, Shane is able to be all things to all people, to adapt his persona depending upon with whom he is interacting. So he can say the things a young boy wants to hear, he can talk Eastern fashion with Marion and, in the famous tree stump episode, he can speak Joe's language of work and struggle. Shane's passage through the novel is important. He arrives out of nowhere. The community takes a chance on him. Both Shane and the community have reservations. He doesn't fight back until the community mandates it. He is entirely democratic in his sensibilities until such times as he feels the need to take the reins for the good of the community, at which point he can act out the role of the heroic leader, sanctioned by the community, to avert the crisis. This quality of recognizable Cold War leadership is apparent in Shane's character from the early stages of the novel. At the beginning, after Bob has watched Shane's approach, Shane commends him:

> "You were watching me quite a spell coming up the road."
> It was not a question. It was a simple statement. "Yes . . ." I stammered. "Yes. I was."
> "Right," he said. "I like that. A man who watches what's going on around him will make his mark." (Schaefer 1984: 69)

As well as acting as an illustration of the way Shane is able to communicate in terms pleasing to a young boy, the exchange is also reminiscent of the Cold War adage, "the price of freedom is eternal vigilance." Shane's own vigilance is constant. He rearranges the dinner table seating, to the annoyance of Marion, so that he "was sitting opposite the door where he could directly confront anyone coming through it." He would never sit by a window, and would always make sure he is positioned with his back to a wall. Bob describes these measures as "part of his fixed alertness." He goes on, "He always wanted to know everything happening around him." He is ever alert to the coming of a crisis:

> This alertness could be noted, too, in the watch he kept, without appearing to make any special effort, on every approach to our place. He knew first when anyone was moving along the road and he would stop whatever he was doing to study carefully any passing rider. (Schaefer 1984: 123–4)

Shane's relationship with the community of homesteaders is crucial. He is involved in the genesis of a new community. It is only through his intervention that the group of homesteaders can come together and become a town. Indeed, there is something of the "big bang" about the genesis of this town: "There's been trouble brewing in this valley for a long spell now. Maybe it'll be good when it comes. Maybe it'll be bad. You just can't tell" (Schaefer 1984: 125).

This burgeoning new community is still very much up for grabs, reinforcing the existential nature of the narrative. The sense of the apocalyptic is strong, and in the mix of these forces is Shane:

> "He's like one of these here slow-burning fuses," I heard an old mule-skinner say one day. "Quiet and no sputtering. So quiet you forget it's burning. Then it sets off one hell of a blow-off of trouble when it touches powder. That's him." (Schaefer 1984: 125)

Shane is here described in terms of a nuclear option, invisible, silent but if put in the right position, lethal. The implied or veiled threat is an important one in Shane's character. Like Theodore Roosevelt walking softly but carrying a big stick, Shane does not carry a gun, although he owns one. Yet he is still perceived as an adept man of violence. Many of these traits are translated into the filming of Schaefer's novel. And it is this combination of characteristics, as presented in the film version in 1953 that contain the character's resonance with John F. Kennedy in the realm of American politics. This analysis will be taken up in Chapter 6, once we have explored the evolution of the cinematic Western.

CHAPTER FIVE

Western Film from Silent to Noir

The constellation of new means of expression and the new language represented by the development of film making technology and the birth of the cinematic art form, both predicated on the evocative notion of motion, of movement, combined with the culture and demography of turn-of-the-century America, and found in the Western narrative a resonance and contemporary relevance, establishing it, in the words of the French film critic Andre Bazin, as "the American cinema par excellence."

Despite the various versions of its closure, elements of the historical frontier did continue into the modern reality of the twentieth century. These elements not only found expression in literary fiction, but were readily exploited by the booming mass media. The exploits of infamous outlaws and bandits, like those that constituted the Wild Bunch Boys, (whose personnel included Butch Cassidy, Deaf Charlie Hanks, Bill Carver, Harvey Logan), and who continued to rob trains into the early years of the century, were presented in romantic terms, reminders of a colorful past. The blurring of fact and fantasy together with the traditional American sympathy for the underdog in the reporting of these figures, figures fighting back against the establishment (such conflict being a key element in Turner's conception of frontier character), was exacerbated by newspaper accounts. These accounts played to this sentiment of the audience and as such provided the ideal ground for the emergence of the myth of the outlaw as a heroic figure. In so doing, they also provided an arena for the exploration of such concepts as right and wrong, good and evil, law and order, which would underpin the American subconscious through the twentieth century. And it was the motion picture which would act as the most effective vehicle to extend and crystallize these values and institutions into the American century.

The emergence of film as an art form was predicated upon the development of new technology. New inventions had been appearing for some time, since the discovery of Camera Obscura in the 1600s to Etienne Gaspard Robertson's Phantasmagoria of 1798 and Emile Reynaud's Pantomime Lumineuses of 1892.

However, perhaps the most significant event, in technological terms, was Thomas Edison's patenting of the Kinetoscope in 1891. The Kinetoscope made it possible to view, through a narrow hole, a sequence of images which simulated movement. It is important to note that Edison's drive to create moving pictures was not an end in itself. In 1878, he patented the phonograph, which made sound recording a reality. The next step was to have moving pictures to accompany his records, to produce, in effect, talkies. Moving pictures then were a by-product of his development of sound.

In its formative stages, cinema existed as a scientific or educational medium; those involved in its development were concerned more with the ability to reproduce the illusion of movement, rather than developing it as an outlet for artistic expression. It is an interesting side note that had it not been for the failure of the Edison Company to assemble the Kinetoscopes, the technology would have been unveiled at the Chicago World's Fair in 1893, the site of much resonance for the development of the American Western. Still, the Western was to play a huge role in the development of American film.

On 23 April 1896, the Koster and Bial Music Hall in New York held the first showing of "moving pictures." Edison's Vitascope was the invention of Thomas Armat, the rights to the manufacture and marketing of the machine Edison purchased when it seemed other inventions and inventors might exclude him from the market he had himself created. The program consisted of six films projected to a large audience and they were described in the *New York Mail and Express* and the *New York Daily News* in these terms:

> The first view showed two dancers holding between and in front of them an umbrella and dancing the while. The position of the umbrella was constantly changed, and every change was smooth and even, and the steps of the dancing could be perfectly followed. Then came the waves, showing a scene at Dover pier after a stiff blow. This was by far the best view shown, and had to be repeated many times. As in the umbrella dance there was absolutely no hitch. One could look far out to sea and pick out a particular wave swelling and undulating and growing bigger and bigger until it struck the end of the pier . . . One could imagine the people running away.

And:

> This was followed by a burlesque boxing bout, in which the contestants were a very tall, thin man and a very short, stout one. The little fellow was knocked down several times and the movements of the boxers were well represented. A scene from "A Milk White Flag" was next shown, in which soldiers and a military band perform some complex evolutions. A group

representing Uncle Sam, John Bull, Venezuela and the Monroe Doctrine got a good welcome from the patriotic. The last picture was a serpentine dancer. The color effects were used in this and it was one of the most effective in the series. (quoted in Musser 2002: 15)

These reviews of the first screening reveal something of the nature and intention of film at its point of origin. What captures the audience's attention is the projection of movement; the repeated references to the fluidity and smoothness of the projected images emphasize this. It is apparent that these films were little more than novelty items, designed to demonstrate the technology, to generate a reaction, rather than existing for their own sake as a new art or narrative technique. Indeed it is telling that the entertainments depicted were part of the vaudeville tradition, a tradition that cinema would ultimately supplant. However, at this stage, such locations of popular culture as vaudeville houses integrated the medium into its programs. Vaudeville houses catered usually for more affluent metropolitan audiences, willing to pay a minimum of 25 cents for a performance. Cheaper, and as a result, more popular venues, such as temporarily erected tents at fairs or rented store fronts (the origin of the nickelodeon), meant that the audience for cinema was from the outset broad and not limited to one class.

Within a decade of the first projection of motion pictures in New York in 1896, film established itself as the dominant mass entertainment medium. In the beginning, though, film continued the trend of making audiences marvel at the effect of the technology, producing travelogues, conveying a sense of motion by placing cameras on trains pulling through stations, showing audiences faraway places or continuing to film theatrical performances. The idea of creating prolonged narratives would come later. There would be ultimately three elements that constituted the film industry: exhibition, production and distribution. In this early period of cinema's development, those engaged with film as a business were developing the exhibition element of the industry, but had not yet grasped the opportunities, or more importantly, the potential profits to be made through developing the distribution and production side of cinema. This development, stimulated by the need of audiences for something more substantial, the businessmen to maintain the audience and experimentation by film-makers to create more realistic and dramatic works, led to the watershed production in 1903 of *The Great Train Robbery*, by Edwin S. Porter.

Porter, after a stint in the Navy began working for Raff & Gammon, the company that marketed Edison's Vitascope. As a result, Porter was one of the projectionists at the historic first screening of motion pictures in New York in 1896. He began making films in 1899, photographing news events for the most part. At the beginning of 1903, he made *The Life of an American Fireman*, a film that was crude, but represented for film historians the first time a motion picture was created in the cutting room. In the same year, Porter filmed an ambitious adaptation of Harriet Beecher Stowe's *Uncle Tom's Cabin*. However, it is for *The Great Train Robbery* that Porter is remembered. It is an important film for two reasons. It is the first American film to use sophisticated editing techniques to convey a more complex, multifaceted story, cutting between a number of locations in space and time, making it arguably the first example of American narrative cinema. The second reason for its importance lies in the fact that within its twelve-minute running time, while by no means the first cinematic Western (the Edison Company produced a large amount of documentary footage with Western settings for the Kinetoscope from 1894, including shots of Buffalo Bills' Wild West, cowboy and Indian scenes and, more specifically, in 1898, the company produced two actuality films, *Poker at Dawson City* and *Cripple Creek Bar-room*) it effectively established the form, structure and, to an extent, given its popularity, the audience for the cinematic Western. The film tells, via a series of thirteen tableaux shots, the story of a gang holding up a train and subsequently being tracked down and killed by a posse. The film was made, not in the West, but in New Jersey but otherwise it exhibits a comprehensive list of tropes that have come to be identified with the Western: outlaws, a train robbery, fights, chases on horseback, gunplay, and even dancing (a recurrent feature in the West of John Ford). John Lenihan offers an interesting observation in relation to the look of the film for modern audiences. Although the film is clearly an evocation of nineteenth century America, *The Great Train Robbery* was for audiences at the time of its release "also a contemporary crime thriller" (Lenihan in Aquila 1996: 110). For a number of years, *The Great Train Robbery* was the nickelodeon's most widely exhibited picture, and it is the film said to have ensured the permanence of the movies. It also acted as a model for the many one-reelers that attempted to emulate the film's success. *The Great Train Robbery* was certainly more complex than any of the half-dozen films that constituted the program at the Koster and Bial Music Hall in 1896, and even among the experiments in the form that had preceded it, Porter's film is a huge leap forward for the possibilities of dramatic narrative cinema. However, *The Great Train Robbery* was lacking in one key area: character. Porter uses long shots throughout with the result that the actors in the film are largely indistinguishable, mere ciphers for action rather than defined, even identifiable individuals. One of the actors who appeared in Porter's film would change that. Bronco Billy Anderson (formerly Max Aronson) would be pivotal in the development of characterization in the Western.

BRONCO BILL ANDERSON AND WILLIAM S. HART

G. "Bronco Billy" Anderson should have been one of the mounted outlaws in Porter's film. However, having no ranch skills, he could barely ride and lost the role because of an inability to stay on a horse, and was demoted to playing a train passenger. However, Anderson was determined and set about acquiring the necessary abilities to become a cowboy. Kevin Brownlow's description of Anderson is illuminating: "[his] inclinations were for the theater; he believed in a strong, simple story, played by colorful, easily recognizable characters, true to melodrama. Nevertheless, he was a pioneer who insisted that his Westerns had to be made in the West" (Brownlow 1979: 249).

Beginning in 1910, with *Bronco Billy's Redemption*, Anderson established himself as a prolific and prominent personality in the Western, making nearly four hundred films in the course of his career. The Bronco Billy films were not a series of connected narratives; he could play an outlaw in one film, a good man in another, he may die at the end of a picture, return undamaged in the next. However, he did tend to play characters on a similar redemptive arc, from outlaw to reformed citizen. In this way he formalized some of the characteristics of the good-bad man character which would be such a familiar figure in later Westerns. His Westerns were not lavish affairs. His costumes were utilitarian, and the focus in the films was on character rather than spectacle. In perhaps his most important contribution to the genre, Anderson set the precedent of identifying an actor with a certain character and generic setting and in this sense was one of American cinema's first stars, and was undeniably the first Western hero. By 1916, however, Anderson's career was effectively over. He attempted a return in 1917, but another star had risen to prominence. As Anderson himself says, "When I came back, they were idolizing Bill Hart, and it was sort of a second beginning. The Westerns I made were good, but they were not good enough to compete with Bill Hart's pictures. So I gave them up" (Brownlow 1979: 252).

Hart was a classically trained theater actor who felt an affinity with the West as a result of an itinerant childhood. His theatrical career, which began in 1899, saw him perform in stage versions of the *Squaw Man*, *The Virginian* and *The Trail of the Lonesome Pine* among the more usual Shakespearean roles. He did not enter the film business until he was 49, in 1914, when he began working for his friend, Thomas H. Ince, an important producer and director whose innovations as head of the Miller 101 Bison Ranch studio, or Inceville as it came to be known, spurred the Western to greater levels of sophistication. Brownlow offers an interesting parallel when he suggests that "the importance of Inceville to the Western might almost be compared to the importance of Detroit to the automobile" (Brownlow 1979: 257). From a couple of bad guy roles in Ince-produced two-reelers, Hart moved toward starring roles and, eventually, directed and sometimes wrote his own films. At the core of Hart's screen persona and the narratives he produced is a deep love of the American West, both in terms of landscape and the values it embodied. Indeed this love, based in his own experiences as a child, meant that Hart's Westerns had a reality, an adult tone and a lack of romance that would set them apart. Hart's West was not a glamorous place, his settings were stark and unadorned. The cowboys were dressed unostentatiously, although he did himself have a distinctive look. However, as Brownlow details, he was able to "justify every last stitch of it," even if his justifications might not be entirely convincing (Brownlow 1979: 267–8). Regardless of any questions about authenticity, audiences believed in Hart and the accuracy of his portrayal was not questioned, even by cowboys. Though Hart believed himself to be accurate in his depictions of Western history and culture, he, perhaps unsurprisingly, was not much more accurate than any other film maker. However, there was a seriousness at the core of Hart's characters and narratives, and also a sense of purpose. Hart was concerned with his function as a role model, so much so that he produced books for boys that emphasized frontier values. In one of them he writes, "I suppose it must be fine for a boy to have something to look up to. A regular hero. It must be healthy for him, and give him a high mark to shoot at" (Brownlow 1979: 270).

In common with Broncho Billy Anderson, Hart played characters moving toward redemption, early versions of the good-bad man that John Wayne will crystallize by the end of the 1930s. This moral dimension to these early cowboy characters and narratives is crucial. The morality displayed in the films of Anderson and Hart have a wider impact in America in the early twentieth century, and further explain cinema's increasing cultural dominance.

THE RISE OF CINEMA

The nickelodeon, a venue specifically designed for the exhibition of films, appeared in 1905. This coincided, at the turn of the century, with a far-reaching social phenomenon: a fresh wave of mass immigration to the United States. In many ways, these early films were the ideal entertainment for mass immigrant communities. In the first instance, they were simple, uncomplicated films, accessible to all, regardless of education or literacy. Secondly, given the five cents admission charge that gave the nickelodeon its name, the movies were an inexpensive activity for a group that would likely have very little money to spare. Finally, and perhaps most importantly, they were silent so there were no linguistic barriers to engaging with the medium. This immigrant context contributed enormously to establishing film as the foremost affordable, accessible entertainment for the masses and in so doing provided the foundation for the future of the motion picture industry. Immigration peaked in the period 1902–3, and movies were, for these reasons, to become a major socializing agent. Frederick Jackson Turner had looked at an American future without the frontier, and was anxious about what would now Americanize Americans. Perhaps the movies held the answer. No longer did an individual become an American as a result of tough interaction with the frontier. The nickelodeon allowed the immigrant to absorb the cultural values of America, to see them in action, from the comparative luxury of a nickelodeon seat.

In order to be effective as a socializing medium, however, the narrative content of film had to become increasingly sophisticated. This development of more sophisticated narrative style altered the status of the nickelodeon itself within American society. Film in its earliest forms had been frowned upon as a corrupting influence, especially by religious leaders who lost congregations to the movies. However, in keeping with the prevailing progressive mood that marked turn-of-the-century America, movies began to project a moral sense and a set of American values which the audience should aspire to. In this way then, although films were silent, there was no doubt that they had the capacity to preach, and the films of this era did acquire a decided moral tone and didactic purpose. On these grounds, social reformers came to approve of nickelodeons as "places of relief for the poor, of enlightenment for the illiterate, of dissemination of culture to the nation at large." As a result, movies became increasingly responsive to the social conditions of modern America and more effective in reflecting them. By 1908, between eight and ten thousand nickelodeons were operating in the country. The power of motion pictures to transmit American myths was not lost on contemporaries of silent film. In 1915, the poet Vachel Lindsay observed of the effect of motion pictures on immigrants:

> He sees alien people and begins to understand how like they are to him; he sees courage and aspiration and agony, and begins to understand himself. He begins to feel himself a brother in a race that is led by many dreams. (quoted in Jowett 1976: 42)

Between 1908 and 1914, the American film industry was marked by two developments. First was the establishment of the Motion Picture Patents Company Trust. The Trust was essentially an economic cartel that sought to monopolize the burgeoning new industry. Its stated aim was to stabilize the business, but the Trust, made up of production companies and distributors, wanted to restrict movie making to only those companies within its number. To this end, they made an arrangement with Kodak to limit access to the raw material of moviemaking, film stock. Furthermore, they worked to prevent the growth of independent film production through litigation. There were two significant outcomes from the actions of the Trust. Firstly, "outlaw" independent companies continued to produce movies. Secondly, and connectedly, the independents discovered Hollywood. Hollywood became a refuge for independent film-makers from the prohibitive and restrictive activities of the Trust, which was based back East. In an image resonant of Turner, to escape the Trust, producers and, indeed, American film, went West. The Trust's attempt to monopolize the industry was destroyed, effectively by 1914, and legally in 1917. The legacy of the Trust though, was, ironically, to establish the independents who escaped to California as the major power-brokers and players in the industry. In Hollywood, five major studios were established and came to dominate the industry: Universal Pictures, Paramount Pictures, Fox Film Corporation, Metro-Goldwyn-Mayer, and Warner Bros. Another effect of the Trust was the emergence of the star system. That is not to say that the studios controlled by the Trust had given any of their actors special prominence. In keeping with their business mentality, they did not want actors to become popular and demand more money or control. However, to compete with the Trust, the independents had to come up with new ways to sell their product, and from this need the "star" as a means of attracting attention to their films developed. It was to be an incredibly successful promotional tool. By 1919 an estimated quarter of a million dollars annually was being spent on correspondence between stars and fans. The Trust's fears were proved correct also. As stars became popular with movies audiences, they pushed for ever more control of their careers. Most famously, Mary Pickford, Douglas Fairbanks, Charlie Chaplin and director D. W. Griffith formed United Artists in 1919 as a means of asserting a greater recognition of their contribution to and independence within the emerging Hollywood studio system. By the mid 1920s stars had indeed assumed a pivotal importance within the industry.

The second development in this period was the introduction of the feature film. The director D. W. Griffith was the figure most responsible for establishing the feature film as central to the movie industry's creative and entertainment enterprise. He was responsible for innovations in the language and vocabulary of film, the creative use of film-making technology and for producing the film that became the model for cinematic narratives, *Birth of a Nation*, released in February 1915 and based on Thomas F. Dixon Jr's novel, *The Clansman* (1905). This was the film that established movies not only as a permanent artistic medium but as a permanent industry. Its influence would be great. *Birth of a Nation* was an epic in every sense of the word. With a running time of three hours, it was the longest American film to date. It extended the audience for film at the expense of the theatre, established and justified the practice of raised admission prices, and went on to gross over $13 million, making it the most successful movie until the advent of the talkies in 1927. *Birth of a Nation* was also epic in its conception of American history. Regardless of its racism and biases, the film demonstrated cinema as a powerful medium with which to represent the nation's past. In all of these ways, *Birth of a Nation* was a revolutionary event in the history of film and film-making, and one that impacted on the Western.

THE SILENT WESTERN EPICS

As an element in the process of turning history into myth, the silent Westerns made a vital contribution. Despite the best efforts and repeated claims by figures like Hart, silent film perpetuated the myths of the West. Yet, the silent Western is simultaneously very closely connected to the West of history in a way that we have seen before, notably in relation to Buffalo Bill's Wild West. Historically, the production of these films overlaps the decline of the Old West, so that it is at once an instrument for mythologizing *and* recording a dying frontier. Indeed it often blurs the distinctions between history and myth in the personages of cowboys-turned-actors, outlaws-turned-directors, and Western landscapes-turned-movie sets. As previously discussed, the silent film was a vehicle well suited for the transmission of myths to American audiences, a large constituent of which were recent immigrants. It is also worthy of note that by privileging action over language, the medium of silent film particularly suited the myth of the West.

The silent Western epics, in relation to the earlier forms of the genre, had an ambition and scale that moved the genre beyond the melodrama and simplicity of those that had gone before. These were films that had a distinct interest in representing, again with the gloss of accuracy, the history and culture of the frontier. The first epic of significance was *The Covered Wagon*, produced by James Cruze in 1923. The film articulates the twin impulse of romantic myth and a more authentic vision in its recreation of the events of 1848, and the movement of pioneers to Oregon. For Cruze this was a very personal project. Having grown up in Utah, where the movie would be filmed, he remembered first-hand watching the procession of covered wagons as a youngster. This memory, combined with stories his grandfather recounted about his own experience of this period, underpin the film's claims of authenticity. The film is undeniably romantic in its vision of the West and the pioneers, but the reality of making the film connects the mythic with the historical. In order to make the picture as realistic as possible, and to the scale he intended, Cruze advertised for Conestoga wagons. Those willing to lend the production their wagons, which were already heirlooms, artifacts of a bygone age, were paid two dollars a day.

Many of the wagons recreated on film the journey they had made for real a few decades ago. This pattern is apparent elsewhere in the film. In one of the most memorable passages in *The Covered Wagon*, the pioneers have to traverse a river. The logistical problems faced by the pioneers were faced in a similar manner by the actors and crew. For example, the wagons proved too heavy on an initial attempt to cross, and two of the horses drowned. The crew had to problem-solve as the pioneers had before them. They came up with the solution of unloading all the gear, fixing barrels to the sides of the wagons for buoyancy, and firing rifles to startle the horses and so pull the wagons and cattle across. This meeting of history and myth gives the film its tone and perhaps underlies the film's success. The critical and commercial reception for the picture was enormous, and *The Covered Wagon* is generally credited with creating a new direction for the Western, with revitalizing the form. An indication of this can be seen in the subsequent production of similarly scaled Westerns: in 1923 around fifty Westerns were made, but a year from *The Covered Wagon*'s release, three times that figure were produced.

The Iron Horse was among the most significant of the Westerns produced in its immediate aftermath. John Ford's epic recreated the construction of the transcontinental railroad, and again, the focus on historical detail and authentic representation was at the core of the production. In a manner similar to Cruze's epic, the film is generally a romanticized account, but the making of the picture embodied fascinating parallels with the actuality of the period. One such example is Ford's use of thirty five Chinese men as extras in the film, men who had actually worked on the old railroad crews some fifty years earlier. This connection to the West of history was further recreated away from the camera. The production was based in Nevada, and during the winter. At the time, the production of *The Iron Horse* represented the largest logistical undertaking for a location shoot in American film history. The conditions were akin to those endured by the previous generation heading West: the train was unheated, and so the actors and crew were forced to live in the sets they built, turning Hollywood artifice into reality, and in keeping with this reality, the community surrounding the production behaved accordingly with reports of fights, conflict and even bootleggers on the set. The critical reception was glowing, and the historical value of the film lay at the center. Critics hailed the film's depiction of one of the greatest national achievements and the way it embodied American values and characteristics. As a *New York Times* editorial declared,

> this ambitious production dwelt trenchantly upon the indomitable energy, resourcefulness, and courage of those who spanned the continent with steel. Little does one realize in these days of modern comforts, the tirelessness of those Americans who shed their life's blood with a smile in the race to get

first to the goal with rails and ties . . . an instructive and inspiring film, one which should make every American proud. (quoted in Pratt 1973: 3)

The audience, however, was equally enthusiastic, though they almost certainly took something different from the film, marveling at the scale, action and drama of the picture. In this way, *The Iron Horse* inaugurated another direction for the Western, one that led towards the action-packed and eventually star-studded reenactments of Western narratives, narratives where history was less important than drama.

The last of these Western epics was produced in 1926 by Henry King. *The Winning of Barbara Worth* portrayed on a magnificent scale the reclamation of the desert for farming in southern California's Imperial Valley, one of the last great pioneer endeavors in the settling of the West, and in that way captures the transition from old West to new. As Brownlow notes, where the other films were set in the nineteenth century, "this is an epic of twentieth-century pioneering" (Brownlow 1979: 245). The movie was made in Nevada's Black Rock Desert, where a tent city was built to accommodate the cast and crew. Yet King felt that they, like those involved in Ford's production, had suffered hardships equal to the experience of the original settlers, including severe temperature changes, sandstorms and baby tornadoes which destroyed sets and caused thousands of dollars of damage. Such was the scale of the production that the inhabitants of the local towns were hired as extras during filming. Brownlow recounts the description of these extras by the editor of Motion Picture Magazine who visited the location:

> There were mountaineers, cowboys, Indians, trappers and ranchers of every description and all in all the queerest looking specimens I have ever encountered. They not only looked and acted their part, but they *were* the part. (quoted in Brownlow 1979: 245)

The film is another documentary recreation of Western history, the climax of which is the devastating flood which occurred in 1906, when the Colorado River burst its banks, wiped out numerous desert settlements, and created the Salton Sea.

The silent Westerns recreated and represented historical moments that lay in the very recent American past and that makes them, in their blurring of the real and the simulated, significant and fascinating documents. These films hired the West's real cowboys and railroad builders to reenact these roles on celluloid. They recorded the last great cattle drives in the region as a backdrop to fiction. In this way they stand as evocative historical documents of value beyond mere entertainment.

THE WESTERN IN THE 1930S AND 1940S

Given the quality of these films, and their huge critical and commercial appeal, it is perhaps surprising that the cinematic Western was about to become, for a time, quite literally a thing of the past. It was to do so for a number of reasons. In the first place, the American public, and consequently the film industry, discovered a new brand of hero. Charles Lindberg made his transatlantic flight in 1927, constructing a heroic type whose daring is associated with modern machinery and modern society, rather than the values and primitive char-acteristics and skills of the frontiersman. The technological advance of the talkies – the first of which, Warner Bros. *The Jazz Singer*, also appeared in 1927 – would aid in the genre's undoing for a time as many of the cowboy stars in the silent period were dismissed as unsuitable for speaking roles. However, the Western would suffer most significantly because of the Great Depression which followed the Wall Street crash of October 1929.

The Depression era marks a significant fault line for the United States and the cinematic Western. In this traumatic time, the resolute, certain hero of the Western practically disappeared from the Hollywood landscape. In his place there emerged a new kind of cinematic hero, or more precisely anti-hero, a figure who emerged from the cycle of gangster movies produced at the beginning of the 1930s. On the surface the ethically constant cowboy is at the opposite end of the moral spectrum from the criminality of the gangster. And yet, the gangster is in many ways connected to the Western hero, containing elements of individualism, violence, outlawry, masculinity and similar codes of dress and generic patterns in form and narrative. Obviously, in almost every instance, these connections to the frontier hero are perverted. The unwavering morality of Gary Cooper's Virginian in the 1929 version of Owen Wister's novel, with a rigid morality that would allow him to hang his friend for cattle rustling, without any qualms, simply because it was right, seemed suddenly anachronistic. As a consequence of the Eighteenth Amend-ment, the prohibition of alcohol, which was introduced in 1919 and repealed in 1933, the early 1930s became a time when a large section of the American population had embraced illegality simply by taking a drink. Certainly, the organized crime culture of violence, that replaced the honor of the gunfight with the random atrocity of the drive-by shooting or the massacre in a restaurant, gave the lie to the simple assurances of the Hollywood Western. Cinema audiences flocked to see the gangster, and for a few hours live vicariously the American Dream enacted by these attractive criminals. That "only gangsters could make upward mobility believable tells much about how legitimate institutions had failed – but that mobility was still at the core of what American held to be the American dream" (Bergman 1972: 7).

In this sense, the gangster is simply updating the traditional American celebration of individual achievement. Criminality and enterprise, not hard work and enterprise, became the gangster's road to success; the goal was the creation of a crime empire instead of the homestead, but the dynamics are much the same. The darker aspects of these movies were not to be forgotten even though the cycle of the gangster movie in this pure form lasted only five or six years. The modifications that the gangster made to the American hero are unquestionably present in the characters of *Jesse James* (1939) and John Wayne's Ringo Kid, in John Ford's *Stagecoach* (1939), the main protagonists in the Westerns that reinvigorated the genre at the beginning of the 1940s. However, as the decade progressed, the mood of optimism and confidence evaporated. Whereas a few years earlier the outlaw had been glamorized, the means by which the frontier was tamed were now beginning to be questioned in a number of films from William Wellman's 1943 adaptation of Walter Van Tilburg Clark's *The Ox-Bow Incident* onwards. Moreover, by the end of the decade, the influence of psychology and film noir would come to throw their shadows over the genre.

These films reintroduced the big themes of the Western, of how the West had been won, and they celebrated Americanness. In their own way they were part of a general response to the Second World War in America, with the nation simultaneously looking inward and celebrating the fight for freedom in Europe and the Far East. If the gangster movie reflected a darkening cultural picture, American involvement in World War II lent this darkness a social immediacy. Although not as deeply traumatized by the Second World War as it was to be by the Vietnam War, the Western necessarily adapted to emerging new attitudes. Along with the psychological trauma for the nation, a significant effect of this period had been the emigration of European artists, film-makers, and intellectuals escaping the emerging evil of German and Italian fascism:

> Immediately after assuming power, the National Socialists purged a once internationally recognized industry of its artistic vanguard and the greater portion of its professional craft and technical expertise. More than 1,500 film-makers – many of whom were Jews as well as progressives and in- dependents – would flee Germany. (Rentschler 1996: 374)

Bringing with them continental styles and forms, new directions that would be of paramount importance in the definition of the visual aspect of American film noir, as well as an awareness of, in particular, Freudian psychoanalysis, which itself would contribute much to the atmosphere and ideology of this cinematic style, the influx is of profound significance. Indeed, by the middle of the forties, as a consequence of the flight of European artists from restrictive fascist regimes, the influence of psychology and film noir was being reflected in the genre of the Western.

Once the initial euphoric mood of victory had subsided, cultural production reflected a new feeling of general disillusionment and cynicism amongst Americans. Tom Englehardt identifies this feeling as one of "triumphalist despair":

> [Post-war society] grasped the pleasures of victory culture as an act of faith, and the horrors of nuclear culture as an act of faithless mockery, and held both the triumph and the mocking horror close without necessarily experiencing them as contraries. In this way, they caught the essence of the adult culture of that time, which – despite America's dominant economic and military position in the world – was one not of triumph, but of triumphalist despair. (Englehardt 1995: 9)

Hollywood played its own part in all of this, an effect of its role as wartime propagandist. The ideal images of America as "white picket fences, cozy bungalows, and patiently loyal families and sweethearts – a pure, democratic society in which Jews, blacks, Italians, Irish, Poles and WASP farm boys could all live and work together"(Cook 1990: 463) were beginning to show themselves as the necessary illusions that they were. Pre-war and certainly during the war, Hollywood produced this type of escapist, socially cohesive and positivist entertainment. There were some exceptions, most notably *I'm a Fugitive From a Chain Gang* (1932), *Fury* (1936), *You Only Live Once* (1937), *Citizen Kane* (1941) and *The Maltese Falcon* (1941), but such films were unusual. Post-war disenchantment stirred in the audience a need for a different type of film.

In 1946 Hollywood had much to celebrate. Victory had opened up huge markets in the war-torn countries of Western Europe and Southeast Asia. Hollywood had already resumed its economic domination of the international film market through its position as the only film industry capable of producing, in sufficient quantity, good-quality films. Domestic audiences eager for diversion had grown to reach a peak of almost two thirds of the population. Hollywood had, then, a vested interest in maintaining the status quo. However, a number of significant obstructions to this began to appear.

A protracted strike in 1945, combined with inflation, led to a 25 per cent pay increase for studio personnel the following year. Hollywood's most important and most lucrative overseas market, Great Britain, levied a huge 75 per cent protective tax on all foreign film profits reducing the American film industry's annual British revenue from $68 million in 1946 to $17 million the following year. Other Commonwealth nations and European countries enforced similar measures. With the end of the War Production Board's price controls in 1946, the industry's major supplier of film stock (Eastman and DuPont) raised their prices, thereby adding $2.5 million to the annual costs for the studios. Most devastating of all though was the adjudication of the anti-trust suit begun by the federal government against five major studios and three minor studios in 1938. This resulted in the "Paramount Decrees" or "consent decrees" in May of 1948. Essentially, these were court orders that forced the companies to divest themselves of the lucrative exhibition circuits, bringing an end to block booking and the guaranteed box-office receipts this practice had created. This consequently signaled the death knell of the studio system, but more importantly, and more positively, a new period of re-structuring and re-organization that would profoundly effect post-war American films.

Production budgets were cut by as much as 50 per cent. Expensive ventures such as costume epics and A-grade musicals were abandoned. Yet this cost-cutting had a vitalizing effect upon the industry. Lavish production values gave way to high quality scripts. The meticulous crafting of each scene of a film, primarily to avoid wasteful retakes, created an unprecedented level of artistry in American cinema. Films that could be shot on location with a small cast and crew were given priority, and it was this style of sparse film-making that lent itself to a deeper, darker realism, a concern for psychological and social issues. This darkening of tone was compounded by the reliance upon a smaller and often-used body of film-makers who now, without the restraints of the studio system, could create films that were more individually expressive. Similarly, the emerging influence of method acting had the effect of allowing actors to take the notion of performance seriously, which in turn impacted upon the very nature and tone of American film. In the silent cinema, acting was often simply gestural, meaning was broadly conveyed. However, with the advent of sound and more complex techniques of film-making, acting moved towards the more naturalistic. This style of acting found its place in America in the 1940s in the Actors' Studio, founded by Elia Kazan and directed by Lee Strasberg.

This combination of a general post-war disenchantment and necessary economic restriction created a resurgence of the genre, or more properly the cycle, of the "social-consciousness" or "problem" picture. The subject of these films would be racism, political or moral corruption, alcoholism, and juvenile delinquency. However important the themes of this cycle of films were, the visual style was equally, if not more, important. Initially, the movement away from the studio allowed for a more documentary feel to the films in the vein of Italian neo-realism. However, there began to emerge a visual style that used both the studio and the location in attempts to depict the rotten core of American life. This was film noir, a name created by French critics in around 1946 upon seeing American films for the first time since the imposition of the Vichy regime and its subsequent ban upon the import of American mass culture in 1940. In some of these films they sensed a new mood of cynicism, darkness and despair. The term film noir derived from the "serie Noire" detective novels that were newly arriving in translation and which were immensely popular in France at the time, encompassing the work of hard-boiled writers such as Dashiell Hammett and Raymond Chandler. These were writers whose works were being adapted into film noir, films concerned with sleazy milieus, grim atmospheres, and a pervading threat of violence that would inevitably and graphically explode.

The pre-war and wartime American preoccupations of love and purity gave way to depictions of greed, lust, corruption and cruelty. At the center of these films lay, however simply portrayed, psychological analyses of criminals, rotten officials and decent people caught up in traps laid for them by a corrupt social order. In this sense, film noir is a "cinema of moral anxiety," the post-war audience able to relate to the conditions in which they found themselves, conditions that ran contrary to those which Hollywood had previously promised in its recurring evocations of the American Dream. "The classic film noir moods [are] of claustrophobia, paranoia, despair and nihilism" (Place and Petersen in Nichols 1976: 327). The moral instability of this world was translated into a visual style of wide-angle lenses, distorted close-ups, of the angular use of light and shadow, of anti-traditional directorial style, of psychological suggestion, character and shadow in the same frame, yet seemingly unconnected. The noir style is a style of distortion and disorientation that paralleled a world in moral chaos. The most important historic feature of film noir is that it held up a mirror to contemporary America in a way that had no precedent.

The American film industry, then, reached the 1950s in an unprecedented mood of introspection, examining and questioning its values and meaning in much the same way as the American people had been forced to do. And this, as Andrew Bergman points out while exploring American film and the Great Depression, is not surprising: "in any period of stress, there are certain tensions which permeate a society and affect the majority of its functioning members, artists and movie makers" (Bergman 1972: xiv).

It is vital to recognize that the Western developed not because of any great intuitive film-makers who could read the national unconscious, but rather because these film-makers felt the very same tensions, were exposed to the very same fears and stimuli as the rest of society and consequently displayed these concerns through their own medium. The Western stood in the middle ground between exploring the concerns of the film-maker (and necessarily the public) and the need to make a profit, to re-create versions of situations that had been popularly, and thus financially, accepted previously.

WESTERN NOIR

This movement toward a darker tone pervaded many genres; it is as visible in *It's a Wonderful Life* (Frank Capra, 1946) as it is in *Notorious* (Alfred Hitchcock, 1946). Most significantly, this film noir style and concern is observable in such Westerns as *The Ox-Bow Incident*, *The Outlaw* (Howard Hughes, 1943), *My Darling Clementine* (John Ford, 1946), and *Red River* (Howard Hawks, 1948). This noir style manifested itself differently in each of these movies. *The Ox-Bow Incident* has a noirish concern with crime and punishment; Jane Russell's character in *The Outlaw* is related to the darker female roles that noir specialized in, specifically the sexually dangerous femme fatale; *My Darling Clementine* is a Western that aims for a more realistic, naturalistic style, eschewing many of the traditional narrative conventions in favor of an all together more direct approach to the material; *Red River* depicts the obsessive nature of man in the Wayne character, as a rancher who begins a cattle drive with a tough-minded determination but leans increasingly toward megalomania.

The 1950s were a particularly traumatic period for the Western. Its territory was being invaded by the "alien" genres of science fiction and horror. Still more damagingly, the small-screen Western was becoming ever more popular and hence common. At the same time, the serial Western and the "B" movie were declining, culminating in the closure in 1958 of Republic Studios, a smaller studio that had specialized in such generically simplistic Western fare – Republic did produce some notable films including John Ford's *Rio Grande* (1950) and *The Quiet Man* (1952) and Nicholas Ray's *Johnny Guitar* (1954). With the arrival of television, the cinematic Western lost the guaranteed box office returns that "A" Westerns had enjoyed since *Stagecoach* and *Jesse James* in 1939, and on through the 1940s; a studio investing in a Western was no longer assured of a healthy return on its investment. This placed the Western alongside any other genre in terms of preference. Yet amid these problematic assaults upon it, the Western in the fifties was at its most interesting. The easy, obvious narratives of the early forties developed into increasingly ambiguous narratives where the hero would question himself and the society that surrounds him, or he would come to be driven by obsessions only dimly understood. Put simplistically, the pre-war Errol Flynn became a film noir James Stewart. Flynn's characters in *Dodge City* (1939) and *San Antonio* (1945) are traditionally heroic, confident and moral. Stewart's characters, especially in his collaborations with Anthony Mann, *The Man from Laramie* (1955), *The Naked Spur* (1953) and *Bend of the River* (1952), are obsessive characters, fallible and angst-ridden.

Westerns, like other genres, became aware then of social issues and reflected them for an audience of a period filled with unease. In contrast to the simplicity of most early forties Westerns, the fifties Western is dark and complicated, yet the form retains a malleability and an openness to narrative and thematic possibility that allows it to remain recognizable and testifies to the genre's vitality. A selection of Westerns made in 1950 offers a good illustration of the genre's flexibility: traditional action Westerns such as Errol Flynn's *Montana* (Ray Enright), and *Rocky Mountain* (William Keighly) and Gary Cooper's *Dallas* (Stuart Heisler) are produced. In the same year, Delmer Daves' *Broken Arrow* radically alters the genre's treatment of Native Americans. Also in 1950, Anthony Mann directs James Stewart in *Winchester '73*, a mature revenge Western. John Ford directs the Western he would claim as his personal favorite, *Wagon Master*. John Wayne appears in Ford's *Rio Grande*, the final installment of their unofficial Cavalry trilogy. And this openness continued for much of the decade.

Thus the Western reached the 1950s in a contradictory manner, both traditionally mythic and moodily introspective. Against this troubled and sometimes contradictory backdrop, Hollywood fashioned many of its finest Westerns. And it is the Cold War that guarantees the genre's political immediacy and sense of purpose.

CHAPTER SIX

The Western and the Cold War: the Gunfighter, Heroic Leadership and Political Culture

It has long been recognized that movies reflect and comment upon the society that creates and consumes them. In 1939, in an early history of Hollywood film, Lewis Jacobs acknowledged that films "reflect . . . the changing temper of the times." The Western has a special capacity to offer this kind of reflection, for a number of reasons. In the first place, no other genre is more American than the Western, more engaged with such fundamental American concepts as individualism, progress, democracy. As a genre it maintained an almost continuous popularity that spans much of the twentieth century. In this way it has remained relevant to aspirations and anxieties of an ever-changing America. As one critic notes, "surely no twentieth century American needs to have the Western's importance as a cultural form demonstrated to him. Uncountable Westerns mark the course of American history." Approaching the Western as the product of a particular social, cultural and political climate unlocks the importance of the form for American society and nowhere is this more fruitful than in the Westerns produced during the anxieties of the Cold War.

Infiltration by Communism, the subversion of the American way, even its destruction by political sabotage masterminded from Moscow, represented the most obvious, certainly the most tangible, threat in this period. Hollywood's depictions of the repulsion of the other, usually Native Americans, and the heroic defense of the American way, provided by far the most numerous cinematic articulations of Western mythology. These movies acted as a focus, recycling depictions of possible resolutions to a pressing concern for Americans. The other or the alien in the Western was vanquished, leaving the American way to be projected as the right way and inviolable. The Western's mythology and perceived historical basis reflected subconsciously upon a psyche yearning for the simple solutions of a time when similar fears had arisen and been resolved. Thus, the Western offered the American people hope in the form of victories of American tradition over previous encounters with an external, alien force. Frederick Jackson Turner articulates this archetypal American conflict in *The Significance of the Frontier in American History* (1893) when he writes:

> The existence of an area of free land, its continuous recession, and the advance of American settlement Westward, explain American development . . . The perennial rebirth, this fluidity of American life, this expansion Westward with its new opportunities, its continuous touch with the simplicity of primitive society, furnish the forces dominating American character . . . In this advance the frontier is . . . the meeting point between savagery and civilization. (Turner 1996: 1–3)

In this passage Turner offers the historical conflict from which the Western movie draws its primary reference. The Indian/Communist dichotomy is not without parallel in this period. As Jon Roper points out in *The American Presidents*, political thinkers were articulating this threat in these terms. Discussing George Kennan's famous "X" article's similarities to Turner's frontier thesis, Roper suggests that, "Kennan's Soviets would fulfill much the same role in the twentieth century as had Turner's Indians in the nineteenth" (Roper 2000: 32). This dynamic can be clearly felt in the language Kennan uses to dramatize the US/Soviet conflict: "To avoid destruction the United States need only measure up to its own best traditions and prove itself worthy of preservation as a great nation. Surely, there was never a fairer test of national quality than this." He goes on to describe how, just as the Indians were essential components in the forging of American identity, the Soviets are now essential in its maintenance:

> He will rather experience a certain gratitude to a Providence which, by providing the American people with this implacable challenge, has made their entire security as a nation dependent on their pulling themselves together and accepting the responsibilities of moral and political leadership that history plainly intended them to bear.

In this conception, the Soviets, like the Indians for Turner, are a force against which to test American exceptionalism. Just as the Indian had acted as a catalyst and a common enemy in the creation of the American in the nineteenth century, acting as a unifying force, so the Soviet would act in the Cold War period, the Communist becoming the new focus for the nation.

However, the Westerns *The Gunfighter*, *High Noon* and *Shane* do not represent the Native American at all. In each case the threat posed to the main characters is recognizably close to themselves: the significantly non-other, white male. The conflicts that drive these narratives are not external in the sense of representing an explicit onslaught of otherness. Rather, the threat is internal, from their own kind. Certainly this could be an articulation of the most paranoid of the period's fear, that American society has already been infiltrated. Yet these Westerns are surely offering more complex representations of less explicit contemporary anxieties and concerns. If the Indian in the Western represents the Communist threat, then these three Westerns, which do not deal with the construct of the Indian, must logically have a different fear at their core.

The other fear in this period, a fear that was less visible than that posed by Communist infiltration, but one that was equally real for the American public was the fear of the atomic bomb and nuclear annihilation. In some ways, the imagery of the two threats, the Indian/Communist and the bomb, were mixed together in the Western. The looming threat of an Indian attack, a stock Western situation, represents not only the fear of Communist invasion but also, perhaps, the looming threat of a devastating atomic onslaught. More often than not, this attack would be deterred or crushed through the superior tactics and/or firepower of the American hero or heroes, the Western again acting as a positive example of America's position as the supreme superpower. But in *The Gunfighter* and *High Noon*, there is another enemy, an enemy that means these films are not merely retreading the familiar Communist paranoia. And this enemy is as paradoxically tangible and abstract as the atomic threat itself: time.

INTERPRETATIONS OF TIME

The use of time as a sinister imagery system in these Westerns of the 1950s represents a clear view of the effects of a new understanding of physics. When the *New York Times* in 1919 ran with the headline, "lights all askew in the heavens/ Men of science more or less agog over results of eclipse observations/ Einstein's theory triumphs" two days after the *London Times* proclaimed "Revolution in science . . . Newtonian ideas overthrown" the comprehension of the workings of the universe was thrown down a shatteringly different path. Einstein's work was not understood in any conventional sense, but elements of it permeated the culture, as this witty limerick printed in *Time*, 1 July 1946, illustrates:

> There was a young lady called Bright,
> Who could travel faster than light;
> She went out one day,
> In a relative way,
> And came back the previous night.

Since the expansion of the railroads in America at the turn of the century precipitated a formalizing of time to allow for timetables, the concept of time had been a solid, tangible construct. Einstein's theory of relativity obliterated the notion of time as an absolute: time only existed when it was being measured, and then that time was relative to the person measuring. This had an important, if inaccurate impact upon culture. The inaccuracy emerged when this notion of relativity in the science was taken as a model of relativism, authenticating a direction the world was heading in any way. Relativism – the concept that truth in whatever sphere exists only in the point of view of the beholder – had very little to do with Einstein. But such thoughts pervaded much of the art and literature of this period:

Art's elimination of semblances to the physical world corresponded vaguely with Einstein's way of seeing time and space, but it really sprung from an atmosphere of change in which Einstein was yoked with Freud, Marx, Picasso, Bergson, Wittgenstein, Joyce, Kafka, Duchamp, Kandinsky and anyone else with original and disruptive ideas and an aggressive sense of the new. (Roseblatt 1999: 56–8)

A central feature, certainly of the writing of this time, is the importance of the first-person perspective, the essential articulation of relativism. This perspective in the Westerns manifests itself in figures that stand apart from society and community. These figures are not necessarily against such institutions, but are ultimately unable to remain within them. They must retain their distance.

Einstein's work reverberated beyond science. On one level, this is perhaps because, as science historian David Cassidy suggests, relativity is a fitting credo for the times, "the incomprehensiveness of the contemporary scene – the fall of monarchies, the upheaval of the social order, indeed, all the turbulence of the twentieth century" (Golden 1999: 36).

On a larger scale, the impact of Einstein's discoveries can be accounted for in the application of his most famous equation $E = mc^2$ in the devastating technology of atomic weaponry. In 1939, after a meeting with Dr. Leo Szilard in which he explained to Einstein the consequences of a chain reaction in uranium that his theory made possible, Einstein added his signature to a letter sent by Szilard to Franklin Roosevelt, dated 2 August 1939, to explain the possibility of not only the invention of the atomic bomb, but also that Germany may be on its way to building one too. Roosevelt acted. This precipitated the gathering of some of the greatest physicists at Los Alamos and the origins of the Manhattan Project. Or as *Time* succinctly wrote in a portrait of Einstein in 1946: "The Manhattan Project, the bomb, the 125,000 dead of Hiroshima and Nagasaki, and the biggest boost humanity has yet been given toward terminating its brief history of misery and grandeur."

The popular connection between time and the atom was cemented in 1947. *The Bulletin of the Atomic Scientists* began its existence as a newsletter. However, in June of 1947, it was printed for the first time with a cover. This cover depicted what would become an icon for the atomic age: "a pay-attention-to-me jack-o'-lantern orange cover. Imprinted over the orange: a boldly simple seven-inch by seven-inch clock face. The hour hand was at twelve; the minute hand at about seven minutes to." The clock, said an editorial in the July 1947 issue,

> represents the state of mind of those whose closeness to the development of atomic energy does not permit them to forget that their lives and those of their children, the security of their country and the survival of civilization, all hang in the balance as long as the specter of atomic war has not been exorcised.

In this way, the Bulletin Clock, first called "the Clock of Doom" and then "the Doomsday Clock," entered American, and indeed global, folklore as a symbol of nuclear peril and "a constant warning that the leaders of the United States and the Soviet Union had better sit up and fly right."

The clock was designed by a Chicago-based artist known as "Martyl." She was married to a physicist, Alexander Langsdorf, one of the bulletin's founders. The decision to place the hands at seven minutes to was one of design, but by placing the hands in the last quarter of the face, the implication was that the end was nigh, time was nearly up. However, if the time was arbitrary in the first issue's cover, it would not be in subsequent incarnations. The hands stayed on seven minutes to until autumn 1949, when news reached Harry S. Truman that the Soviets had successfully tested an atomic device. In the October issue of that year, the hands moved forward to three minutes to. On 31 October 1952, the United States tested its first thermonuclear device, a device that had a yield nearly a thousand times greater than the atomic bomb that had devastated Hiroshima. The islet of Elugelab in the Pacific, the site of the detonation, disappeared, leaving nothing but a crater 160 feet deep and more than a mile wide. Nine months later, in August 1953, the Russians exploded a less powerful but still awesomely destructive thermonuclear device. The cover of the September 1953 bulletin was remade at the last minute, as soon as word of the Soviet test reached the United States: the minute hand moved to two minutes to midnight:

> In the following issue – October 1953 – Editor Rabinowitch said: "the hands of the Clock of Doom have moved again. Only a few more swings of the

pendulum and, from Moscow to Chicago, atomic explosions will strike midnight for Western civilization." (Moore 1995, *Midnight Never Came: the History of the Doomsday Clock*)

The Doomsday Clock would change another thirteen times between 1953 and 1998, variously reflecting slackening tension and tightening anxiety. In the image of the Doomsday Clock, culture found a shorthand for the atomic threat.

The use of the time motif in the Westerns *The Gunfighter* and *High Noon* is an indication of the vaguely, but intuitively understood connection that existed between the "new" version of time and the atomic bomb. Time is now a sinister relation to immense violence, rather than the orderly construct it was perceived to be before Einstein pulled the rug away. The countdowns depicted in both films are not neutral; time is not to be trusted. Time brings violence, confrontation and death once the clock reaches twelve. The extent to which this evocation of time as a symbol of nuclear anxiety informs American culture can be seen in its manifestation in the Western. Henry King's *The Gunfighter* imports this use of time and the imagery of the clock face to suggest a sense of an approaching apocalypse for its eponymous character who, like a Cold War superpower, constantly faces the threat of violence.

THE GUNFIGHTER (1950)

One of the strongest constructs of the Western in this period is that of the gunfighter. A stock character of the Western since its inception, the gunfighter rose to special prominence in the late 1940s and 1950s.

The background for this change of status lies in the movement toward a psychological cinema, the emergence of cinema noir. The "big themes" of the 1940s gave way to a concentration upon "a particular kind of abstraction and stylization" (Slotkin 1992: 380). Previously, the gunfighter's skill had been simply one element in the overall skill set of a cowboy. In the pattern of the late 1940s and 1950s Western, a single element would be removed from its traditional context, exaggerated and made the focus. This kind of stylization of the hero, and necessarily the Western itself, is directly related to the problems of the post-war/Cold War transition. Slotkin suggests that the link between the formal character of the gunfighter and the changes in ideology created a "cinematic resonance and made the heroic style of the gunfighter an important symbol of right heroic action for film-makers, the public, and the nation's political leadership" (Slotkin 1992: 380). In this statement, Slotkin opens a fascinating field of connections, one he does not develop satisfactorily. His idea can be taken much further. What audiences took from these gunfighter Westerns was more than simply a symbol of heroism. The new gunfighters, the gunfighters of *High Noon* and *Shane*, became "plans" for heroic leadership, containing the necessary elements of direct action and psychological complexity for Cold War society.

That in *Shane* and *High Noon* the gunfighter would come to represent a model of existentialism, a character that could "transcend the narrative," was in no way obvious. That Shane and Kane are able to make choices, where to go, when to leave, which side to fall in with, is a new direction for this stock Western character. *The Gunfighter's* Jimmy Ringo is not able to transcend this narrative. Rather he is locked into a fate that is from the opening moments of the film, inevitable.

The idea of the individual who is capable of forging a new identity through interaction with fresh environments has its roots once more in the work of Frederick Jackson Turner. On the frontier, Turner suggests, the individual, the American, could strike out and carve for himself a place. This self-direction was initially refused the gunfighter in the movies. His life was at the mercy of an already mapped fate. If he had committed some crime, it would have to be paid for, usually in his death, mirroring the inevitable fate of that other classic screen outlaw, the gangster. The gunfighter could be the hero, but his fate was pre-destined. However, as the gunfighter myth developed, he came to define his own future; he would not allow events or history to lead him. The change in the conventions of the gunfighter is made apparent in the gap between *The Gunfighter* on one side and *High Noon* and *Shane* on the other, a gap which Slotkin, far too simplistically, naturally classifies as a chronological, generic progression. This transition seems largely dependent upon altruism, something Slotkin does not see. Where Ringo is unable to move beyond his reputation as an outlaw, and can only try and protect himself, Kane and Shane can both use the skills of the gunfighter to work for the community, rather than against it. In this way, by gaining the trust and respect of the community, the gunfighter can become a hero.

The Gunfighter is the story of Jimmy Ringo, a gunfighter with an infamous past who attempts to buck his fate by returning to the town in which his wife, Peggy, and son live. This is an attempt to escape his legend and reconcile their relationship, wrecked precisely because of his past. Ringo is locked into an inevitable destiny of having his position constantly challenged, a situation that will only end when he loses. In his dying scene, he realizes the reality of his existence in the revenge he bestows upon Hunt Bromley, the "squirt" who shot him in the back: rather than allow his friend, Marshal Mark Strett, to bring Bromley to justice, Ringo passes on his infamy via the construct of "the-man-who-shot-Ringo." In so doing, Ringo condemns the youngster to the same life of constant threat and movement that Ringo had brought upon himself.

The Gunfighter begins in the outdoors, a lone figure riding through the landscape, heading towards a nameless frontier town. The significance of this image is twofold: first it acts as a contrast, because most of the film physically and psychologically takes place, claustrophobically, indoors. But it also becomes a signifier for Ringo's revenge when, in the last scene of the movie, another lone rider, the successful pretender to Ringo's crown, crosses the open plains in silhouette. This repetition in the representation of the characters is indicative of their inability to transcend their pre-destined role in the gunfighter cycle. This is not the only such use of repetition to give the notion of inevitability. The rider at the beginning of the film, Ringo, enters a nameless town's saloon. Immediately, the saloon begins to buzz in recognition of him. A young cowboy looks at Ringo and says to his friends, "he don't look so tough," and begins to taunt him. This phrase is repeated throughout the film. Ringo laments, "How come I got to run into a squirt like you nearly every place I go these days. What are you trying to do? Show off to your friends?" This feeling of resignation is important. On the one hand, Ringo no longer enjoys his renown. On the other, he recognizes in the young cowboy something of himself in the early days, a youngster trying to make a name for himself. The young cowboy draws, but Ringo is faster. The pattern of the scene, though not the shooting, will be reproduced later in the film, in another saloon, between Ringo and Bromley. It is through this technique of repetition that the audience comes to sympathize with Ringo's world-weariness.

Ringo is forced then to move on toward the town of Cayenne. En route, he betters the brothers of the young punk from the saloon. His super-heroic legend is neatly expressed here when one of the brothers articulates his belief that a gunfighter should not fire on a kid. Ringo incredulously replies, "What was I supposed to do? Let the kid shoot me full of holes?" Running off their horses rather than killing them, Ringo unwittingly puts into motion the film's central concern with time through a slow burning showdown motif, as the brothers make their way toward Cayenne. The brothers' misplaced thirst for revenge invites the audience to question the extent to which Ringo's legend is myth or reality, by laying bare the process of a gunfighter existence. It is a technique that will also be repeated later.

Once in Cayenne, Ringo again heads for the saloon. The pattern of the earlier sequence reappears: he is recognized by the bartender, word travels of his presence and an impressive crowd forms. The bartender sends the stable boy to get the marshal. There is a very important relationship between Ringo and the marshal, Mark Strett. They ran together in the early days, which makes his presence as lawman a great surprise to Ringo. The marshal comments upon the men and school children, all boys, who have gathered outside the saloon as voyeurs, fascinated by his legend, but also perhaps eager to see him in action, even be killed. He goes on, "That's the way you wanted it, wasn't it? Top gun of the West." Resignedly, Ringo replies, "Yep, I guess I've got more people wondering when I'm gonna get killed than any other man in the country." The marshal responds, "You don't sound as happy about it as you did the last time I saw you."

This exchange is vital. That the marshal could escape his criminal youth and become, of all things, a lawman, and equally that Ringo has not been able to escape his younger days at all, offers insights into the scale of the two men's exploits, and the energy with which both went about "making a name" for themselves. This conversation suggests a version of the young Ringo as an infinitely more successful incarnation of the young, cocky, punk cowboy from the beginning of the film.

As well as the vengeful brothers, the main threat to Ringo lies in the form of the town "squirt," Hunt Bromley, a replica of the young, dead cowboy. He goes through the same routine of posturing in front of his friends, and confronting Ringo in such a way as to precipitate confrontation. Ringo defuses the situation with a bluff, but comes again to lament, "It's a fine life, ain't it, just trying to stay alive, not really living, not enjoying anything, not getting anywhere. Just trying to keep from getting killed. Just waiting to get knocked off by some tough kid." On a simple level there is again here a resignation to his lot and an ironic recognition of his own part in that lot through his origins: Ringo was once "some tough kid." This is supported in the marshal's recognition that his ability to escape his origins lies in his lack of prominence. Mark recounts a shoot-out in which a little girl is killed. He may or may not have fired the bullet that killed her, but significantly the incident did not attach itself to him. Undoubtedly, the marshal was a bad man, but he lacks Ringo's clinging infamy. However, at a far more complex level for the audience, there is in Ringo's words an articulation of the oppression of living under the constant threat of the atomic bomb. In this moment, a Cold War audience can identify with Ringo's oppressive situation.

Throughout the film, Ringo has waited to see his estranged wife. Almost as time is about to run out, she agrees to see him. He tries to tell her that he has changed and he wants to settle down, using the typical articulation of a ranch as a focus for this dream. There is in this articulation some ambiguity. A cowboy who does not recognize Ringo discussed the same dream earlier in the saloon, so it is likely he is simply repeating the generic cliché of a lifestyle apart from society. Sincere or not, she realizes it is not for him to decide if he has indeed changed. Ringo asks her to give him a year and he will return. In that year, he'll prove he is no longer the "gunfighter." She agrees and finds Jimmy, Ringo's son. While he is talking to his son, although he does not acknowledge the relationship in those terms, the brothers arrive in town, find where he is and prepare to kill him. As Ringo makes ready to leave, a deputy finds the brothers in a barn, thus seemingly neutralizing the threat that has been signified in terms of the countdown motif. Ringo mounts his horse, but Bromley jumps from the shadows and shoots him in the back before he can turn. Immediately the kid is caught and arrested, but Ringo tells Mark he does not want traditional justice, saying he, Ringo, had drawn first. Initially, the people around are incredulous, but Ringo explains, in his dying breaths, that he has imposed upon Bromley a worse punishment than prison or hanging. His legacy, his reputation, has been passed to the man who killed him. Bromley is now open to the constant threat and challenge that Ringo has been. The film ends again with a lone figure riding the open country, Bromley now physically taking over from Ringo in the opening credits, his punishment made real.

JIMMY RINGO TO WILL KANE

The Gunfighter is representative of the nature of the transition from the classic style of Western, like Jesse James and Stagecoach, to a darker, more complex Western. While rooted firmly in the tradition of The Ox-Bow Incident, introspective and claustrophobic, it goes further and opens up a dialogue between tradition and threats to tradition that will be taken up more explicitly in later Westerns. The Gunfighter in this way is explicitly a Cold War Western, that is, a Western that is concerned with and readily illustrative of the nature of existence under a looming threat, only vaguely glimpsed if seen at all, but still tangible. Jimmy Ringo can be seen to represent an American nation weary of conflict but aware of the existence of and the need for readiness against new threats. This theme is expanded through the seemingly constant attention paid to Ringo. A United States in a period of strange contradiction – of controlling massive power while existing in a state of vulnerability – is reflected in the oft-repeated phrase, "he doesn't look so tough." Ringo exists in an atmosphere of almost constant threat. He is ever alert to possible attacks. He is the dominant figure in contemporary gunfighter myth, "top gun of the West," in the same way as America is politically dominant, yet he cannot prevent confrontations, as America in the thermonuclear age is unable to shape the course of crucial events. Ringo represents a parody of the Cold War situation, "at once the most powerful and most vulnerable man in the world" (Slotkin 1992: 390). It is in these terms then that The Gunfighter is most valuable. The Gunfighter presents the gunfighter character as unable to avoid destiny, unable to transcend the narrative, and unable to play the hero. And this is in many ways a negative message, certainly a message steeped in pessimism. Audiences were not shown a threat repelled; the threat, the fear, was in fact victorious. Just at the point at which the audience comes to understand Ringo's predicament, and truly sympathize with him, he is killed. There is a useful ideological parallel to be made here. If the Western in this period is traditionally invoked to repeat the endless victory of cowboys (America) over Indians (Communism), an optimistic meta-narrative of traditional American democracy and spirit, *The Gunfighter* seems to be exploring the opposite political extreme. In this view, *The Gunfighter* is forcing the audience to ask, "what if?" What if Marx is right, that Communism is the only way, that the forces of history are set on a path that cannot be averted, indeed, that America may be on the wrong side of history? More precisely, what if the notion of American exceptionalism is bogus? *The Gunfighter*'s ideological function seems to create the need to change the form of the gunfighter character. This kind of questioning by the film of the audience would certainly illustrate an ideological divide between it and *High Noon* and *Shane* that renders Slotkin's analysis of these films simplistic. Examples of Ringo at the mercy of these "forces of history" are manifest.

Through contact with Peggy, a version of the generically common redemptive woman, Ringo intends to re-establish links with tradition. But Peggy cannot redeem him as she cannot believe that he can change, and that change or not, he will still be Jimmy Ringo, the champion to be challenged. Indeed, Ringo cannot change, like his friend from the old days did to become marshal, because his profile is too high. For Ringo, like America in this period, there is no going back to a better past, to a perceived "age of innocence." The logic dictates that he must die. That he dies at the hands of a punk pretender is typical of the genesis of Ringo's career too, a notion that moves very far away from the accepted heroic and romanticized histories of the conventional cowboy hero.

The narrative, although beginning and ending in the wide open spaces, largely takes place inside. Combined with the inherent feeling of psychological claustrophobia and oppression, there is this pre-occupation with clocks and time. Characters, especially Ringo, have a kind of hyper-awareness of time. People in the saloon look at and check clocks constantly. In many shots, the clock is present even in the metonym of a swinging pendulum, or a moving minute hand. Ringo extends time throughout until it runs out. Time ultimately kills him. Significantly, *The Gunfighter* is not a Western concerned with Communist plots. Rather its concern is a looming threat that is only vaguely recognized, almost little more than something in the air. Ringo is a victim of fate. Regardless of any plans he makes, events and history will always overtake him, pushing him towards his unavoidable conclusion. Throughout the narrative, although he seems to believe he is creating his own future, his fate is already set. Time is certainly not the ally, the healer Ringo wishes it to be. Rather it is an enemy, symbolically a more potent one than the Indian, a silent countdown towards annihilation. This use of time as metaphor is taken up, and indeed is stronger and far more apparent, in *High Noon*.

As a legend, Ringo holds a certain heroic place in the public imagination. He is locked into the momentum of history. Due to his dark past, he has no chance to prevent, ultimately, his own death. This is the only means of redemption available to his character. That Ringo will be killed by a young pretender is a given of his future. Will Kane, the heroic center of *High Noon*, however, continually affects his future throughout the course of the narrative. The model of gunfighter hero in *High Noon*, a hero who can to some extent determine his future, inaugurated in the Western a fundamental characteristic of the gunfighter as the Cold War accelerated – a characteristic that the American people could, unlike with Jimmy Ringo, take hope from based upon the perceived history of their frontier heritage. The gunfighter's new-found ability to shape the course of his existence was a metaphorical protection and endorsement of American nationalism and exceptionalism at a time when society needed to be so reassured. The narrative patterns of the early, traditional Westerns up to *The Gunfighter*, with heroes who were trapped in a particular series of predictable events, held little appeal to a nation which did not want to be told of its lack of control over its destiny, that it was powerless in an era where power and control could mean destruction or survival.

For Richard Slotkin, *High Noon* represents the middle ground between *The Gunfighter* and *Shane*, a progression in his notion of the "cult of the gunfighter." He considers them simply as a triptych of foundation Westerns that would spawn countless imitations. The movies then are linked, a linear "train" of similar films. Certainly, there are such straight connections to be made. *The Gunfighter* and *High Noon* can be usefully linked, in terms of the time motif and the articulation of a tangible, looming threat, and similarly, the character of the gunfighter as represented in Ringo and Shane do have some important parallels in terms of personal history, and the wish to escape from an ill-defined past. However, Slotkin's easy description of the continuity between these three Westerns must be disputed insofar as it ignores much of these movies' individual importance. *High Noon* is *not* naturally connected to *Shane*. Rather than being the middle feature in a trilogy, *High Noon* is a unique Western, one that speaks of closure, of endings, and in so doing acts to throw into relief exactly the newness and difference of *Shane*. And it is in this notion that a crucial political connection is foregrounded. Just as *High Noon* illustrates the difference of *Shane*, so Eisenhower illustrates the difference of Kennedy, and even the 1950s illustrates the difference of the 1960s. By examining the film's representations of closure, the interaction between the film's social and political concerns and those of the larger American society in this period will be made manifest. In the early 1950s then, these two Western narratives, *High Noon* and *Shane*, appeared, which represent pivotal developments in the cinematic Western form. In *High Noon*, released in 1952, and *Shane*, released the following year, these connections can be taken further: both Westerns can be usefully read as strong representations or models of presidential leadership.

High Noon is specifically redolent not only of the nature and atmosphere of Eisenhower's presidency but in the central figure of Will Kane, of Eisenhower's character. *Shane* is less directly connected to a particular individual, setting up as it does a model for leadership that would find many and fascinating parallels initially within the presidency of John F. Kennedy. But of greater significance is this model's subsequent ability to be successfully and relevantly re-worked and re-defined, creating a dialogue with aspects of presidential leadership and surrounding circumstances from 1960 onwards (see Chapter 8). There emerges from this an important first question: why does *High Noon*, the first released, and the first to offer striking associations with the character of a president, not carry on as the allegorical Western form to be re-worked and reformed as comment on the contemporary political era, or the current presidency? The answer lies in the film's concern with closure, a concern that can be traced back to the literary source of *High Noon*, the short story *The Tin Star*.

THE TIN STAR BY JOHN M. CUNNINGHAM

As Jon Tuska suggests in the introduction to *The Western Story: A Chronological Treasury* (1995):

> the Western story grew up with our nation and passed through all those painful periods of internal or external conflict which have shocked, torn and divided, as well as united and made bold and visionary, the people of our land." (Tuska 1995: x)

The seriousness with which Tuska treats the Western story offers a profitable approach with which to analyze John Cunningham's *The Tin Star*, a short story which was published in *Colliers*, 6 December 1947, and which became the basis for Fred Zinneman's *High Noon*. This date is interesting, given that it places the story's appearance within just over a year of the original appearance of Jack Schaefer's *Shane*, as a serial in the magazine *Argosy* under the title *The Mysterious Stranger*, in 1946. It is illustrative to begin with the short story to demonstrate that *High Noon*'s thematic concerns are not just those of the film-makers. Rather, the short story that acts as source material already contains much of the political and social comment that made the 1952 Western so unique. Recognizing the central importance of the story strengthens the cross-currents of the cultural and political in what is on the surface a popular genre and little else.

Cunningham had had quite some success in the short story format, selling his work to pulp Western magazines like *Adventure*, *Dime Western* and *Fifteen Western Tales*, but with *The Tin Star* he broke into the better quality magazines such as *Colliers*, *Redbook*, *Saturday Evening Post* and *Cosmopolitan* (Work 1996: 67). That this story should be recognized as something unusual, above the typical pulp Western is readily understandable. The story concerns the ageing sheriff, Doane, and his deputy, Toby. The two are watching the younger of the Jordan brothers from the sheriff's office. Doane sent down Jordan's older brother for murder. Although he was originally sentenced to death, that judgment has been overturned. Young Jordan and some of his friends are getting drunk in the saloon, awaiting the arrival of the elder Jordan on the 4.10 p.m. train. The town mayor, Mettrick, comes to see Doane to try and persuade him to resign, something he has attempted before, but Doane continues to refuse. Doane is a widower, and it has been his ritual on Sundays to lay fresh flowers on his wife's grave in the cemetery at the edge of town. Toby tries to dissuade him, suspecting young Jordan may try something, but Doane is adamant. As he makes his way to the grave, the very drunk Jordan tries to provoke Doane into a confrontation, but Doane does not respond. At the graveside, Jordan, to prove he is not so drunk that he cannot fight, tries to shoot a flying bird but misses. He leaves, running off Doane's horse. Doane tends the grave and begins to make his way back to town when several shots ring out. In an instant he realizes that the earlier shot and the empty horse could be misinterpreted by Toby: Jordan has shot Doane, and the horse has ambled back to town on instinct. He hurries back to town. In the ensuing gunfight, Doane and Jordan are killed, leaving Toby to take over the reins of authority.

Although in many ways, Cunningham's story obeys the generic conventions laid down by the pulp Western formula, there is at the center a fairly complex political and social discussion that offers several clues about the similar thematic make up of *High Noon*. From the first line, the story is concerned with endings and closure, with death:

> Sheriff Doane looked at his deputy and then down at the daisies he had picked for his weekly visit, lying wrapped in newspaper on his desk. "I'm sorry to hear you say that, Toby. I was kind of counting on you to take over after me." (Work 1996: 68)

Doane is certainly not the typical Western hero. He is pre-occupied with death, overtly in the case of his wife but also in his awareness of approaching the time when he ought to retire. There is an important sense in which he conceives the role of sheriff as not simply a job; Doane will not give up the tin star until he is dead, and until then he will continue to do his duty. An early conversation between the old sheriff and the younger deputy articulates clearly the story's concerns with the nature of leadership, duty and sacrifice. If Doane considers the position of sheriff as a calling, Toby is unable to reconcile the importance of the role and the lack of respect and monetary reward such a role engenders:

> "I been working for you for two years – trying to keep the law so sharp-nosed money-grabbers can get rich, while we piddle along on what the county pays us. I've seen men I used to bust playing marbles going up and down this street on four-hundred dollar saddles, and what've I got? Not a damn thing."
>
> There was a little smile around Doane's wide mouth. 'That's right, Toby. It's all for free. The headaches, the bullets and everything, all for free. I found that out long ago." The mock-grave look vanished. "But somebody's got to be around and take care of things." (Work 1996: 68–9)

In this sentiment Doane offers a parallel with Jimmy Ringo. Doane is similarly unable to transcend the narrative, to move out of his role, and yet paradoxically, it is his decision to stay and face the Jordan gang. He has the chance to leave, and nobly, through resignation from the job that he should have retired from a number of years back. He is as locked in to an inevitable narrative as Ringo, albeit an inevitability based upon his personal conception of civic responsibility rather than the "forces of history":

> [Doane] looked out of the window at the people walking up and down the crazy boardwalks. "I like it free. You know what I mean? You get a thing for it. You've got to risk everything and you're free inside. Like the larks. You know the larks? How they get up in the sky and sing when they want to? A pretty bird. A very pretty bird. That's the way I like to feel inside." (Work 1996: 69)

By associating Doane's inevitable end with the town's people walking up and down the boardwalk, Cunningham sets his sheriff up as a sacrifice. The freedom represented by the movement of the community requires Doane as a sacrifice. Doane is a man giving his all to protect the security, the freedom of the larger community.

This notion of Doane's time coming to an end is enhanced in the physical descriptions of the man: "Doane began kneading his knuckles, his face set against the pain as he gently rubbed the misshapen, twisted bones. Using his fists all these years hadn't helped the gout" (Work 1996: 68). In a manner similar to Jimmy Ringo, Doane's past is represented by the use of guns. But where Ringo is cut off in his prime, Doane has lived to be an old man, arthritic, but wise, and yet he is still unable to give in, to retire. However, Doane's heroism, unlike his sense of duty, is not assured. Cunningham presents his sheriff as simultaneously stubborn yet wracked with anxiety:

"Shut up, shut up," Doane said. "For God's sake, shut up." He sat down suddenly at the desk and covered his face with his hands. "Maybe the pen changes a man." He was sitting stiff, hardly breathing.

"What are you going to do, Doane?"

"Nothing. I can't do anything until they start something. I can't do a thing . . . Maybe the pen changes a man. Sometimes it does. I remember – "

. . . Doane's hands came up again in front of his face, but this time he was looking at them, his big gray eyes going quickly from one to the other, almost as though he were afraid of them. He curled his fingers slowly into fists, and uncurled them slowly, pulling with all his might, yet slowly . . . Doane's eyes came again to the flowers, and some of the strain went out of his face. Then suddenly his eyes closed and he gave a long sigh, and then, luxuriously, stretched his arms. "Good God!" he said, his voice easy again. "It's funny how it comes over you like that." (Work 1996: 70–1)

Doane is an essentially human character in an exceptional situation. Because of his moral stance, the community is protected. The townsfolk's lack of comprehension of the debt they owe Doane for maintaining security, as displayed by Mettrick and Staley, a cowardly deputy who resigns his tin star before any shooting begins, does not deter the elderly sheriff – he will carry out his role with or without popular support:

[Mettrick] jabbed a pen out at Doane. "Sign it and get out of town."

The smile left Doane's mouth. "This is an elective office. I don't have to take orders, even if you are mayor." (Work 1996: 70)

Evidently Doane has been repeatedly elected for some years, and given his own views on his role, he emerges as a paternalistic figure, making the town safe and taking personally the maintenance of that safety. But with his career coming to an end, who will take over this role? Toby seems to be the typically irreverent youth. He will stay and help Doane, but once the Jordan situation has been remedied, he is going to quit as deputy. He does not feel the same sense of responsibility or calling, being concerned with more material things like money and social position. However, in the climactic gunfight, he goes through something of a rite of passage:

[Doane's] breath was coming hard, in small sharp gasps.

"There's nothing in it, kid," he whispered. "Only a tin star. They don't hang the right ones. You got to fight everything twice. It's a job for a dog."

"Thank you, Doane."

"It's all for free. You going to quit, Toby?"

. . . Toby shook his head . . . He took Doane's gun in his hand and took off Doane's star, and sat there in the street while men came out of stores and circled about them. He sat there unmoving, looking at Doane's half-averted face, holding the two things tightly, one in each hand, like a child with a broken toy . . . He looked up at the men, and saw Mettrick.

"I told him he should have resigned," Mettrick said, his voice high. "He could have taken his horse – "

"Shut up," Toby said. "Shut up or get out." His eyes were sharp and his face placid and set. He turned to another of the men. "Get the doc," he said. "I've got a busted leg. And I've got a lot to do." (Work 1996: 81)

In this lengthy passage, Toby seems to literally grow up in the presence of the dying Doane. He moves from being, as Cunningham describes him, like a child holding broken toys to become the new Doane, the next protector of the community. Toby has now entered into the pattern of existence and morality to which Doane adhered and from which he was unable or at least unwilling to escape. Toby's evolution does not suggest change though. Rather it represents the closure of a circle, the onset of the same cycle. The status quo is maintained as though Doane was still in office. The climax of the story represents a significant departure from the screenplay. Where Doane dies, Kane lives. Where Doane lives on in Toby's taking up the tin star, in *High Noon*, Kane throws his star into the dust and leaves town. Both stories have at heart a concern with the nature of paternalistic leadership and the responsibility of community to support it. Where ultimately, in *The Tin Star*, this representation is mythically heroic, *High Noon* tempers its representation in something more substantial.

Ten years after the publication of *The Tin Star*, a Western movie of the same name was produced. The friction between age and experience, lying at the heart of both the short story and *High Noon*, is compounded in Anthony Mann's 1957, *The Tin Star*. Philip Drummond in the *BFI Classics: High Noon* asserts "Mann's *The Tin Star* [is] based on Cunningham." This is misleading. The screenplay and the story are nowhere attributed to Cunningham in the credits (credit for the story is attributed to Barney Slater and Joel Kane). It is more accurate to suggest that the film uses Cunningham's story as an influence rather than a source (*High Noon* and *Rio Bravo* are also notable points of reference). The one aspect of the story it borrows most noticeably is the relationship between the sheriff and the deputy, an aspect that was less prominent in *High Noon*. However, even if the story and the Western are not connected by source material, they are certainly connected in their political allegories. Starring Henry Fonda as a former sheriff turned bounty hunter, Morg (Drummond incorrectly cites James Stewart in the role), and Anthony Perkins as Ben, the movie depicts a young sheriff who is finding the role difficult. He wants to retain the tin star, but his age and inexperience are against him. He turns to Morg, an older, wiser man who teaches him the job, and who essentially moulds the young Perkins into his image. Unlike Toby, Ben wants the role of sheriff, he enjoys the respect. Unlike Doane, Morg has given up the tin star. Yet the relationship is very similar to that depicted in Cunningham's story: the youth who grows into the role adopting the style and characteristics of the mentor. In an attempt to persuade Morg to stay on as sheriff, Ben offers to be his deputy but the offer is declined. Like Kane in *High Noon*, Ben is required to stand against the wishes of the town to ensure legal justice, as opposed to frontier justice, is done. And like *High Noon*, the narrative closes with Ben in place as sheriff and Morg riding off with a new family to settle down. Although Anthony Mann's Western was not nearly as successful, critically or commercially, as *High Noon*, it demonstrates that the Doane/Kane figure found a resonance in Eisenhower. The redolence that this story has to the contemporary political landscape lies in aspects of the relationship between Eisenhower and Nixon, and is specifically highlighted in the events of 1955–7, and Eisenhower's heart attack and stroke. Nixon talks of this period of the president's illness, and his handling of it in *Six Crises*, published in 1962. Nixon indicates his awareness of a seemingly common perception of the conflict between Eisenhower's age and his own more youthful persona:

> Hundreds of thousands of words had been written in 1952 about my youth as a vice presidential nominee, questioning my ability to assume the duties and responsibilities of the presidency if required to do so. I had long been the whipping boy for those who chose not to direct their political attacks against Dwight D. Eisenhower, the most popular president in recent history. (Nixon 1962: 134)

In *Affairs of State: The Eisenhower Years, 1950–1956* (1956), Richard Rovere considers Nixon's political career and his youth in unusual terms:

> if Nixon misses in 1956, he will be conspicuously available in 1960. Indeed, almost as far as one can see down the corridors of time – 1956, 1960, 1964, 1968, 1972, 1976, 1980, and even 1984 – Nixon will be available. With giant strides being taken every day in the field of geriatrics, it is even conceivable that Nixon will be a hard man to count out in the Republican convention of 2000 – held, perhaps, at some pleasant American resort on Mars. (Rovere 1956: 295)

The sense that emerges most clearly from Nixon's accounts of the events in *Six Crises* is the degree to which, on the one hand, he was careful not to be seen to be "brash or timid in meeting the emergency" but equally on the other, the extent to which he acted as an interim president:

> My own position as Vice President called for maintaining a balance of the utmost delicacy. On the one hand, aside from the President, I was the only person in government elected by all the people; they had a right to expect leadership, if it were needed, rather than a vacuum. But any move on my part, which could be interpreted, even incorrectly, as an attempt to usurp the powers of the presidency would disrupt the Eisenhower team, cause dissension in the nation, and disturb the President and his family. Certainly I had no desire or intention to seize an iota of presidential power. I was Vice President and could be nothing more. But the problem was to guard against what I knew would be easy misinterpretation of any mistake, no matter how slight, I might make in public or private. This crisis was how to walk on eggs and not break them. My problem, what I had to do, was to provide leadership without appearing to lead. (Nixon 1962: 144)

There is an interesting conflict within Nixon's sentiments. He talks of the team, but he feels he must lead. He has no wish to be misinterpreted but is still prepared to walk on these most fragile of eggs. Given Nixon's later acute awareness of his being "one heartbeat from the presidency" and his continuous narrative of personal action throughout the crisis, the above account becomes increasingly disingenuous. Nixon saw the ill-health of Eisenhower as an opportunity to promote himself as a possible future presidential candidate, a prospective leader. At two points in his account, something of the sheriff/deputy relationship emerges. At one stage he talks about Eisenhower's methods of demonstrating his appreciation for a job well done:

> At the Cabinet meeting [Eisenhower] thanked us all for our "perfect" performance during his absence. But to my knowledge, he did not thank anyone personally. He felt that all of us, no matter how hard we worked, were merely doing our duty, what was expected of us under the circumstances . . . This was characteristic of Eisenhower. Only when he believed someone had gone beyond what the job called for did he express personal appreciation to that individual. (Nixon 1962: 133)

He proceeds from this to tell of three specific occasions on which the president thanked him personally and in general expressed further personal gratitude for his foreign visits. The final phrases of this passage are telling:

But after this most difficult assignment of all – treading the tightrope during his convalescence from the heart attack – there was no personal thank you. Nor was one needed or expected. (Nixon 1962: 152)

In a book that seems concerned with a search for acceptance this passage stands out. Nixon feels that he should have been thanked because, as he illustrates, the president's ill-health was *Nixon's* crisis. Nixon here seems to be the deputy, yearning for acceptance from the mentor, and is secretly hurt when it is not forthcoming.

The other incident occurs around the time that Eisenhower decides to offer himself as Republican candidate in 1956. He is oblique about Nixon staying on as vice president and Nixon does not like it. The sense is that he has surely done enough to warrant the respect and support of the president, and when again it does not seem to be forthcoming, his reaction is akin to the petulant youth:

The public announcement [that Eisenhower would stand as Republican candidate in 1956] was made at his press conference of February 29 and when he had completed his statement, the first question was: would Richard Nixon be his running mate? The president evaded a direct reply . . . In politics, however, not speaking out can be another way of speaking out, and the president's words set off a wave of speculation by the public and a furor among my own friends and supporters. This in turn caused embarrassment to me . . . At the next weekly press conference, on March 7, the president delivered his now famous answer: "I told him (Nixon) he would have to chart his own course and tell me what he would like to do." His statement was telephoned to me soon after the press conference in a somewhat garbled version. The impression I got was that he was really trying to tell me that he wanted me off the ticket. I told Vic Johnson . . . that the only course of action I could properly take under the circumstances was to call a press conference the next day and announce that I would not be a candidate for the vice president so that Eisenhower would have a free hand to select his running mate. It seemed to me it was like the fund controversy all over again. But then Eisenhower had not known me well and had every justification for not making a decision with regard to keeping me on the ticket until all the facts were in. Now, he had had an opportunity to evaluate my work over the past three years, and particularly during the period after the heart attack. If he still felt, under the circumstances, that he wanted me on the ticket only if I insisted on seeking the post, I concluded he should have someone else in whom he had more confidence as his running mate. (Nixon 1962: 164)

The dynamics of the older sheriff and the deputy, seeking to become sheriff himself, and Eisenhower and Nixon, seeking the general's confirmation, offer a persuasive parallel between *The Tin Star*, *High Noon* and political personality.

Perceptions of youth underpin the description of Nixon's third crisis. He talks of Eisenhower's conception of the presidency and suggests that, initially, Eisenhower saw himself as a one-term president because of his age:

> Eisenhower frequently told his associates that he wanted to be a one-term president. He thought that in four years he could substitute his concept of a moderate federal government, a free economy, and a balanced budget for what he considered the Democratic Party's drift toward welfare state. He wanted to build up the Republican Party into a moderate, responsible majority party, and then turn over the reins to a younger man. (Nixon 1962: 152)

The theme of retirement is a recurring feature and as a result, the telling is imbued with the sense that Eisenhower is a dying man and, as such, his death, and implicitly Nixon's ascendancy, is only a matter of time. Richard Rovere, writing about Nixon in 1955, echoes such a notion:

> Nixon is pretty certain to be Vice-President again – which is a way of saying that he is likely to be President, since Mr. Eisenhower, between 1957 and 1961, will not have the life-expectancy tables in his favor. (Rovere 1956: 293–4)

This awareness of Eisenhower's age and health problems manifested themselves elsewhere too. In his memoirs, Nixon remembers how such thoughts were used against him in the campaign of 1956: "The underlying issue of the campaign was . . . Eisenhower's health and the fact that if anything happened to him I would become President" (Nixon 1978: 178). He goes on to quote an article from *Newsweek*, August 1956, reporting the Democrat's National Convention:

> From the opening crack of the gavel in Chicago until the last lusty cheer echoed and died, Nixon was the target . . . In attacking Nixon, the Democrats . . . were asking, "Do you want a man like this in the White House? Remember, he'll be president if you re-elect Mr. Eisenhower and Ike dies." (Nixon 1978: 178)

Nixon presents his relationship with Eisenhower in positive terms. While Eisenhower was deciding whether or not to run again, Nixon describes a conversation he has with the president regarding the vice presidency:

> He tried to reassure me of his satisfaction with my work as Vice President. "There has been no job I have given you that you haven't done to perfection

as far as I am concerned," he said. "The thing that concerns me is that the public does not realize adequately the job you have done." (Nixon 1962: 159)

However, these glowing words are not echoed in the popular media, and as such, conflict between the generationally separated men is manifest. Nixon is probably right in his complaint that he was a whipping boy for a country that did not want to attack a figure as popular as Eisenhower.

HIGH NOON (1952): THE EISENHOWER WESTERN

A large measure of *High Noon*'s uniqueness as a Western rests in its capacity to be "read," to contain meaning above its generic status. In this way, *High Noon* is a Western that has been taken "to mean different things to different people" (Zinneman 1992: 96). It has been read as an allegory of the Korean War, equating "Will Kane with America, Frank Miller with international Communism, Amy Kane with isolationists, and the town of Hadleyville with nations content to let the United States go it alone in Korea" (Mitchell 1996: 192). Far more persuasively, Carl Foreman, the film's scriptwriter, explicitly shaped it as an allegory of his own experience of political persecution in McCarthy era Hollywood, such that Will Kane may be seen as a portrayal of such men as Dalton Trumbo and Alvah Bessie. Conversely, it has been read as an allegory commending the strong individual who refuses to compromise. This reading would suggest the hero acts very much in the vein of Senator Joseph McCarthy, who continued to fight against enemy infiltration even when others fell back on "do-nothing" policies. For Fred Zinneman, the director, it was more generally an attack upon the growing silent majority:

> It was a story of a man who must make a decision according to conscience. His town – symbol of a democracy gone soft – faces a horrendous threat to its people's way of life. Determined to resist, and in deep trouble, he moves all over the place looking for support but finding there is nobody who will help him; each has a reason for not getting involved. In the end he must meet his chosen fate all by himself, his town's doors and windows firmly locked against him . . . It is a story that still happens everywhere, everyday. (Zinneman 1992: 97)

Regardless of these different interpretations, it is clear from the outset that *High Noon* was intended and, equally, perceived as a political film, a film that is firmly rooted within a variety of contemporary political circumstances. There is evidence for this in the way that the film was named. Stanley Kramer, the film's producer, explains: "We already had the title . . . So when Carl Foreman suggested a rousing little Western thriller he'd read in a magazine, we finally had a chance to use it" (Kramer quoted in Spoto 1978: 99). The title then seems almost organic, with a meaning that is not fixed in any one particular narrative. Rather it acts as a comment upon the era, perfectly expressing a period in which a final destructive conflict is tangibly approaching, like a silent countdown. But the film-makers take this contemporary frame of reference and from this anxiety create a tale with a moral, a tale that offers the American public valuable lessons and possible resolutions. In *The Culture of the Cold War*, Stephen Whitfield discusses at length *High Noon*'s political claims. He suggests that the message of *High Noon* "better than any other film of the 1950s, exemplified political criticism in the shadow of the blacklist" (Whitfield 1991: 146). He connects this analysis of *High Noon* with a speech Eisenhower delivered in 1953 upon receiving a Democratic Legacy Award. In the speech that followed his acceptance, Eisenhower ad libbed some objections to McCarthyism:

> The President mentioned his own origins in Abilene, Kansas, where "Wild Bill" Hickok had served as marshal. "Now that town had a code," Ike reminisced, "and I was raised as a boy to prize that code. It was – meet anyone face to face with whom you disagree. You could not sneak up on him from behind – do any damage to him – without suffering the penalty of an outraged citizenry. If you met face to face and took the same risks he did, you could get away with almost anything, as long as the bullet was in front." The frontier moral that Eisenhower applied was that "in this country, if someone dislikes you or accuses you, he must come up in front. He cannot hide behind the shadow. He cannot assassinate you or your character from behind without suffering the penalties of an outraged citizenry." (Whitfield 1991: 146)

Even if Eisenhower's administration did not act upon this code and allowed relatively unchecked the continuation of McCarthyism, this speech is vital. In the first place it locates Eisenhower's persona within the frontier past. This in turn offers the possibility that those listening (the speech was broadcast over three television networks) may have moved from perceiving Will Kane as an abstract model of leadership to having a resonance in the political arena. As Whitfield's analysis begins to hint at, *High Noon* and Eisenhower are fundamentally linked.

Initially, the film fared indifferently at the box office, despite the boost of the Academy Award for Gary Cooper and another for Dimitri Tiomkin's signature ballad. In the 1950s, at the height of McCarthyism, its subversive nature was widely recognized. The scene at the end of the film, in which Kane throws down his tin star, the symbol of federal authority, was famously (mis)quoted by John Wayne, who found the film wholly objectionable:

> It's the most un-American thing I've ever seen in my whole life . . . The last thing you see in the picture is ole Coop putting the United States Marshall's badge under his foot and stepping on it. (Roberts and Olsen 1995: 349)

This reaction borders on the hysterical: Cooper throws down the star, but he does not step on it. The exaggeration in this articulation of the fear of subversion in some ways goes beyond the political and into the realm of the mythical as Zinneman recognizes:

> the nervousness about subversion was perhaps not even political, but rather a subconscious worry that the classical myth of the fearless Western hero, the always victorious superman, was in danger of being subverted. (Zinneman 1992: 108)

Howard Hawks' response to *High Noon* is illustrative of this:

> I saw *High Noon* . . . and we were talking about Western pictures, and they asked me if I liked it, and I said, "Not particularly." I didn't think a good sheriff was going to go running around town like a chicken with his head off asking for help, and finally his Quaker wife had to save him. (McBride 1996: 161)

This reading of the film is as paranoidly exaggerated as Wayne's. As counter to *High Noon*, Hawks and Wayne made *Rio Bravo* four years later, the "exact opposite to Zinneman's film," a Western devoid of complexity but timeless in its mythology.

Given its overtly political nature, that *High Noon* did come to capture the public imagination then is perhaps surprising. The film's peculiar appeal warrants further investigation. Zinneman has his own theory, a theory with important implications for the role of the Western in the coming decades. He says: "Interestingly, its popularity waxes and wanes; people become aware of it at times of decision, when a major national or political crisis is threatening" (Zinneman 1992: 108).

High Noon, like Cunningham's story, does not boast a particularly complex narrative. It is the story of Marshal Will Kane, who at the start of the picture has married his young Quaker wife. He turns over his tin star and looks towards retirement. News arrives however that Frank Miller, the leader of the gang who terrorized the town of Hadleyville until Kane "cleaned it up" is being released, having had his death sentence overturned. From this moment, the film moves into almost real time, one minute for the audience is one minute nearer noon for Kane, and the arrival of the train carrying Miller. Kane tries to raise a posse, but apart from an old man, a drunkard and a kid (the same character types Hawks uses in his response to *High Noon*, *Rio Bravo*), no-one will aid him. Ultimately, Kane, a figure wracked with fear and doubt, faces Miller and his gang alone.

In the character of Marshal Will Kane, *High Noon* offered an anxious public a hero made-to-measure for the times: a hero slow to anger but quick to action, and a hero with a recognized history of achievement and victory. The name "Will Kane" is, as is the case with many Western heroes' names, worthy of examination. Slotkin suggests that "Kane" is "a homonym of the bible's first murderer"(Slotkin 1992: 393). So if the Western hero offers the American public models of leadership, then one of the most significant aspects of this model is the insistence upon the legitimacy of violence. This reference is common place in the Western. In John Ford's 1962 film, for example, *The Man Who Shot Liberty Valance*, James Stewart's character, Ransom Stoddard, becomes a successful senator and a prospect for the vice-presidency because of his eponymous act, the action of the killing being verbalized in the movie in the scenes where the senatorial candidate is being chosen as his having upon him "the Mark of Cain." Although this is intended as an attack upon his candidacy, it becomes a positive issue: the heroic leader who can act decisively, who can make the big decisions, if the need arises, promises security in any future confrontations. Similarly it is useful to note, as Ricardo Quinones does, that *Shane* too has the phonetic connection to this biblical image of violence. The prominence of violence in the character of the Western hero instills violence as a virtue; to become a heroic leader, he must be seen to be capable of violence, to actively embrace the prospect of violence. In this sense, murder in the defense of liberty is no sin, a necessary attitude in the Cold War climate of threat and stand-off.

Of equal importance in this impressionistic characterization of Kane is his first name, Will. Slotkin equates this with "a drive to power." This can be usefully taken further. The idea of "Will" as it impacts upon the narrative of *High Noon*, and the character of Kane, can be equated with the Nietzschean concept of the "will to power." Nietzsche challenges the Darwinian notion that a "will to live" is a driving desire. The concept of the "survival of the fittest," as Nietzsche points out in *The Ascent of Man* (1871), is merely a struggle for life rather than death and leads only to the continuation of the herd, "the average and below average types." Characters like Kane and Miller who deliberately place themselves in situations of great risk negate this impulse. In figures like these, Nietzsche sees the "will to power." He posits that there is no such thing as truth, and therefore "everything is permitted." In this way, the Nietzschean conception of society is one given over to disaster and decline. Nietzsche tempers this nihilism with this concept of "will to power." Only in the quest for power, and the pain and suffering this quest brings to great men, "supermen," over the masses of "the bungled and the botched" could life be affirmed. In this sense, the characters of both Kane and Miller are working models of Nietzsche's philosophy: only through their conflict does the rest of the community realize it is alive.

Furthermore, Hadleyville also becomes a model of Nietzschean thought: this fledgling, frontier society, apt to be riven with violence and disorder if left to the mass of "average" people, requires the efforts of figures like Kane and Miller. The townsfolk are different from Kane and Miller; they have only the "will to live." Nietzsche's ideas have a strong association with the philosophical and ideological underpinnings of the Nazi party, connecting this notion of the "superman" and "will to power" with fascism. In the movie, all of this throws up two important and connected issues. In narrative terms, there is Kane's determination to remain and fight against the wishes of much of the community of Hadleyville. And for the audience watching, there is the fact that they identify positively with this figure who is blatantly operating within an autocratic manifestation of leadership (because the audience relate to Kane as a leader, even if the inhabitants of Hadleyville do not). The nature of this fascistic system needs qualification. The town of Hadleyville as a society seems prepared for nothing more or less than autocratic control. They do not want Kane to stay and fight, but neither do they want to involve themselves in pushing him out, and although the thought of Miller returning fills many of them with dread, they are prepared to suffer his authority and its inevitable consequences rather than act. Whatever the outcome of the Kane/Miller showdown, they are allowing the will of one man to rule over the majority.

Although the narrative may be fairly simple, Will Kane is a complex character, and complex in a way that *The Gunfighter*'s Jimmy Ringo, and even Doane/Toby are not. Kane, a lawman, is crucially not innocent or morally safe. Kane has a "dark side" that is represented in his name, in the elements of his history that are recounted during the film, and symbolically in the relationship he has had with Helen Ramirez, the significantly "dark" Mexican woman, in the past. Her "darkness" is twofold. In the first place it is a reference to her color, her otherness. But it is also suggested in her relationship with Miller before he was sent for execution. That Kane has not spoken to Ramirez for a year is a good indication of his commitment to a traditional concept of duty, the negation of this "dark side" in deference to his role as public servant. But the symbolic union that exists through the Mexican woman between Miller and Kane cannot be underestimated. The marshal who held the position before Kane confirms at one point in the story that Kane could have turned out "bad" if he had not picked up the badge. This underlying capacity for violence, this "darkness," the capacity to be like Miller, is the essence of his power, his strength. Having been married minutes before the telegram announcing Frank Miller's pardon and release from prison arrived, Will Kane reluctantly gives up his tin star, ready to move on. Upon hearing of Miller's impending arrival, the community tries to persuade Kane to leave town. Although he does begin to leave town, Kane decides to go back, to stay on as marshal for an extra day, by which time the new marshal will have arrived. Kane's refusal to leave town despite the efforts of the largely craven community is in some ways a reassuring image for a nation in the grip of contradictory political and social conditions. So the film acts simultaneously as an attack upon the ever-growing silent majority and also provides a sense of center; a solid hero that provides his qualities of leadership as a focus in a time of uncertainty. The crucial thing about the heroic Kane is that his response to the problem faced by the town is traditional, in frontier narrative terms, and based upon similar events and resolutions in the past. Like Doane, there is very little about Kane that is exceptional save his bravery and courage. In terms of ability, Kane and Miller are equally matched, different sides of the same coin. He is not some version of a mythical Western super-hero. Kane is afraid, frustrated, put simply, he is human. Kane reflects the notion that a simple, straightforward response, a response that had worked in the past should be supported by the public as a common sense measure. In Hadleyville, the townsfolk's lack of support offers the American audience a timely lesson.

When Kane looks at his tin star and says, "I'm the same person with or without this badge," he goes even further in suggesting the role of an individual in a community. It suggests that civic responsibility is the domain of everyone, not simply paid civil servants. Simultaneously, it also lends further support to the ideal of the heroic leader; that leadership and duty transcend mere employment but the necessary strength of character is rather a very real calling, something born to rather than trained for. This is duty as articulated by Sheriff Doane and, as will be discussed, Eisenhower. In this sentiment, Kane becomes Cain, positioning himself as a sacrifice for the greater good of the community. The idea of Cain as a sacrifice requires qualification. The story in Genesis has Cain, a farmer, and Abel, a shepherd, making offerings to God. Abel's is accepted, but Cain's, for no specified reason, is not. After God offers Cain some moral advice, Cain rises up and kills Abel in a field. The crime is discovered by God from Abel's blood, which "crieth unto me from the ground," and he confronts Cain. He denies any knowledge of the murder, and, as punishment, God condemns him to walk the earth. Cain pleads for mercy, which is granted by God placing upon him an unspecified mark. This mark means that no-one can kill or attempt to kill him without visiting upon themselves God's wrath. Within this story, the sacrificial element seems to reside in the mark – a symbol of violence and vengeance that will attract the same in others as he wanders the earth. Cain, although roundly recognized as the Bible's first murderer is also a victim, he is manipulated by God, practically set up to commit the act of murder as an example, as a lesson. In the Western, the character with the "mark of Cain" typically positions himself between the forces of "good" and "evil," deliberately sacrificing himself, knowing that once violence is visited upon him, he will retaliate with an Old Testament wrath. Will Kane, as one with the mark, provided the type of solid, loyal and righteous leadership that the American people needed in the immediate aftermath of one war and the onset of a new one. And it was a type mirrored in the contemporary race for the White House.

High Noon's presidential link is far from tenuous. As a cultural artifact, High Noon emerges as a pivotal cultural response to the anxiety of the Cold War and the atomic age in much the same way as Eisenhower's election is a political response. The construct of the gunfighter is, as Slotkin suggests, a Cold War construct. And like the gunfighter, the heroic president is a Cold War construction:

> The image of the gunfighter as a professional of violence, for whom formalized killing was a calling and even an art, is . . . the reflection of Cold War-era ideas about professionalism and violence and not the mores of the Old West. (Slotkin 1992: 384)

This would certainly explain the distance between Wayne and Hawks, the Western mythologizers and High Noon. Considering this, High Noon is exceptional in so far as it is not concerned with Western myth but rather using that myth to a more explicitly political end. This twisting occurs on a variety of levels. On perhaps the simplest level is the choice of Gary Cooper for the role. On one level, his personal politics align him with Eisenhower: Cooper was a fervent Republican. His testimony to HUAC was a high profile, if pointless exercise, but his presence was a ringing endorsement of their activities. On a physical level, Cooper was specifically chosen for his age or, more precisely, the ability to play the character in terms of that age. Cooper imbued the role with a stiffness, a world-weariness of a man who has lived a long time, and is physically ready to retire, even if his sense of duty tells him otherwise. Cooper plays the scene where Kane and his deputy punch it out in the stable with an arthritic strength. Although he knocks his deputy out cold, he emerges from the stable bloody and bruised, clearly in pain, not only from the blows but also from the sheer exertion.

The relationship between Kane and his much younger deputy is an interesting one. *High Noon* has a cast made up of old-timers. Although there are
children in Hadleyville, its population seems predominantly middle aged or
older. The young deputy is willful and petulant, largely because he has been
passed over for the position Kane is to vacate, another interesting diversion
from Cunningham's story. The character is a version of the stereotypical punk
that has appeared in so many Westerns: Hunt Bromley, the kid who shoots
Ringo in the back in *The Gunfighter*; the character of Chris in *Shane* (more
precisely in the novel than the movie); the Schofield Kid in *Unforgiven*. What
makes this character important is his specific relationship with Kane. The
power relationship resembles the relationship between Eisenhower and his vice
president, Richard Nixon, most explicitly in the conflict of youth and experience. One of the pivotal scenes in *High Noon* is the brawl between Kane and his
deputy in a stable. Kane has acted as a father figure to the deputy, guiding him.
But, and this is similar to Toby in *The Tin Star*, he does not understand the level
of commitment the role of marshal requires. The deputy wants the prestige and
the authority of the role but has not the sense of civic responsibility, the sense
of duty that the role entails. He wants to be Kane: he even, at least for part of
the movie, has Helen Ramirez as a partner, though she tells him that compared
to Kane he is barely even a man. The deputy feels he can do the job of marshal,
and has not challenged Kane out of his respect for him.

Kane established a model of leadership that resonated in the similar qualities
of Eisenhower. By far the most important commonality between Eisenhower
and Kane is their nature as heroes of their specific time and place. Put another
way, the leadership they proffer is from the outset understood, they are known
quantities. Indeed they are only in the position of power because their qualities
are tried and tested, their personae established. They do not have to define
themselves from within this leadership role. Based upon a renowned history of
success and victory, which acts as the platform for their election, the two can be
relied upon to win through again. In times when the need for security is at a
premium, this kind of leadership is attractive. It also acts as a straitjacket.
Neither of these characters have anywhere to go. Once their time moves on, so
the demand for their abilities vanishes and they have nothing new to offer.

David Caute describes this time and place, America in the 1950s, as the age
of the "Great Fear" in his book of the same name. Caute suggests that the
Communist purges and the paranoia over the perceived threat of infiltration
are the keys to understanding the national psyche at the beginning of the
decade. Certainly, there can be no doubt that the rhetoric and high visibility of
Senator Joseph McCarthy and the subsequent atmosphere of fear and oppression in this era are central. McCarthyism had far-reaching effects. But more
horrific than this, and more ambiguous, was the fear that had been created by

America's emergence into the atomic age. The burgeoning threat of nuclear Armageddon at the hands of the Soviet Union perhaps turns Caute's "Great Fear" into the "Wrong Fear." The threat of Communism was something that at least had a form, and a highly visible system in place to deal with it. The atomic fear was a great fear precisely because it was an unknown, intangible, and ambiguous.

In the Western generally, these tensions are played out over and over again. Structurally, Communist metaphors would include versions of the alien, of infiltration, of betrayal, of fear and paranoia regarding some external threat. Necessarily, the threat of nuclear annihilation can be represented by some of these images. Yet the atomic metaphors are perhaps more subtle, most often taking the form of allusions to or images of time, borrowing the image system from "Martyl" and the Bulletin Clock. Time seems in many ways the best means of alluding to the atomic threat. At a most basic level, time, like the atom, exists intangibly, though both have the power to devastate mankind.

If Henry King's *The Gunfighter* was the first Western to significantly reflect an anxiety with the onset of the atomic age through the use of time as a metaphor, its time imagery system is not as central or explicit as *High Noon*'s would be two years later. From the very first image of railroad tracks pointing forever toward the horizon, the audience is made aware of a threat. The image acts as "a symbol for an enormous, looming event" (Zinneman 1992: 100). Throughout the film, this idea of oppression is highlighted through the "real time" narrative and, as in *The Gunfighter*, the repeated use of the clock face motif. This tension can easily be superimposed upon the fears of the Cold War generation, the living day to day in fear of the looming and much publicized invasion by Communists and nuclear attack. The time motif is crucial to Eisenhower's presidential narrative, especially in and around his second term. With his health failing and retirement becoming an increasingly real prospect, the link between Eisenhower and the characters of Doane and Kane and their narratives of retirement and death make concrete the notion of time running out. In a sense the impending return of Frank Miller to his gang and the threat it poses to the peace, both economic and political, of Hadleyville, also suggests Miller as, possibly, a version of the threat that could be the first stage of the feared Communist invasion of the United States or perhaps more vitally, a devastating nuclear onslaught. Will Kane stands as a counter to this threat, feeling it his responsibility, despite having no legitimate platform, to defend Hadleyville. The American need to find right solutions, to create a version of the present that would act like a protective bubble, would not only create a new or more receptive audience for the Western but would lead to strong parallels with the election of Dwight Eisenhower as president, and a new era in American politics.

EISENHOWER AS KANE

The manner of Dwight Eisenhower's ascendancy to the presidency ultimately rested upon his unique capability to face a specific crisis. Whatever he projected as president, it was his performance during the election campaign that foregrounded interesting parallels between his character and that of Will Kane. The pressing issue of the campaign was American involvement in Korea, a conflict that was being described as "Truman's War." The cost of American involvement in the Korean War was the arrival home of dead American boys and the subsequent public wish to extricate itself from the conflict. As Richard Rovere suggests, "the Korean war was the most unpopular war we have ever fought. Its purpose was understood by fewer people than that of any other war in our history, and not all of those who understood approved of it" (Rovere 1956: 195). In a speech delivered in Detroit, 24 October 1952, Eisenhower made an announcement that was to have great symbolic effect.

> Where will a new administration begin? It will begin with its President taking simple, firm resolution. That resolution will be: to forgo the diversions of politics and to concentrate on the job of ending the Korean war – until that job is honorably done. That job requires a personal trip to Korea. I shall make that trip. Only in that way could I learn how to best serve the American people in the cause of peace. I shall go to Korea. (quoted in Donovan 1956: 17)

In the speech, he made the promise that if elected he would "go to Korea the following January and . . . determine for myself what the conditions were in that unhappy country" (Eisenhower 1963: 72). This was a promise that he alone could legitimately make and more importantly be trusted to keep. The belief that Eisenhower alone could end American involvement in Korea is illustrated in the media's reaction to the announcement. In his memoir, Eisenhower remembers one newspaper reporter "went so far as to say that the promise made the outcome of the election a certainty" (Eisenhower 1963: 73). Talking of the impact of the speech, Sherman Adams, Eisenhower's campaign manager wrote:

> When mimeographed copies of it were distributed to the reporters on the train, they said to us excitedly, as soon as they saw the "I shall go to Korea" line, "that does it – Ike is in." The speech had the same immediate effect on the audience in Detroit and on the television and radio audiences across the country. As Jack Bell, the Associated Press political reporter wrote of the Detroit speech later, "For all practical purposes, the contest ended that night." (Adams 1961: 44)

In this act, the perfect alignment of Eisenhower's past achievements, the contemporary problem and his signature solution virtually guaranteed his victory. It is important that his Korean promise became his election "ace in the hole" as it goes a great distance towards explaining why Eisenhower was so right for the spirit of his time and, further, why he was unable to move beyond it. The sense that, given Eisenhower's past achievements, he could be relied upon, trusted to do his best is a fundamental quality of his presidential character, a phenomenon explored by James David Barber in his book *The Presidential Character: Predicting Performance in the White House* (1992). Barber sets out in this work to predict and explain how a given president might act or why a given president acted in the manner that he did:

> To understand what actual Presidents do and what potential Presidents might do, the first need is to know the whole person – not as some abstract embodiment of civic virtue, some scorecard of issue stands, or some reflection of a faction, but as a human being like the rest of us, a person trying to cope with a difficult environment. To that task, the candidate brings an individual character, worldview, and political style. None of that is new at campaign time. If we can see the pattern set already for the candidate's political life, we can, I contend, estimate better the pattern this person brings forth to the stresses and chances of the Presidency. (Barber 1992: 1–2)

Barber's framework for analyzing the president in this way comes in layers. He considers in general the president's personality; he establishes how that personality is patterned, how "his character, worldview, and style fit together in a dynamic package understandable in psychological terms"; he explores how the president's personality "interacts with the power situation he faces and national 'climate of expectations' dominant at the time he serves"; and he considers how the president's early biography, up to the first independent political success, explains how the personality was created. From this analysis he applies a label to the president that runs along two axes: the first from active to passive and the second from positive to negative (Barber 1992: 8–11).

Within this framework, Barber suggests that Eisenhower is a "negative-passive" president. Eisenhower, as Barber portrays him, does not want the responsibility of leadership, but will carry the burden; he will not pro-actively pursue policy, but rather would be inclined to act as and when the need arises. His election promise in Detroit demonstrates the second element of this equation of Eisenhower's presidential personality: he could readily project himself as a man of action. But the reluctance to accept such a position as president is amply illustrated in his journey to the nomination as presidential candidate for the Republican Party. If this negativism is accurate, then why would Eisenhower take on the position? Barber answers this question:

> Why then did Eisenhower bother to become President? Because he thought he ought to. He was a sucker for duty, and he always had been . . . Eisenhower did not feel a duty to save the world or to become a great hero, but simply to contribute what he could the best he was able. Throughout his life . . . Eisenhower felt, amid questions about many things, that duty was a certainty. (Barber 1992: 181–2)

Eisenhower was born to serve; his character is such that he will do nothing more or less than his best in carrying out his duty. Just as Kane does not really want to face Miller's gang, Eisenhower does not want to be president. However in both men's character lies an inviolable code that allows neither man to turn his back on his own conception of duty. Just as the townsfolk of Hadleyville will not help Kane defeat Miller, the election of Eisenhower could be considered a similar attempt by the American public to keep themselves safe. Eisenhower is elected because he, without any undertaking on their part, can "win." This is what is illustrated in his election promise to visit Korea personally once he is elected. In this dynamic is a useful illustration of Nietzsche's notions of "will to live" and "will to power," of the herd and the "superman."

The communities of the United States in the 1950s and Hadleyville have much in common: they have a similar political atmosphere and outlook and a similar kind of leader/hero guaranteeing security. In *The Presidential Papers*, Norman Mailer discusses the heroism of leadership in terms that have resonance with Eisenhower's presidency and the heroic core of *High Noon*: "An unheroic leader is a man who embodies a time but is not superior to it" (Mailer 1964: 6). Taking this as a useful starting point, a heroic leader must be defined as the opposite of the above statement; a heroic leader necessarily embodies a time but is crucially superior to it, is able to transcend the time. Mailer's definition very closely resembles the Eisenhower/Kane notion of the hero with a closed narrative, a hero who represents the spirit of his age, a hero locked into a finite journey. America had always required heroes of some variety, not simply in the political arena: America is, as Mailer points out, "a country which had grown by the leap of one hero past another" (Mailer 1964: 16). Within these differing versions of heroism lies the reason why *High Noon* is a narrative of closure rather than a beginning. A further examination of Eisenhower's journey to the presidency makes readily apparent another aspect of the similar nature of his heroism in relation to Kane.

Robert Divine discerns two ways of understanding Dwight Eisenhower's ascension from Supreme Commander to Chief Executive. The first is to see "his selection as President as almost an inevitable result of his role in World War II" (Divine 1981: 3), to accept that his taking on the role was nothing more than the call to duty that a soldier must obey. The second is to see Eisenhower as actively advancing his interests in the presidency, as following "a deeply held but carefully concealed ambition and a shrewd manipulation of men and events." That Divine posits that "the truth probably lies somewhere between these two versions" (Divine 1981: 4–5) is, for the present purpose, irrelevant. In his memoirs, Eisenhower describes his rise to the presidency very much in terms of the first version of events, and certainly contemporary reports and public opinion would subscribe to the "inevitable" model.

Thus, that General Dwight D. Eisenhower was elected thirty-fourth president of the United States in 1952 was an almost inevitable consequence of World War II. The idea of inevitability is an important one. In the years immediately following the war, the American people were in a position to take advantage of the unparalleled prosperity of the economically strongest country in the world. The rugged individual of the frontier doctrine gave way to a more complex system of society. The state that replaced individualism finds form in Norman Mailer's "totalitarianism," a psychic need to belong in mind, body and deed. This progression has its most telling example in the exodus from the inner city into the suburbs. Education was moved further away from research and there emerged the practical discouragement of free thinking. Education was taken from the so-called "eggheads" and moved to classes which explained how best to fit in. This down-sizing of research and education was a trend that was to have serious repercussions in Eisenhower's second term of office. Of greater significance, between 1953 and 1961, the American people were "alternately piqued and threatened by the Russians" (Albertson 1963: xxi) and lived in the uncertain atmosphere of the Cold War. It was precisely this complex and confusing mix of contradictory forces at a time when, historically, the American people wished for quiet simplicity that made Eisenhower the inevitable choice for president.

The United States as Hadleyville

Eisenhower as president has been described as a "decent but soft leader." A leader who symbolized:

> both the essential decency and love of ease of a great nation . . . If so, the symbol may also indicate an anti-climax for the nation which speaks rather pretentiously and glibly of its "moral leadership in the free world," while living complacently in a hell of insecurity, consoled by its innumerable

comforts, and failing to take political measures requiring discipline and courage which would make that leadership effective. (Albertson 1963: x)

The American society described here is very similar to Hadleyville. The relationship between the community, whether it be the town or the country, and the hero who will protect it has very obvious parallels in the presidency and *High Noon*. Where the United States charged Eisenhower to protect the country, Hadleyville is simply prepared to allow any form of control from above, whether it be Kane or Miller. Its citizens' only requisite is that they avoid personal involvement. What both communities are craving is a state of government that finds a close approximation in what Norman Mailer, one of the most astute commentators upon the 1950s and 1960s, labels "psychic totalitarianism."

Mailer, who proclaims himself "novelist, philosopher, essayist, journalist, personality, cathartic, spark or demiurge" (Mailer 1971: 7), was from his earliest work concerned with totalitarian societies. As Christopher Brookeman points out, "his first treatment of a mass society inexorably submitting to totalitarianism was in his war novel, The Naked and the Dead (1948)" (Brookeman 1984: 150). This use of the term "totalitarianism" is not directly connected to the common definition, which found its greatest evocation in Hitler's Germany or Stalin's Soviet Union. Rather Mailer, suggests Brookeman, "uses the term totalitarian to describe a process of dehumanization that was . . . evident in the culture of American capitalism" (Brookeman 1984: 153).

This version of "totalitarianism" is less a political state, although there is an element of such control, than a social one, a state of mind Mailer sees as alarmingly prevalent in post-war America. Perhaps the best way of understanding his construction of "totalitarianism" is to consider briefly his view of the challenge of Kennedy to Eisenhower:

> In the fifties, every subliminal political sense was ready to tell us that the country was being run by the corporations, the FBI, the CIA and the Mafia . . . In the sixties, that cancer seal began to crack – Kennedy's election was the hairline split to the American totalitarianism of the fifties. (Mailer 1964: 7–8)

Eisenhower's administration was, for Mailer, a "tasteless, sexless, odorless, sanctity in architecture, manners, modes and styles" (Mailer 1964: 43). In an interview in 2000, he talks of the "totalitarianism" of the 1950s being akin to the "totalitarianism of plastic," with all of the substance's qualities of monotony, repetition, and ease of manipulation. Yet it was exactly this dullness, the ability to maintain a period of uneventfulness that was Eisenhower's strength in this moment.

A mixture of post-war apathy, discontent at the onset of another war in Korea, and the need for a sense of security in the post-war atmosphere of anxiety generated by the Cold War, created among the general populace a society ready to actively pursue the ideal of the heroic president, a character who could guarantee the safety that Mailer's "totalitarianism" seemed to promise. This ideal found its form in Dwight Eisenhower. Literary voices, like Mailer's, or Arthur Miller's, or those of the burgeoning Beat Generation, against such "totalitarianism" were in the minority, for the most part the concerns over its negative aspects were expressed by the few intellectuals not cowed by McCarthy. Writing in 1966, in *The Intellectuals and McCarthy*, Michael Rogin suggests, "McCarthy's power, if overwhelming, was comparatively short-lived. But his impact on the intellectual community has lasted far longer. There are those who charge that the McCarthy atmosphere continues to stifle intellectual dissent" (Rogin 1967: 2). For the majority of the American public, "totalitarianism" offered the benefits of being led, of having little to worry about, less to do. It provided a form of security for the masses, safe in the knowledge that someone else was steering the country. Regardless of whether or not "totalitarianism" is a force that "beheads individuality, variety, dissent, extreme possibility, romantic faith, it blinds vision, deadens instinct" (Mailer 1964: 184), it was a condition that the American people supported, a support that allowed the unchecked emergence of McCarthy, the House Un-American Activities Committee and the Communist witch hunts.

This vogue of "totalitarianism" resonates in a variety of places in the 1950s. The sociological studies of this period provide essential evidence of this. Chief among them is David Reisman's *The Lonely Crowd* (1950). In this work, Riesman attempts to define the ideology and social character of 1950s, post-industrial America. What he charts is the movement of the American character away from the tradition-directed values of the feudal system in which "ritual, routine and religion" serve "to occupy and orient everyone." Once capitalism begins to break up feudal structures, such tradition-directed characters must evolve with the times. The next stage he discusses is the inner-directed character, a character that must remain flexible and capable of "adapting himself to ever changing requirements and in return requires more from his environment." Riesman offers the metaphor of a "psychological gyroscope" to represent the notion of the kind of movement the individual must be capable of, "to receive and utilize certain signals from outside" while also simulating the restrictions to that movement, "the limited maneuverability his gyroscope permits him." From this context, Riesman describes the other-directed character (Reisman 1970: 11, 16). As Brookeman points out, Riesman considers "the main agencies of 'other-directed' post-industrial social character [to be] the culture of school, of the peer group, of the mass media and of corporate bureaucracy" (Brookeman

1984: 108). His analysis of schools and education is illuminating. Inner-directed schooling is a system where "the sexes are segregated from each other" and "the focus is on intellectual content that has for most children little emotional bite." The role of other-directed schooling was to expound the virtues of conformity and "totalitarianism": "what matters is not their industry or learning as such, but their adjustment in the group, their co-operation, their (carefully stylized and limited) initiative and leadership." At this time in America, Riesman suggests, the children "will probably conclude that to be unco-operative is about the worst thing one can be" (Reisman 1970: 58, 62, 63).

Christopher Brookeman assesses the contemporary effect of *The Lonely Crowd* in these terms: "A major impact of Riesman's investigations was to reinforce the image of post-war America as a society fast achieving alarming proportions of conformity. His master metaphor of a 'lonely crowd' had overtones of totalitarianism" (Brookeman 1984: 111). Arthur Brodbeck Jr is more precise in his analysis of Riesman's title:

> A "crowd" is a group of people without continuity with past or future, a throng acting upon the temporary stimulant of the moment. It conveys a portrait of men turned animals and running in a herd, pushing and crowding against each other blindly, taking direction from whatever sudden, frightening or comforting event is accidentally encountered. (quoted in Brookeman 1984: 111)

Riesman's was not the only such analysis of "totalitarianism." C. Wright Mill's *The Power Elite*, published in 1956, examined how the power in a post-industrialist society had passed into the hands of three connected groups: corporate capitalists, militarists and politicians, three groups that have parallels in Riesman's agencies of other-direction. Stephen Whitfield sees these socio-logical studies as essential reference points for the Western movie: "The Western film is far more intelligible when fixed within a certain critical tradition that began with Tocqueville over a century ago and was invigorated in the 1950s: the exploration of the pressures of conformity" (Whitfield 1991: 148). Indeed, Whitfield too connects these analyses to *High Noon*: "*High Noon* raised the question of how strongly the private sense of right and wrong – and of personal honor – can resist 'the tyranny of the majority'." He suggests that,

> everyone in Hadleyville but Marshal Will Kane seems to agree that the town will be more secure if he leaves, yet his arguments for remaining are as principled as they are practical. Though fearing for his life, he holds one truth to be self evident – that dangerous evil must be faced and routed rather than evaded and denied.

Whitfield goes on:

> In making the case for personal honor, *High Noon* challenged the semi-
> official ethos of the era, which film director Robert Rossen put most
> succinctly. "I don't think," he told HUAC in 1953, "that anyone can
> indulge himself in the luxury of individual morality or pit it against what
> I feel today very strongly is the security and safety of this nation." But
> "individual morality" is precisely what Kane pits against the townspeople,
> who fear for their "safety and security" should the lawman remain among
> them. (Whitfield 1991: 148)

Zinneman's intended attack upon a growing silent majority is certainly
accounted for in this analysis. So too is the connection between Hadleyville
as a microcosm of the United States. Kane the individual, as Whitfield portrays
him, is an attack upon the contemporary political scene as articulated by Rossen,
a force of deconstruction. Yet, in the film's famous church scene, the townspeople acknowledge that they are being naive if they believe that Miller will not
return the town to its prior hellish state, their "safety and security" is not
guaranteed either way. In this sense then, *High Noon* is an attack upon the tenor
of the times, but is also didactic. Kane is a man who should be supported. That
the people of Hadleyville do not do so allows the depiction of a community not to
be emulated. The community is not worthy of a figure like Kane. Hadleyville
then represents Mailer's "totalitarianism" and as such supports his concerns.
Given the politics of the film-makers, it is not surprising that *High Noon* rails
against the specific ideas set forth by those like Rossen. Yet the film also offers
comfort, in the shape of Kane, that there is a figure who can represent the needs
of his age, the spirit of his time. Unlike *The Gunfighter* which is unable to offer any
sense of hope in its articulation of contemporary anxiety, *High Noon* tempers its
worries by setting up the ideal of the heroic leader, an established figure and one
uniquely suited to react to the problems of the times. This is significant because
what Kane offers is not a commitment to change, but rather to stasis. He fights to
protect the status quo, not to create anything new. This was to a great extent the
mandate Eisenhower was charged with.

As a result, the Eisenhower years were described by Eric Goldman as an era
wherein,

> we've grown unbelievably prosperous and we maunder along in a stupor of
> fat . . . We live in a heavy, humorless, sanctimonious, stultifying atmo-
> sphere, singularly lacking in the self-mockery that is self-criticism. Probably
> the climate of the late Fifties was the dullest and dreariest in all our history.
> (Goldman 1960: 27)

New York Post editorialist William V. Shannon gauged the era in much the same terms:

> The Eisenhower years have been years of flabbiness and self-satisfaction and gross materialism . . . [The] loudest sound in the land has been the oink-and-grunt of private hoggishness . . . It has been the age of the slob. (quoted in Albertson 1963: x)

From such perspectives, the immediate post-war period is marked by the willing acceptance by American society of the kind of "totalitarianism" discussed by the likes of Mailer and Riesman. In this version of "totalitarianism," just as in the traditional version, there is one pivotal construct, and that is the fundamental necessity of a strong personality, a heroic leader who can be seen to offer answers to problems, whilst also demonstrating the definiteness of purpose that engenders respect, faith and security. Although in America, "totalitarianism" is not so much a political system as a mass daydream to mask the true anxiety of the age, the need for a strong leadership figure is still central. In a time of trouble or unrest, the people crave the reassurance of a heroic leader, they "require national discipline of a sort best stimulated by a powerful personality" (Schlesinger Jr 1960: 3).

The Eisenhower Siesta, as William Manchester has labeled it, or the Eisenhower Trance, to quote Arthur Schlesinger Jr, came to an abrupt end in November 1957 when news arrived of the Soviet launch of the first satellite, Sputnik 1. The shockwaves from this event were immense. No longer could Americans delude themselves about their technological superiority. The events in Little Rock the month previous shook the belief that America was a land of the free, of individuals born in equality.

Eisenhower's supporters did not feel particularly strongly about the increasing social malaise that was setting in. However, large elements of the coming generation would look to distance themselves from the inertia of Eisenhower and come to stand behind the youthful figure of John F. Kennedy. Norman Mailer gave credence to this movement when he said that Kennedy challenged the Eisenhower legacy of "false security in the power and panacea of organized religion, family and the FBI" (Mailer 1964: 43). In an interview given to *Esquire* magazine in 1986, Mailer recalls this moment of change:

> in the sixties there was a feeling that we were finally coming out of the Eisenhower era, and that there was an army of us who were sort of young, or still young . . . who were passionate and who were infuriated at the way we'd been held down and felt there was a world to gain. (Lennon 1988: 342)

As Brookeman puts it, "Mailer's qualified support for Kennedy rests on the idea that he represents the only alternative to an intensified totalitarianism in American society" (Brookeman 1984: 159).

That Sputnik should mark the end of the Eisenhower era is portentous. The idea of newness, of technical and scientific advancement at the turn of the decade is crucial. On one level it mirrors Eisenhower's increasing anachronism. On another level, the booming media industry, which had been increasingly evident in American politics since the advent of Roosevelt's radio fireside chats, and which, with the television press conference during the Eisenhower years, had become an important political tool, was by 1960 truly essential to any and all political discourse. It is crucial too that the two men who were to fight the 1960 election were to use this technology to project themselves as young, aggressive and strong.

Post-war American society, in the new shadow of the Cold War, yearned for a hero, at the same time as mourning the loss of Franklin Roosevelt. However, this was a much different hero from any that had been craved in the past. In a sense, what the American people craved in the Cold War, nuclear era was a "super-heroic" president. Not simply a strong, charismatic politician who could lead a country through a crisis, as had been sought in the past, but an individual leader who could steer the country safely, leaving the people with nothing to worry about, a capable barrier between the twinned threat of Communism and nuclear holocaust and themselves.

General Dwight D. Eisenhower was generally credited as the man who "won" the Second World War and as such was ideally and uniquely qualified for the job of president in this particular period of history; a safe, paternalistic leader, who had also demonstrated formidable strength of character in war, a leader whose past promises had been universally followed through. The heroic president no longer was simply an individual with exceptional political skill or a figure related to a single crisis at a particular moment. Rather, he became an icon, something to look up to and to place faith in. He became a center, a focus for a society constantly bombarded with the fear and paranoia generated by the Cold War. Eisenhower was a hero who became president precisely because of that previous heroism and his promise to end the Korean War in a similar manner. Any leader who fulfilled the heroic criteria would be given absolute authority. One of Eisenhower's strengths was that he was able to use this power to do very little. Indeed, as Sherman Adams reports: "He once told the cabinet that if he was able to do nothing as president except balance the budget he would feel that his time in the White House had been well spent" (Adams 1961: 28). Although this is perhaps a valid political goal, it certainly portrays Eisenhower as a leader of little vision or purpose, lacking any sense of the pro-active drive that the Cold War and the approaching decade of the 1960s seemed increasingly to demand. Norman Mailer is typically outspoken in his opposition to this inertia: "Eisenhower could stand as a hero only for that large number of Americans who were most proud of their lack of imagination" (Mailer 1964: 43). However, in a period when the American people wanted a return to quieter times, this does not sound so harsh a criticism.

Eisenhower was able to tap into the feeling of the masses, that something had gone wrong for America. His platform was not a partisan one; a vote for Eisenhower was a vote for the man. Eisenhower was unique among twentieth-century presidents in that his political experience lay in international affairs; he had little knowledge of domestic policy (Divine 1981: vii). Eisenhower's appeal lay in his previous international victories. At a time when the American economy was thriving and standards of living were increasing, but internationally there still existed conflict, perceived and real, Eisenhower can be seen to be the nation's hero. Eisenhower, the general, was a people's hero and if as a general he had the qualities to defend the world from tyranny, surely Eisenhower could transfer his abilities to the office of Chief-Executive and maintain the status quo.

This status quo, the vaguely benevolent "totalitarianism" as described by Mailer, was a fundamental feature of the 1950s. Yet the 1950s was also the point of origin for much of the coming counter-culture. "Totalitarianism" represents a mass day dream, a dream that exists as much for the country as the individual. Talking of this notion of day-dream in 1950s and 1960s Britain, Christopher Booker explains:

> The full workings of fantasy in society are, in fact, both so complex and yet so simple that they can only be fully appreciated and understood by looking at their evolution in detail, in one society in particular, over one particular period of history. Only thus is it possible to appreciate fully the way in which fantasy works like a disease; the way in which all forms of fantasy are highly contagious, feeding on and attracting each other; and the way in which, a society or individual infected by one form of fantasy is all the more susceptible to others. (Booker 1992: 79)

This is an interesting version of the pattern of post-war American history, how McCarthy's Communists led to Eisenhower's heroic inertia, which in turn led to Mailer's "totalitarianism." The emerging counter-cultural trends are the first attempts to question this state of affairs. The public response to the writings of the Beat Generation strongly illustrates their minimal contemporary effect. The 1950s was the decade wherein the day-dream was stronger than the attempts at rebellion. The 1960s represents the inversion of this; a decade where the mass day-dream is corrupted and ultimately destroyed, both individually and nationally. The links between the two decades are crucial, the fifties coming to represent something of a dry run for the sixties. One of the strongest images of the national day-dream was that America existed as the chief defender of democracy in the face of the heinous, Moscow-driven Communist onslaught. This was the thinking that led to American involvement in both Korea and Vietnam. The Beat writers of the fifties, although largely insignificant in their immediate time, created the arena in which a counter-cultural voice could be accepted and listened to, a voice that would be more spectacularly taken up by the likes of Bob Dylan. The 1960s peeled back the skin of the fantasy life, the day-dream that was so crucial to America in the 1950s. The Western, the ultimate American day-dream, was uniquely able to represent both sides of this dream/reality equation simultaneously throughout this period. The 1950s represent a contradictory mix of cultural tradition and revolution, a harking back to times past and the beginning of the movement toward the 1960s. This combination of old and new is essential to an understanding of the 1950s, and is typified in the period's Westerns. The Western was the perfect medium to channel the twin concerns of tradition and contemporary society. Stated boldly, no other cinematic genre has the ability to handle these dual concerns. Other genres were inadequate, often too elitist, or not popular enough. The Western made the "new" more palatable by associating it with and exploring it in relation to the "old."

It is because *High Noon* is ultimately so redolent of Eisenhower that it is unable to speak of or for anyone or anything else. Eisenhower's presidency was timely, of its time, serving a very particular need in the country's history. Reactions to his presidency in the latter days beset both narratives with problems. Ultimately, *High Noon* is unable to transcend Eisenhower, just as Eisenhower is unable to transcend his era. Eisenhower's is a circumscribed narrative. Once he leaves office, there is no more to the story, and certainly his failing health lends weight to this perception. This parallels Kane hurling his star into the dust and moving on with his Quaker wife. His riding off is not a suggestion of new adventures, but rather retirement and resignation, a narrative closure. In both narratives there is the conclusion to a larger story, and as such, there emerges the point at which a new narrative must begin.

SHANE (1953): THE KENNEDY WESTERN

Released in April 1953, *Shane* had been in production almost from the moment of the novel's publication. Paramount bought the screen rights to Schaefer's book in 1949, merely weeks after it appeared, and offered it to George Stevens on 1 June 1950. Stevens accepted the job and set about finding a screen writer. Significantly, Schaefer was not even considered among the seventeen names that were submitted. Stevens lured A. B. Guthrie Jr away from his classes at the University of Kentucky with a lot of persuasion and $1500 a week, for four weeks work on the script. Work began on the screenplay on 11 January 1951, and was completed by April of the same year.

The cinematic version of *Shane* differs from the Schaefer original in a number of ways. The narrator, Bob Starrett in the novel, becomes Joey Starrett, taking on his father's name. Fletcher, the cattle baron, becomes Ryker. Torrey, who is just another settler in the novel, is transformed by the film into a Confederate, and nicknamed Stonewall. In the shoot-out at the climax of the movie, Shane is shot in the arm, suggesting a relatively straight-forward recovery. In the novel he is gut shot, suggesting the possibility of survival is far more ambiguous. Perhaps the most significant difference lies in the perspective of the narrator. In the novel Bob has the dual perspective of a grown man remembering his childhood. In the film, an overall narration is not apparent, although Stevens does skillfully portray much of the film through the young boy's eyes.

The near dismissal of Schaefer's authorship of *Shane*, evidenced in the recent study of the film by Edward Countryman and Yvonne von Heussen-Countryman, is simply a continuation of the pattern that was apparent contemporaneously to the film's making. Schaefer had no part in the scripting of his novel for the screen. Indeed, although he was aware *Shane* had been optioned shortly after its 1949 publication, he learned about the actual details of production only when they appeared in a newspaper article:

Paramount bought the film rights and there followed, insofar as I was concerned, a prolonged silence broken only by a note seen in a paper that A.B. Guthrie, Jr. was doing the screenplay. Time passed and I read an article in the New York Times stating that George Stevens was filming an epic called Shane in the Jackson Hole country of Wyoming. I wrote to him . . . saying that I was curious what he was doing with my story and wondered if I could see a copy of the script. No reply, not even from an office boy's assistant.

So Schaefer was completely divorced from the film-making process, but he was also to be disconnected, by the studio, from the source material itself:

Then the publicity build-up started, keyed to the dominant note that George Stevens, in virtually single-handed genius, had created a masterpiece. Mr. Guthrie, a one time Pulitzer Prize winner, was occasionally mentioned. Once or twice I even came on my own name – misspelled and coupled with such fascinating misinformation as the assertion that the story was a short which had appeared in Esquire. Then even that faded and reached the point at which, in various ecstatic previews and in an article in Colliers, the flat statement was made that Mr. Guthrie wrote the story.

In an interesting piece in INFO, dated October 1953, headlined "MAN WITH A GRIPE," Schaefer responds to some of the more outlandish claims made by the publicity machine surrounding the release of *Shane*. The basis of the article is a press release relating quotes from a letter Schaefer supposedly sent Stevens which contained some jarring comments. One of these was Schaefer "expressing surprise . . . over Stevens" ability to "extract such thunder from my plain and simple yarn." Another inaccuracy has the magazine editor who bought *Shane* referring to Schaefer as "a lucky idiot who didn't deserve a break into print" because he had single-spaced his manuscript. Schaefer's reply to all this is simple and to the point: "nuts!" Again though, the article makes apparent Schaefer's key gripe with the production of the movie. Schaefer was not especially incensed over the content of the release as such, but he took exception to it as a prime example of the picture's publicity campaign which, he stated, carried a deliberate and obvious slant aimed "to inflate George Stevens as the master-mind who, virtually single-handed, created a masterpiece." According to Schaefer, the fact that Stevens "had a reasonably good book to start with and that almost everything of value in the film was directly suggested by and in many instances carefully spelled out for him in that book, has been ignored."

Countryman taps directly into this misinformation surrounding the authorship, a situation that Schaefer counters effectively:

> Against that background, it begun to be somewhat aggravating to note, in those previews and later in the regular reviews, that most of the things cited, beyond point of physical film technique, as evidences of Mr. Stevens' genius and Mr. Guthrie's subsidiary assistance, were derived directly from the book.

Schaefer seems eminently even handed in his criticism of the way he was excluded from the film's production. He talks of how he recognizes that keeping the author out of the equation makes sound sense given that the author's ownership of the source material may preclude an objective adaptation or elision of dialogue or incident. He comments upon the technical quality of the film, stating that Stevens had "not only capable, but eminently qualified assistants." However, and this is the source of his chagrin, he believes that

> it would have been pleasant and somewhat on the fair side if he [Stevens] or any of the others, in the voluminous publicity and interviews, had also let slip a stray hint or two that they had fairly good material with which to work – a book that was the original impetus for the whole enterprise and which

gave them, not just the story which was relatively unimportant because composed of old familiar ingredients (though it did strip these down for them into the lean, concentrated, classical form they use), but also the attitude towards those ingredients, the manner of treatment, even the method of presentation which helped give the film maximum impact.

Schaefer's aggravation at a lack of proper recognition, given that it is perpetuated in Countryman's study, is well placed. However, this does not prevent him from giving an interesting, in-depth opinion on the movie adaptation of his novel. In general, he says of the film, "It was remarkably faithful, not only in story, but in tone, in approach, in treatment, in effect sought, to the book." In effect, Schaefer can see himself, his authorship, his intentions for the story brought to the screen. The differences that exist for Schaefer are stylistic not thematic. He is not a great admirer of the Stevens technique:

> I think that Mr. Stevens made a fine film, a very fine film, within the limits of his somewhat limited use of the medium (which he shares for probably sound commercial reasons with most American producers) and of his own rather recently developed personal "style" . . . There were sequences that were slow and dragging, result of that "style" with its over-use of dissolves and tendency to try to draw too much out of certain scenes . . . And there were times when, for me, the film seemed to jump a bit in and out of focus as if Mr. Stevens had not quite made up his mind whether he was doing a genre or period piece or a symbolic epic. But that too is part of the "style" – a quiet authentic realism in which slow tension builds to burst into the release of violent impressionistic action. All that is picking on picayune points, simply adding up to the conclusion that I am not a devotee of Mr. Stevens' style.

He does not begrudge Stevens a style, "a man making a film has as much right to his style as a man writing a book." And in his final analysis of Stevens' movie, Schaefer is complimentary:

> He translated my book into a film in which all major components, script and settings and music and photography and casting and performances, combined to offer frequent sequences as fine as I have ever seen, a film which, on the whole, had an epic sweep that was refreshing, dependent not on mere size and scope but on a consistent attitude towards and treatment of the material. He worked not only with a definite style but with an overall concept, that of presenting the basic Western legend, a blend of history and folklore, in its simplest and most human and dramatic form. (all quotes from unpublished essay, Jack Schaefer collection).

Shane, the movie, is so good because it has as a foundation *Shane*, the novel. Regardless of Countryman's reading of events, Schaefer cannot be divorced from the movie adaptation of his novel. All the qualities with which Schaefer imbued his novel are present in Stevens' Western, and, most importantly, the character of Shane himself translates practically untouched. The resonance he has in the novel is thus brought to a far wider audience. Indeed, the quality of the movie was instantly recognized by the critics and the movie-going public alike.

High Noon was immediately recognized as having political overtones, whether it be an allegory of the Korean War or an attack upon McCarthyism. *Shane* has no such political connotations attached to it. Rather it was immediately understood in the realm of mythic revision and Western folklore. *Time*, 13 April 1953, writes:

> It tells the familiar old Western yarn about the good guy v. the badmen . . . This conventional screenplay has been filmed in entirely unconventional style by Producer-Director George Stevens.

Look repeats this analysis in a photo spread, 19 May 1953:

> [Stevens] has performed the near miracle freshening up familiar prairie folklore (honest homesteaders terrorized by villainous cattle barons) by sensitively making his characters real and understandable human beings instead of the usual symbols of virtue and evil.

In the same piece, a headline reinforces *Shane*'s mythic credentials: "A homeless cowboy St. George slays the homesteaders' evil dragon." Otis L. Guernsey Jr in another review from 1953 defines *Shane* as:

> an exciting and spectacular Technicolor drama built to Western specifications, but adding a unique point of view and an element of good sense to the good old story of hot-headed Americans carving a civilization in the glorious wilderness.

Rose Pelswick writing in the *New York Journal* (1953) says:

> "Shane" is not a conventional sagebrush saga. A rousing story of the old West at the turn of the century, the picture is consistently sound in its workmanship and characterizations and relies on none of the time-worn, wide-open-space clichés.

Alton Cook, in the *World Telegram*, 24 April 1953, articulates a similar sense of the film:

> Director George Stevens has reworked standard Western story and character material but he has given it a rugged vigor and sincerity it does not often carry. His people are engaged in an ordinary, industrious struggle to subdue a new land. If heroism is needed they can briefly become heroes but they prefer to be left to their plodding, hard work.

It is significant that *Shane* should be received in this way. *High Noon's* political readings lock it into a specific time and place. Any subtext is fundamentally attached to that period in American history. *Shane*, seen as an updating of traditional mythic and generic patterns, is not so bound up in its age. Rather, by establishing something new within the mythology of the Western, *Shane* is archetypal, timeless. This sense of timelessness is important in connecting *Shane* to *The Gunfighter* and *High Noon*. Where time is an integral theme in the narratives of the latter two, acting as a central symbolism, *Shane* is not concerned with time at all. The novel begins with a date, 1889, but the movie has no such connection. There are no clocks and even the passage of time through the day does not give a sense of conventional chronology.

Jack Schaefer's *Shane* cannot be underestimated. It is his construction of the character that was transferred, practically unchanged into the more familiar movie. This is not to say that the film version does not have anything to add to *Shane's* relation to the political culture. Indeed, the cinematic rendering of the source novel acts to strengthen the novel's portrait of heroic leadership. Given that so much of what appears in the film comes directly from the novel, Countryman's designation of Stevens as author, or Fiedler's outright dismissal of Schaefer and his novel, are demonstrably misjudged. The film then does not represent the origin of *Shane*, but the film is vital to the understanding of the links between *Shane* and American political culture.

Shane established in the popular imagination a further archetype of leadership and heroism, one significantly different from that set up in *High Noon*. *Shane*, either in its literary or cinematic form, necessarily could not have been about Kennedy in any direct, deterministic way. However, so compelling a mythical archetype was the film's central character, the ultimate articulation of the right leader at the right time, that it becomes a valid point of reference in examining matters of leadership. Given Schaefer's composition of Shane, the model of leadership that the character represents resonates with the Kennedy image.

Shane created an example of a very different type of leadership for the times. Pauline Kael described Shane as "Galahad on the range" (Kael 1983: 526) and it is this allusion to chivalry that is crucial to his "different" heroism. The costume of the cowboy hero had always been a significant feature of the Western from William Hart through Tom Mix, Gene Autry and Roy Rogers. However, as the Western entered its more realistic phase, so the clothes became less conspicuous, less ornate and more utilitarian.

Shane's garb is like that of a knight, regimented and ornate yet purposeful. His manner is courteous, chivalric. This aristocratic air is taken directly from Jack Schaefer's novel. His origins are ambiguous, neither Easterner nor Westerner, he just belongs in this environment at an elemental level, his surprise at the price of clothes suggesting a distance from society. It is also evoked in the choice of actor for the role. Alan Ladd did not make very many Westerns in his thirty year career. Standing only five foot five inches high, his was not the rugged frontier persona. Robert Warshow sees the choice of Ladd "to play the leading role [as] an indication of [*Shane*]'s tendency":

> Actors like Gary Cooper or Gregory Peck are in themselves, as material objects, "realistic," seeming to bear in their bodies and their faces mortality, limitation, the knowledge of good and evil. Ladd is more "aesthetic" object, with some of the "universality" of a piece of sculpture; his special quality is in his physical smoothness and serenity, unworldly and yet not innocent, but suggesting that no experience can really touch him. Stevens has tried to freeze the Western myth once and for all in the immobility of Alan Ladd's countenance. (Warshow 1970: 150)

Better known by audiences as a hard-boiled tough guy, Raymond Chandler offered an insightful description of Ladd's appeal: "he is after all a small boy's idea of a tough guy" (Gardiner and Walker 1962: 217). However, with *Shane*, he became one of the major faces of the genre. His softer features, more classic leading man looks, added to his sense of distance from those around him, both within the narrative and amongst other Western actors. His look was not one made for the Western, though. He would come back to the genre later in his career, but without significant success.

Similar to Kane, Shane is not quick to temper or violence, but when it is called for he is amply prepared. *Shane* presented the American public with a hero of truly mythical proportions, exceptional in a way that Kane is not. Kane was made the way he was through work and guidance. He could easily have gone over the line that distinguishes good and bad. Shane has none of this background. He appears at a time when the society needs him, when the society is on the brink of a new era, with new versions of old rules and problems, chief among them, the shift from pastoralism to small farming. This idea of the new era is best illustrated in the name of the family Shane adopts, Starrett, pronounced "start" through most of the film. This, combined with the film's simpler narrative perspective, that of the young boy, Joey Starrett, makes Shane a leader for the new era, a man to be followed. The inevitability of action or violence in High Noon becomes mixed with a boyish anticipation of such action and violence in Shane. A society has gone from idly sitting back and waiting for the inevitable to yearning for confrontation, actively, and, through the heroic leader, pursuing it as a means of progress. The acceptance of violence for a leader like Shane is central. For Shane, the gun is "just a tool," a necessary evil that is just one element of his ability to lead and inspire men. Shane is young, but has a charisma that draws people to him, especially Joe's wife, Marian, but it is also worth noting the incident where Chris Calloway, one of Ryker's men who has already picked fights with Shane and, ultimately, lost heavily, comes to tell him of the trap that is planned for Joe. When asked why he is proffering this information, he replies, "Something's kinda come over me."

The version of democracy presented in/by Shane is interesting. He symbolically changes his exceptional clothes, from buckskins to blue jeans, to fit in with the society, to hide his own exceptionalism. His tasseled buckskins do not make an appearance again until he has to go to town to face Wilson and Ryker's men. By far the most explicit illustration of Shane's democracy lies in the protracted stump scene. Without being asked he begins to attack a huge, gnarly tree-stump on Starrett's land, a stump that Starrett himself had been battling against for some time. Shane knows what the problem is and how to deal with it. Starrett joins him and together they finish the job, a symbol of unity that is repeated in the brawl in the bar. In both instances, Shane takes the initiative, Starrett following. And in both instances, the bonding and co-operation result in victories. The fight at the end between Shane and Starrett over who should go to town to face Ryker and Wilson, offers the notion of the battle between leader and public: there may be moments of internal disagreement and conflict and it may be painful in the short term but it is ultimately for the public good. This final fight between Shane and Joe is important, because it shows Shane's selflessness and reinforces the idea of him as a knowing, willing sacrifice, instrumental to progress. The fight is surrounded by a tumult of natural sound giving it the feeling of a titanic clash. Toward the end of the fight the two men seem inseparable. Exchanging blows equally, they tumble toward the stump of the tree that was removed at the beginning of the narrative. Once against this stump, Shane is able to regain his balance and knock Joe unconscious with the butt of his revolver. If the stump represents the democratic union of leader and public in a common cause, then Shane's "use" of the stump may well signify a leader relying upon a past victory or right decision to explain or justify a present or future conflict. Shane, despite an initial disagreement regarding the method of incapacitating Joe, is vindicated when he asks Marian to say sorry on his behalf. "He already knows," she replies. Heroic leadership requires the making of some difficult, possibly painful decisions, but the resolution, in this case the death of Wilson and Ryker and thus a cessation of further interference from "big business," makes the pain and difficulties worthwhile.

JOHN F. KENNEDY AS SHANE

Shane represents a vastly influential model for heroism and leadership that would find a permanent place in the American psyche. Examining this model alongside Kennedy's emergence in the 1960 election campaign offers some striking reflections and resonances. However, in the broader context, the continued significance of this Western as a truly political narrative lies in its reworking over the next four decades; each version of the *Shane*-myth acting as an excellent barometer of and window on social, cultural and political feeling in the United States.

Kennedy was the first president to be deliberately marketed and represented in terms of a film star. This has no better illustration than in his success against Richard Nixon in the series of live debates. As a consequence, the Kennedy presidential campaign began to receive the kind of attention and hysteria usually reserved for movie stars. Theodore H. White, in *The Making of the President 1960* (1962) describes vividly Kennedy's "star quality":

> Any reporter who followed the Kennedy campaign remembers still the quantum jump in the size of the crowds that greeted the campaigning Senator from the morrow of the first debate . . . His crowds had been growing for a full seven days before the debates, but now, overnight, they seethed with enthusiasm and multiplied in numbers, as if the sight of him, in their homes on the video box, had given him a "star quality" reserved only for television and movie idols. (White 1962: 291)

Later in the campaign, numbers and enthusiasm still growing, White records scenes that would seem more suited to The Beatles' famous Shea Stadium gig in 1965:

> One remembers being in a Kennedy crowd and suddenly sensing far off on the edge of it a ripple of pressure beginning, and the ripple . . . would grow like a wave, surging forward as it gathered strength, until it would squeeze the front rank of the crowd against the wooden barricade . . . One remembers the groans and moans; and a frowzy woman muttering hoarsely . . . "Oh, Jack I love yuh, Jack, I love yuh, Jack – Jack, Jack, I love yuh" . . . One remembers, of course, the jumpers . . . The jumpers were, in

the beginning, teen-age girls who would bounce, jounce and jump as the cavalcade passed, squealing, "I seen him, I seen him." (White 1962: 330–1)

Kennedy came to represent a new virility in American politics. The president went from an icon of control and power, of political safety, to aggressively youthful and pro-active in the pursuit of American interests and an end to the Cold War. This was something totally new. Once again, Norman Mailer provides insight: "that he was young, that he was physically handsome, and that his wife was attractive were not trifling accidental details but, rather, new major political facts" (Mailer 1964: 26). Kennedy's campaign success lay in precisely the way he offered a means of escaping from the deadening effect of "totalitarianism," this escape coming to represent a major defining feature in the transition of 1950s to the 1960s. As Mailer suggests:

regardless of [Kennedy's] overt politics, America's tortured psychotic search for security would finally be torn loose from the feverish ghosts of its old generals, its MacArthurs and Eisenhowers – ghosts which Nixon could cling to – and we as a nation would finally be loose again in the historic seas of the national psyche which was willy-nilly and at last, again, adventurous. (Mailer 1964: 27)

Kennedy's electoral platform was a direct appeal against the inertia of the Eisenhower administration, embodied in the campaign slogan, "I think it's time America started moving again" (White 1962: 287). By moving forward domestically, Kennedy believed that the United States could move forward internationally. What Kennedy was able to do was to tap into the vague fears and paranoia that existed, offering himself as a leader who would not only protect the individual as Eisenhower had done, but actively pursue these concerns to some kind of resolution. That the American people perceived some kind of intangible threat to come, and that further, Kennedy was best suited to deal with that threat was his mandate.

Close readings of four texts illustrate the ways in which Kennedy can be seen to be constructing a persona, and significantly a persona that has resonance with the character of Shane. These are: a speech delivered to the National Press Club in Washington, D.C., 14 January 1960 entitled, "The Presidency in 1960"; the Arthur Schlesinger Jr book, *Kennedy or Nixon: Does it Make Any Difference?*; the context and effect of the debates between Kennedy and Nixon, broadcast live on radio and television between September and October 1960; and the account of the Kennedy style and persona as it emerged at the 1960 Democrat convention, that is presented in Norman Mailer's *Superman Comes to the Supermarket*. These texts are connected by the fact that they offer versions of Kennedy before he becomes president. They act as witnesses to the nature of his arrival on the global political scene and provide a number of useful insights into the creation of a persona, his promise and the manner of his acceptance.

THE PRESIDENCY IN 1960

On 14 January 1960, John Fitzgerald Kennedy delivered this speech to the National Press Club in Washington, D.C. Although his nomination as Democratic presidential candidate would not be made until July, in the speech Kennedy established several aspects of his conception not only of what the presidency should be, but also what the presidency has been, during the two terms of the Eisenhower tenure. He prefaced the speech by stating:

> the public is rarely alerted to a candidate's views about the central issue on which all the rest turn. That central issue – and the point of my comments this noon – is not the farm problem or defense or India. It is the presidency itself.

Kennedy seems to be conscious from the outset that his presidency would be different, and that this difference would mark him out as poles apart from Eisenhower.

> The history of this nation – its brightest and its bleakest pages – has been written largely in terms of the different views our Presidents have had of the Presidency itself. This history ought to tell us that the American people in 1960 have an imperative right to know what any man bidding for the Presidency thinks about the place he is bidding for, whether he is aware of and willing to use the powerful resources of the office.

In some ways this is an ideal approach to damage Nixon's run for the presidency. Kennedy is overtly dealing with precedents, "whether his model will be Taft or Roosevelt, Wilson or Harding." All the while, he is implicitly suggesting through his recognition and discussion of his conception of the presidency, that he follows no model, but is rather leading the way, creating a new model. Nixon in this sense is unable to compete, having been Eisenhower's vice-president for eight years, he is in no position to talk against this model, and in fact, must defend it.

It is not long before Kennedy moves from the general concept of a prospective candidate discussing his views of the office of Chief Executive towards a more specific attack upon the Eisenhower years:

During the past eight years, we have seen one concept of the presidency at work. Our needs and hopes have been eloquently stated – but the initiative and follow-through have too often been left to others. And too often his own objectives have been lost by the President's failure to override objections from within his own party, in the Congress or even his Cabinet.

The American people in 1952 and 1956 may have preferred this detached, limited concept of the Presidency after 20 years of fast-moving, creative Presidential rule. Perhaps historians will regard this as necessarily one of those frequent periods of consolidation, a time to draw breath, to recoup our national energy. To quote the State of the Union message: "no Congress . . . on surveying the state of the Nation, has met with a more pleasing prospect than that which appears at the present time." Unfortunately this is not Mr. Eisenhower's last message to the Congress, but Calvin Coolidge's. He followed to the White House Mr. Harding, whose sponsor declared very frankly that the times did not demand a first-rate President. If true, the times and the man met.

In this way, Kennedy, quite subtly, tars Eisenhower with the same brush: a president right for the times, not greater than them. This is a clear articulation of the notion of Eisenhower, the heroic leader whose heroism is established before he becomes president, the hero who cannot transcend the narrative. After this smoothly damning description of Eisenhower, Kennedy asks the fundamental question: "what do the times – and the people – demand for the next four years in the White House?" His response to his own question is clearly his conception of himself as leader: vigorous, active, heroic. And it also offers many resonances with the nature of Shane as a leader, as a hero:

[The times and the people] demand a vigorous proponent of the national interest – not a passive broker for conflicting private interests. They demand a man capable of acting as the commander in chief of the Great Alliance, not merely a bookkeeper who feels that his work is done when the numbers on the balance sheet come even. They demand that he be the head of a responsible party, not rise so far above politics as to be invisible – a man who will formulate and fight for legislative policies, not be a casual bystander to the legislative process.

This is almost a call to action, one which resonates with his famous inaugural demand of "ask not what your country can do for you, ask what you can do for your country." But Kennedy goes further in offering what is essentially a reversal of the Eisenhower style:

Today a restricted concept of the Presidency is not enough. For beneath today's surface gloss of peace and prosperity are increasingly dangerous, unsolved, long postponed problems – problems that will inevitably explode to the surface during the next four years of the next administration – the growing missile gap, the rise of Communist China, the despair of the underdeveloped nations, the explosive situations in Berlin and in the Formosa Straits, the deterioration of NATO, the lack of an arms control agreement, and all the domestic problems of our farms, cities and schools.

This passage from the speech is crucial to the image Kennedy was establishing for himself and, less explicitly, it demonstrates how he would seek to establish his heroism from within the presidency itself. These are the words of an active leader, highlighting issues that need to be tackled, issues that "this administration has not faced up to." This immediately, then, places him at odds with Eisenhower, the invisible, casual bystander. But more telling is the language he uses. Twice he uses the idea of explosion to articulate the danger of these foreign policy situations, immediately invoking the anxiety of the bomb, and, through his fearless confrontation with these issues, pushing himself forward as the man who should control the button. This application of the fear of atomic war is further compounded in the listing of the missile gap and the lack of an arms agreement, which are essentially the same thing, but the double mention increases its centrality to the concerns of the 1960s, the next president and, by necessity, the American people. In all of this Kennedy is coming to a single conclusion:

In the decade that lies ahead – in the challenging revolutionary sixties – the American Presidency will demand more than ringing manifestoes issued from the rear of the battle. It will demand that the President place himself in the very thick of the fight, that he care passionately about the fate of the people he leads, that he be willing to serve them, at the risk of incurring their momentary displeasure.

Kennedy, again, highlights the newness of the coming 1960s, that the times are changing. Crucially, he articulates this in terms of violence: this is a battle, wherein the president must be in the thick of the fighting. The combat imagery is far removed from the notion of siesta attached to Eisenhower. Kennedy repeatedly suggests that the 1960s will be a time of unnamed radical shifts. When he quotes Woodrow Wilson, "the President is at liberty, both in law and conscience, to be as big a man as he can," Kennedy establishes something of the nature of the frontier hero. Couple this with a sentiment he articulates regarding the nature of the presidency as an institution, and there emerges a pattern that resembles quite specifically Shane's heroism:

Ulysses Grant considered the President "a purely administrative officer" . . . But that is not the place the Presidency was meant to have in American life. The President is alone, at the top – the loneliest job there is, as Harry Truman has said. If there is destructive dissention among the services, he alone can step in and straighten it out – instead of waiting for unanimity. If administrative agencies are not carrying out their mandate – if a brushfire threatens some part of the globe – he alone can act, without waiting for the Congress.

While he acknowledges that such action may bring the charge of dictatorship, Kennedy suggests that the next occupant of the White House may have to act in such a way, "if the times demand." The "turbulent sixties" he envisions will require a new kind of president:

> [we cannot] afford a Chief Executive who is praised primarily for what he did not do, the disasters he prevented, the bills he vetoed – a President wishing his subordinates would produce more missiles or build more schools. We will need instead what the Constitution envisioned: a Chief Executive who is the vital center of action in our whole scheme of government.

This version of the president creates an image which resonates with *Shane*: a new leader, like Shane, who arrives afresh and takes up the challenge. A president who will act decisively in government as Shane acted decisively in 1880s Wyoming. The new president for these new times "will need a real fighting mood in the White House." He must be "a man who will not retreat in the face of pressure." Kennedy's vision of the president is one where he works pro-actively in the political arena. But he must also be a moral leader, the White House "must be the center of moral leadership":

> For only the President represents national interest. And upon him alone converge all the needs and aspirations of all parts of the country, all departments of the government, all nations of the world. It is not enough merely to represent prevailing sentiment . . . We will need in the sixties a President who is willing and able to summon his national constituency to its finest hour – to alert the people to our dangers and our opportunities – to demand of them the sacrifices that will be necessary.

In all of this, Kennedy has one model, a model that will endow the office of president "with extraordinary strength and vision":

> We must act in the image of Abraham Lincoln summoning his wartime Cabinet to a meeting on the Emancipation Proclamation. That Cabinet has

[sic] been carefully chosen to please and reflect many elements in the country. But "I have gathered you together," Lincoln said, "to hear what I have written down. I do not wish your advice about the main matter – that I have determined for myself." And later, when he went to sign, after several hours of exhausting hand shaking that had left his arm weak, he said to those present: "If my name goes down in history, it will be for this act. My whole soul is in it. If my hand trembles when I sign this proclamation, all who examine the document hereafter will say, 'He hesitated.'" But Lincoln's hand did not tremble. He did not hesitate. He did not equivocate. For he was the President of the United States. It is in this spirit that we must go forth in the coming months and years.

Kennedy's speech seems to have made an impact because Richard Nixon, in a press conference in Miami Beach, Florida, two days later, responds to some of Kennedy's remarks:

In looking at Senator Kennedy's statement, I disagree with his tendency to characterize leadership too much in terms of the personalities of the individual Presidents involved rather than in terms of what they accomplished. An appraisal of leadership cannot be put down and described in terms of absolute, rigid, black-and-white categories. To say that one man is a strong leader and another man is a weak leader may be, on the basis of a whole record, a fair appraisal. But whether a man is a strong or weak leader is determined by the results rather than the methods. Now looking to the 60s. I believe the American people in their President are looking for a number of characteristics, whether he is a Democrat or a Republican. Among these are: first, that the President of the United States be a man who knows the great international and domestic issues . . . That knowledge, it seems to me, must then be combined with leadership qualities. The President must have the ability to gain support for the policies he believes are in the best interests of the nation. When we speak of strong leadership, there is sometimes a tendency for people to say that we need, whenever some kind of crisis comes up, is for somebody to rush out and charge and lead the people in the proper direction . . . But in the '60s . . . the American people and the free world need in the American Presidency a man who has sound and sober judgment – a man who in a crisis will be cool, a man who won't go off half-cocked. (Nixon 1960: 135–6)

In this response, Nixon is essentially signaling a major distinction between the personalities of himself and Kennedy. Where Kennedy is supporting a model of leadership that can operate pro-actively, existentially almost, Nixon is advocating calm, learning, study. Even in this one passage, the difference between the two men is manifest: Nixon is the politician, ground out through the system. Kennedy is the new boy, young, idealistic, intelligent, and vigorous. Indeed, in the run up to the election, the comparisons and contrasts between the two men become more clearly defined.

KENNEDY OR NIXON: DOES IT MAKE ANY DIFFERENCE? (1960)

In an attempt to boost Kennedy in the 1960 presidential election campaign, Arthur Schlesinger Jr posed the question, *Kennedy or Nixon: Does it Make Any Difference?* Schlesinger's intention was to put to an end the "favorite cliché of 1960 . . . that the two candidates . . . are essentially the same sort of men, stamped from the same mold, committed to the same values, dedicated to the same objectives – that they are, so to speak, the Gold Dust Twins of American politics." His reasons for undertaking this analysis of the two men's difference are familiar: "this difference may be vital to the safety and survival of our nation in the troubled years ahead" (Schlesinger Jr 1960: vii). Indeed, one of Schlesinger's conclusions in the book is "if everything is fine in the United States, then Nixon is the man for President." Schlesinger argues his case in much the same terms as Kennedy's speech. Kennedy is a man of action, Nixon is a hangover from the Eisenhower era:

> Nixon remains a characteristic figure of the Eisenhower period – concerned with externals rather than substance, indifferent to the merits of issues, generally satisfied with things as they are. There is no reason to suppose that a Nixon administration would be much different from an Eisenhower administration . . . Kennedy, on the other hand, stands for a new epoch in American politics. He understands that we can't go on as we have in the last decade. He understands that our nation must awaken from the Eisenhower trance and get on the march again. He understands that this requires purpose and sacrifice. (Schlesinger Jr 1960: 50, 33)

In defining the personalities of the two men, Schlesinger creates two radically differing, almost bipolar political portraits. Nixon is described as a man with ambition, but no policies. His concern is nothing more or less than Nixon, his preoccupation is image. Schlesinger offers a telling illustration in this regard. In a newspaper article in the *New York Herald Tribune*, 7 August 1960, it is written that Nixon, who is not a "natural smiler" or glamour boy "can turn [such] Kennedy assets into liabilities, contrasting his own humble, plodding, serious, lonely – he would like it to be called Lincolnesque – manner with that of the wealthy, flashy, handsome, sometimes imperious Kennedy clan." Schlesinger offers this as an example of Nixon's misplaced priorities: "Can one think of any President who began his campaign for high office conducting fascinated discussions of his own 'image' and entreating that his personality be thereafter described as Lincolnesque?" (Schlesinger Jr 1960: 17).

From such a perspective, Schlesinger attacks Nixon's reasons for running for president. His running represents quite simply the logical next step of a highly ambitious career man. Nixon believes in nothing and everything, and as such can change his mind without damaging his public persona; Schlesinger goes as far as to suggest that the public expect such chameleon-like qualities from him. Nixon is not natural in any sense. Schlesinger offers the famous quote he made to Ralph de Toledano, "the only time to lose your temper in politics is when it's deliberate," as evidence of the "fantastic energy and solemnity" Nixon expends on analyzing his image. Nixon is constructed, artificial:

> Issues for him are subordinate and secondary, to be maneuvered and manipulated. What matters is stance, not substance: what matters is a felt righteousness of motive, a sentence of humility on the lips, a look of dedication on the face.

Given this portrait of Nixon, Schlesinger begins Kennedy's by immediately underscoring the whole point of the exercise: "it is clear that Kennedy could hardly be more different" (Schlesinger Jr 1960: 16, 18).

Kennedy is natural: a natural scholar, a natural hero, a natural politician, a natural leader. Kennedy is a candidate who stands for something. He is a man with real interest in a range of real issues, a range in which popularity is not a consideration. Whereas Nixon's image is created from Nixon's careful crafting of it, Kennedy's is derived naturally, any sense of image (which is of course as crucial to Kennedy) coming second to policy. When Schlesinger discusses Kennedy's image, he does so in terms of exceptionalism:

> He cannot disavow his age, his money, his looks, his college, his father, his intellect, his religion, his self-possession, or even his sense that he can achieve what needs to be achieved more effectively than almost anyone else on the scene. Therefore he presents himself with exactitude as he is, giving his critics who cry "cold" and "machinelike" the target they desire, but gradually accustoming the rest of us to the particular strengths of his brand of personality. (Schlesinger Jr 1960: 28–9)

Kennedy is different, but, Schlesinger seems to be saying, that difference needs to be embraced. Kennedy is dynamic and vigorous, the herald of a new age in American politics. Schlesinger quotes Kennedy defining this new era:

Whereas in Nixon's view the times demand only a continuation and mild enlargement of the measures of the Eisenhower administration, Kennedy asserted that we stand "at a turning point in history." "The old era is ending," he said. 'The old ways will not do." The Republican pledge "is a pledge to the *status quo* – and today there can be no *status quo*." The times, he said, "demand invention, innovation, imagination, decision." (Schlesinger Jr 1960: 37)

Throughout Nixon is presented as a figure out of time, with little imagination, a phony. Meanwhile Kennedy has a real, easy heroism and vigor. These portraits were amply crystallized in the debates which were simultaneously televised and broadcast over radio.

THE NIXON–KENNEDY DEBATES

If the speech of January 1960 and Schlesinger's book reached only a limited audience, (although it would surely have effected media coverage of the candidates) then the televised debates did the same job, expressed the same elements of Kennedy's arrival and difference, but on a much grander scale. The presidential debates that were broadcast between 26 September and 21 October 1960 are crucial to an understanding of the new political style at the turn of the decade. More precisely, the debates are central in the examination of the emergence of Kennedy as a possible heroic leader with Shane-like qualities.

The use of television in the electoral process represented a new and powerful means of campaigning. It created new issues and new problems. Perhaps most significantly, the content of the debates illustrate the lack of issues in the 1960 election as far as the electorate were able to discern. This kind of campaigning requires a fair level of political awareness on the part of the audience. It has been argued that the American electorate would have been ill-prepared for such demands (see Lubell 1977: 151–63). If this is the case, then all that is left for the majority of viewers is a debate in which the central issue is nothing more or less than image.

Eisenhower was able to operate a presidential campaign by projecting an image of leadership based upon a combination of his past deeds and current crises. Nixon attempted to invoke his vice-presidency, with its implicit political experience, as his presidential platform. Kennedy had little as grand to call upon as a measure of his political abilities. Indeed, it has been suggested that Kennedy's mystery, his lack of public reputation, presented his greatest obstacle. What was known was barely helpful: he was young, and he was Catholic.

Most analyses of the debates allow Kennedy the victory, and even if he did not win in some final sense, he certainly emerged the stronger candidate in many ways. This was his triumph in the debates. He presented himself as every bit Nixon's equal politically, thus seriously damaging Nixon's vice-president-experience card. Nixon, apart from his televisual problems, seemed unable to get on top of Kennedy, certainly in the first and most crucial debate. Where Kennedy would aim the answer to a question at the audience, at the electorate, Nixon could only address himself to Kennedy. For the most part, Nixon agreed with the goals Kennedy set out, his difference emerging in the methods employed to achieve them. But the persona Kennedy presented, the image of this cool, smart young man was crucial.

The image of Nixon as the old hand, representative of the old order, in the face of a charismatic and exceptional newcomer is a pivotal one. The frontier imagery Kennedy used in his "new frontier" rhetoric and the now visual aspect of this newcomer has resonances in *Shane*. His youth, charisma, his relative anonymity, immediately links him to the tradition of the hero in the *Shane* myth: the mysterious stranger who emerges almost from nowhere at a time of flux, change or danger to guide the community safely through the crisis. Watching the debates, Americans witnessed the "arrival" of a new force in politics, startlingly different from Eisenhower, a figure as new and unknown as the 1960s.

SUPERMAN COMES TO THE SUPERMARKET (1964)

Mailer is keenly aware of the newness of Kennedy. Indeed, he is perhaps one of the harshest, most sustained critics of the Eisenhower years. In his account of the 1960 Democratic Convention in Los Angeles, he presents the mixture of feelings the delegates, as representatives of the greater American public, have about the nomination of the frighteningly different Kennedy. He describes the overall atmosphere of the convention as one of mystery, and Kennedy himself as "the edge of the mystery":

> The man it nominated was unlike any politician who had ever run for President in the history of the land, and if elected he would come to power in a year when America was in danger of drifting into a profound decline. (Mailer 1964: 28)

In this sentiment, Kennedy does look a little like Shane, coming out of nowhere, different, exceptional, and a force that can correct and steady the community's course. Mailer's account acts to subliminally connect Kennedy and Shane in two main ways. In the first place, he creates a Ryker-type in Eisenhower, and by implication, Nixon becomes his henchman:

Came the Korean War, the shadow of the H-bomb, and we were ready for the General. Uncle Harry gave way to the Father, and security. Regularity, order. And the life of no imagination were the command of the day. If one had any doubt of this, there was Joe McCarthy with his built-in treason detector, furnished by God, and the damage was done. (Mailer 1964: 40)

Eisenhower acts to mark out and control the territory, albeit psychological, in the same way that Ryker wants to retain control of the grazing rights from the homesteaders. McCarthy in this sense acts like a heavy, a symbol of the violence and damage perpetrated in Eisenhower's name. It is from this vantage point that Kennedy comes to look like a Shane. Just as the homesteaders need a hero in order to move forward, so, Mailer argues, does America:

It was a hero America needed, a hero central to his time, a man whose personality might suggest contradictions and mysteries which could reach into the alienated circuits of the underground, because only a hero can capture the secret imagination of the people, and so be good for the vitality of his nation. (Mailer 1964: 41–2)

In this idea, Mailer is describing the process by which a figure in the political realm is attached to one in the cultural; how Kennedy's qualities can be linked in the popular imagination with Shane's similar characteristics. Mailer continues to map a political heroism that resonates with Shane:

a hero . . . is larger than life and so capable of giving direction to the time, able to encourage a nation to discover the deepest colors of its character. At bottom the concept of the hero is antagonistic to impersonal social progress, to the belief that social ills can be solved by social legislating, for it sees a country all-but-trapped in its character until it has a hero who reveals the character of the country to itself. (Mailer 1964: 42)

For Mailer then, the political hero acts very much in the mould of the Shane hero. He endorses action rather than endless debate and in so doing reveals the power and strength of vision that already exists within the community. Along this line, Mailer is unequivocal about Eisenhower's heroism: "Eisenhower has been the anti-hero, the regulator." A crucial feature of Shane is the mark of violence that is upon him, the capacity for violence, and this is something Mailer recognizes about the hero who will come and overturn the preceding eight years of "totalitarianism." Talking about how such a state could leave America powerless against the forces of Russian totalitarianism, he invokes the "first maxim of the prizefight manager . . . 'Hungry fighters win fights' " (Mailer 1964: 43–4). This is also, though, a representation of the tenacity of the hero as Mailer conceives him. And it is in this that Kennedy and Shane come even closer. Looking at Kennedy, Mailer sees something of the mark that can be sensed in Shane:

> Kennedy's most characteristic quality is the remote and private air of a man who has traversed some lonely terrain of experience, of loss and gain, of nearness to death, which leaves him isolated from the mass of others. (Mailer 1964: 48)

This could be Joe Starrett describing Shane. In the novel Shane says to Bob to explain why he must leave, "A man is what he is, Bob, and there's no breaking the mold" (Schaefer 1984: 263). Mailer similarly describes Kennedy as having "the wisdom of a man who senses death within him and gambles that he can cure it by risking his life." In this conception, Cain is about to become president. The hero, if he makes it into office, will be the one, Mailer argues, who will re-engage "the myth of the nation," and Kennedy's "New Frontier" rhetoric seems to do just that. With the Kennedy nomination comes the promise, as Mailer sees it, of a new direction for America:

> the possibility that the country might be able finally to rise above the deadening verbiage of its issues, its politics, its jargon, and live again by an image of itself. For in some part of themselves the people might know (since these candidates were not old enough to be revered) that they had chosen one young man for his mystery, for his promise that the country would grow or disintegrate by the unwilling charge he gave to the intensity of the myth, or had chosen another young man for his unstated oath that he would do all in his power to keep the myth buried and so convert the remains of Renaissance man as rapidly as possible into mass man. One might expect them to choose the enigma in preference to the deadening certainty. (Mailer 1964: 48, 49, 58)

As with Shane, the placing of the community's faith in Kennedy is dangerous, uncertain. However, it is better, as far as Mailer is concerned, than the status quo. Mailer constructs a version of Kennedy as a hero, a war hero and also a mythic hero. And Mailer places Kennedy squarely in the landscape of the "New Frontier." But once again, Kennedy and Shane occupy a similar space here. Slotkin discusses a contradiction at the heart of Kennedy's political style: "The paradox of the New Frontier was that it aimed at achieving democratic goals through structures and methods that were elite dominated"

(Slotkin 1996: 500). Just as Shane emerges into a community in which he does not belong, so Kennedy emerges and leads, not from within the community, the masses, but as separate from them. Kennedy, like Shane is not a populist figure, certainly not "one of us" as perhaps Joe Starrett, and *High Noon*'s Will Kane are.

Kennedy's inaugural address categorically locates him within the West of Turner, the corner stone of the West of the imagination. A significant aspect of his inaugural address was the reading by Robert Frost of his poem, *The Gift Outright*. The poem speaks of Westward expansion and the acceptance of the violence that was necessary to facilitate it:

> Such as we were we gave ourselves outright
> (The deed of gift was many deeds of war)
> To the land vaguely realizing Westward,
> But still unstoried, artless, unenhanced,
> Such as she was, such as she would become. (Frost 1969: 202–3)

Kennedy may be speaking of the "New Frontier," but it is rooted firmly in the traditional one, a place of idealism and righteous violence. The expansion into the "New Frontier" with Kennedy at its head located JFK, the Easterner, within Western mythology. Much had already been made of his wartime heroism, a soldier's heroism as opposed to Eisenhower's general's heroism. Eisenhower's "act only when necessary," became Kennedy's pursuit of action embodied in the rhetoric of his inaugural address:

> In the long history of the world, only a few generations have been granted the role of defending freedom in its hour of maximum danger. I do not shrink from this responsibility; I welcome it. I do not believe that any of us would exchange places with any other people or any other generation. The energy, the faith, the devotion which we bring to the endeavor will light our country and all who serve it, and the glow from that fire can truly light the world.
>
> And so, my fellow Americans, ask not what your country can do for you; ask what you can do for your country.

The Kennedy era was an era of activism, social and political, his aggressively kinetic style of leadership inspirational for a society ready to move forward. Kennedy's heroic leadership had its foundations in inspiration and initiative, where Eisenhower's was grounded in security and protection. Both presidents offered the population a means of handling contemporary events and conditions.

The 1960s saw major shifts in American politics, a visible collection of "new" issues, and as a result, a period of heightened political activism. Now Americans looked to a young leader, virile and exceptional, a leader seemingly capable of change, of a movement forward. The template for the type of leader Kennedy was, or at least was perceived to be, then had very definite origins in the archetypes of Western movies and particularly, in Shane.

CHAPTER SEVEN

New Western Perspectives: History and Literature

THE NEW WESTERN HISTORY

Historically speaking, Frederick Jackson Turner's *The Significance of the Frontier in American History* was the basis for the study of the West for much of the twentieth century. Turner's ideas did become unfashionable, as the cinematic Western had, in the 1930s and 1940s, as a result of the Depression. The trauma the nation experienced, the devastating economic difficulties and resulting hardships, did not marry with the historian's narrative of abundance and opportunity. In addition, Turner was being criticized on intellectual terms by those historians who found his explanation deficient in explaining how America, by this time distinctly urban, had become a leading industrial power. However, while Turner's thesis "lost its preeminence, it did not die" (Walsh 2005: 4). The circumstance for a revisioning of his ideas was the economic strength and national confidence at the end of the Second World War. The war facilitated the recovery of the economy and a new wave of exceptionalism. The historian Ray Allen Billington is largely responsible for the repackaging of Turner's frontier history in *Westward Expansion*, first published in 1949. Unlike Turner, who forewent footnotes and evidence and produced what Worland and Countryman call a "prose-poem that hymned westering whites" (Buscombe and Pearson 1998:182), Billington gathered detailed information and provided research that tested aspects of Turner's frontier framework.

By the 1960s, the concept of the frontier had established itself firmly as a term with great rhetorical significance, best evidenced in John F. Kennedy's appropriation of it in his "New Frontier" of the 1960 election campaign. By the 1970s, Western history in this mode was becoming staid. Surrounded by "new histories" in other fields of inquiry, offering revisionist views of urbanism, economics, politics and ethnicity, Western history was merely uncovering further evidence to support the status quo. However, there emerged in the mid-1980s a new collection of voices that began to frontally challenge Turner's ideas on the role of the frontier on American history and the formation of American character. This challenge was unprecedented; historians may have considered his thesis inadequate in certain areas, and perhaps not *the* explanation of American history Turner suggested, but the frontier was accorded some measure of historical merit throughout. This history came to be known, quite self-consciously, as the New Western History and this sense of self-consciousness is important.

The emergence of the Old Western History has a fixed point of origin: the evening of 12 July 1893, when Turner delivered his paper at the Chicago convention of the American Historical Association. There is, as a result, an authoritative founding text in Turner's paper and subsequent pamphlet, *The Significance of the Frontier in American History*. Finally, Western history has a single founder in the person of Frederick Jackson Turner himself. The New Western History does not exhibit the same certain origins. Perhaps unsurprisingly, the New Western History has a genesis that resonates with the inflections of what might be called the postmodern condition. Here was a new school of historical inquiry that emerged inadvertently, a new perspective that came into being through a questioning of its own legitimacy as a field for historical debate. This resonance with postmodernism is further compounded in the relationship its birth has with the reaction of the mass media. From its self-conscious and tentative beginnings, that it would claim to have a mission is striking and gives an early indication of the character of this way of thinking about America's Western past.

If there is a point of origin for the New Western History, it was 1989. Patricia Limerick had published *The Legacy of Conquest: the Unbroken Past of the American West* in 1987. In it she offers at times an almost journalistic synthesis of Western history that emphasizes continuity and diversity over the Old Western History's finite and ethnocentric version of the frontier. The most significant aspect of the book's new perspective was, as the title suggests, to present conquest as the defining experience of the region, and subsequently to explore the consequences. The debate stirred by the book, which in the words of the author it was "passionately loved by some, passionately hated by others, and creatively revised and responded to by many more" (Limerick 1991: 85), established Limerick as the leading exponent of this type of new history. In 1989 she was organizing a symposium on this topic of New Western History, to be held in Santa Fe, New Mexico, but was concerned about the implications of the title she had given the event. The title she had come up with was "Trails: Toward a New Western History." Her dilemma was whether or not to drop the "toward," the word making the difference between suggesting a new direction for historical inquiry into the West and proclaiming the creation of a new historical school. Limerick contacted academics who were to attend the conference to collect their opinions on the possible titles. Understandably, she received the reply from one participant to define what this New Western History might mean. When the conference convened, Limerick distributed an answer in a brief one-page statement entitled "What on Earth is the New Western History?" Significantly, she added after this title, in brackets, "Not a Manifesto." In her response she offers a number of important defining features, and it is worth exploring this text at length.

Firstly, she suggests that New Western historians understand the West as a place, as a region with fuzzy boundaries, "because nearly all regional boundaries are fuzzy." She goes on to state that historians of this type "do see a 'process' at work in this region's history," though this process is not exceptional as it is a process that has "affected other parts of the nation as well as other parts of the planet." However, she forcefully states that such a perspective "reject[s] the old term 'frontier' for that process" because, when the term "frontier" is defined, it is a term that only has meaning in relation to nationalistic and racist connotations: "in essence, the area where white people get scarce." Without this ethnocentric perspective, she argues, the frontier loses an exact definition. Rather, the New Western History characterizes the process with terms like "invasion, colonization, exploitation, development of the world market." She defines the process, in New Western History terms, in this way: "the process involves the convergence of diverse people – women as well as men, Indians, Europeans, Latin Americans, Asians, Afro-Americans – in the region, and their encounters with each other and with the natural environment." This attention to minorities who do not have a voice in the Old Western History is important to the new, and she suggests that the New Western historians "admit that it is OK for scholars to care about their subjects, both in the past and the present, and to put that concern on the record."

From offering an alternative process to Turner's frontier, she then challenges another of his central tenets. New Western historians reject the notion of a clear cut "end to the frontier," in 1890, or in any other year. Where Turner had used the findings of the census in that year to mark the end of the first period of American history, Limerick's New Western historian sees continuities, and considers the attempt to divide old and new Wests unnecessary. In terms of the tone New Western History would take, a tone that would receive significant attention, Limerick's description of the New Western historians' intention to "break free of the old model of 'progress' and 'improvement,' and face up to the possibility that some roads of Western development led directly to failure and injury" is crucial. This perspective "makes it clear that in Western American history, heroism and villainy, virtue and vice, and nobility and shoddiness appear in roughly the same proportions as they appear in any other subject of human history." All of this, she concludes in an almost confrontational manner, "is only disillusioning to those who have come to depend on illusions"

(Limerick 1991: 87–8). This new breed of Western historian, then, took it as their mission, and that is a phrase that Patricia Limerick uses, to "widen the range and increase the vitality of the search for meaning in the Western past" (Limerick 1989: 88). The use of the word "mission" to explain their objectives is provocative. It implicitly suggests an evangelical bent, that these historical missionaries have in some sense the correct version of this history, that they wish to convert others to their way of thinking and to disagree is to be, quite simply, wrong.

Several reporters acquired copies of Limerick's one page summation and quite understandably took the "Not a Manifesto" subtitle to mean that, in fact, it actually was one. Articles appeared in the *New York Times*, the *Washington Post*, the *Los Angeles Times*, the *Denver Post*, the *Boston Globe*, the *Christian Science Monitor*, the *New Republic* and even national public radio. She recalls "an improbable rush of media coverage. A variety of news organizations picked up the story [and soon] the new Western history started to exist." It is certainly unusual for the mainstream media to pay much attention to an academic symposium. However, a glance at the perspective taken in The *Arizona Republic* explains the interest and gives substance to her comment on the nature of illusion: "why can't the revisionists simply leave our myths alone?" The same article went on to assert, "Westerners – and most other Americans, for that matter – are quite content with our storied past, even if it tends to fib a bit" (Limerick 1991: 87).

Whether or not the article is correct about America's attachment to the mythic West, New Western historians certainly were not prepared to leave the old model alone. In another essay, Limerick attempts further definitions of New Western History. In it she considers Turner's frontier thesis as demonstrating "considerable intellectual courage," Turner himself a figure willing to boldly assess his own time, "standing on the edge of the future and forecasting mega trends." However, she goes on to bluntly state, "Turner was also wrong" (Limerick 1991: 83). The strength, conviction and directness of the challenge to established ideas lie at the core of New Western History's mission.

The nature of the newness of the New Western History was at the forefront of the reaction to it. The mythology of the West was being interrogated as it had never been before. No longer was the story of the frontier one of heroism and progress. The New Western historians were producing critical histories that saw the frontier as synonymous with conquest, in ethnic, cultural and environmental terms. As Elliott West says in his evocatively titled essay, *A Longer, Grimmer, But More Interesting Story*:

> Western history . . . feels different . . . when told through these themes. Under
> the older frontier interpretation, the story shimmered with a romantic, heroic

glow. Suffering and tragedy were redeemed by the glorious results presumed to have followed – the nurturing of American individualism and democracy and the coming of a civilized order into a wilderness. The new themes, by contrast, emphasize a continuing cultural dislocation, environmental calamity, economic exploitation, and individuals who either fail outright, or run themselves crazy chasing unattainable goals. (Limerick 1991: 105)

The New Western historians aim to reinscribe the history of the region from the points of view of those that had been excluded from Turner's history. To allow, in the New Western History's terms, the oppressed, the colonized and conquered the opportunity to articulate their experience would require a number of shifts in perspective away from the Old Western History. Considering Turner's history as one of suppression, a history that represses the truth, New Western History turns the story from a celebration of democracy and progress brought about by white males to a tragedy that laments the treatment of the marginalized. In that sense, New Western historians reject the top-down perspective, and seek to offer a history that operates from the bottom up. As Daniel Worster puts it: if we "look at the West from the point of view of the Indians, what could it look like but a failure?" (Robinson 1998: 4–5).

This sense that New Western History demands a shift in perspective takes other forms. Richard White, in the essay *Trashing the Trails*, usefully illustrates this point in describing the different ways the Old Western History and the New would see the pioneer trails:

> much of the difference between the new and old Western historians is revealed by what they make of the garbage so lavishly strewn along the trails. Old Western historians looked past the garbage and saw "nature" . . . They wanted to see wilderness because from it they derived the culture of the West. Many new Western historians . . . have an affinity for trash as the evidence of human actions, the relics of culture. Where old Western historians see nature, new Western historians see the debris and the consequences of human use. (Limerick 1991: 27)

Put simply, the New Western historians "see the garbage first." This altered perspective has been at the core of much of the critical reaction to New Western History. White notes that one of the problems New Western History faces in establishing itself as the proper interpretation of Western history, is that it cannot match the imaginative qualities of the older story. He says, "One reason the New Western History has failed to displace the Old Western History in the popular imagination is that it lacks an equally gripping and ultimately satisfying narrative" (Limerick 1991: 32).

The history of the New West is a story with an unhappy ending. White suggests the different versions of the history can be seen in terms of comedy and tragedy: "The Old Western Historians usually write comedy, in the sense that they provide a happy resolution . . . [the New Western Historian] writes tragedies. Things don't end well . . . we confront our own fatal flaws" (Limerick 1991: 31–3). Critics of New Western History argue that this focus, which led Larry McMurtry to describe the New Western History as "failure studies" insofar as such a perspective negates "the quality of imagination that constitutes part of the truth" (McMurtry 2005: 37), prevents the celebration of the attainments of Westward expansion. They go on to suggest that this new perspective, focusing as it does on the victims of Westward expansion, is just as unreal as Turner's view precisely because it negates the importance of a group or groups. Gerald Nash offers an extreme perspective of the New Western History, suggesting it is a vision driven by ideology. In his essay, *The Global Context of the New Western Historian* he questions, on a number of levels, just how new the New Western historians actually are. He sees in this history of the underside of the West a negativism, a moral righteousness, an intolerance and a romanticization of the victim, which has resonances with the production of history in the totalitarian circumstances of Nazism and Stalinism. More importantly, he discerns in New Western History the focus of the New Left. The New Left's condemnation of capitalism as the engine of racism, the oppression of minorities, poverty and the destruction of the environment is what underpins the New Western History:

> In condemning much of the American experience in the past, they also ascribed special virtues to the masses of oppressed people, whether poor, ethnic and racial minorities, or anyone outside the mainstream of a white male-dominated society. (Gressley 1997: 153)

In this way he proceeds to refute their claims to newness: "to claim that NW historians were the first to challenge the Turnerian synthesis is to ignore major figures of the previous generation and to make unwarranted claims" (Gressley 1997: 150). He goes on:

> There was little that was new in the content or interpretation of many New Western historians. Revisionists of Native American history had begun to multiply after 1960; historians of the much neglected African-American experience surfaced just a few years later. And by 1970 Chicano history was gaining its well-deserved recognition. That was also true of the history of Asians in the West. And some of the most challenging works about women in the region began to appear at the same time. It was simply not true that

the NW group was the first to give attention to these subjects – scores of other had preceded them. (Gressley 1997: 159)

For Nash, then, the New Western History is an ideological history, "or history as propaganda to reflect current political or social agendas" (Gressley 1997: 150). Nash's observation about the importance of the political ferment of the 1960s is a crucial aspect of the New Western History and one that links their perspective to the wider political culture. Although the New Western History emerged in the 1980s, its origins lie in the universities of the 1960s and 1970s. The generation to which Limerick, White, Worster and the rest belong was a generation who have been portrayed as rebellious and idealistic, not prepared to be silent and accept the world their parents bequeathed them. Resonating with Kennedy's call to "ask not what your country can do but what you can do for your country," millions of young men and women enrolled at the nation's universities. As the sixties progressed, they became increasingly alienated from what they perceived to be an unjust society. They were involved in the struggle for civil rights, were shaken by the assassination of John F. Kennedy and above all they protested against the war in Vietnam. The sense of idealism shone through their actions, through which they believed change could be effected using democratic means, and that by doing so, they could make America better. This idealism was shattered by the events at Kent State University in May 1970, where four protesting students were killed by American police officers. The realization that they were not going to change America saw the generation turn their attention to other causes, specifically the treatment of minorities, feminism and a concern for the environment, the basic constituents of the New Western History as written by "historians who had been undergraduates in the 1960s" (Gressley 1997: 4). This connection is given weight by Daniel Worster when he writes, "perhaps the single most important, most distinguishing characteristic of the new Western History is its determination not to offer cover for the powers that be – not to become subservient, by silence or consent, to them" (Gressley 1997: 22). It is this basis in the tumultuous decade of the 1960s that provides a continuity of connections and resonances between the concerns of the New Western History and similar perspectives in film and literature.

NEW WESTERN PERSPECTIVES AND WESTERN LITERATURE

In a talk given to the Western Literature Association at Durango, Colorado, 11 October 1975, Jack Schaefer made an interesting and surprising comment:

Innocence lost, blinders gone, of course, I could no longer write – certainly not as I had written before. How could I write another *Shane* with the same innocent attitude toward him, even though using again the device of the perspective of a hero-worshipping boy? Inevitably I would be troubled by the realization he was aiding the advance of settlement, giving his push to the accelerating onrush of the very civilization I find deserving contempt.

For Schaefer, the character of Shane no longer had a place in modern, post-Vietnam America. Schaefer's concern is environmental, his attitude to the character, and the way in which he helped the very civilization who would so ravage the West lying behind his contempt. In any event, that he has come to question Shane, perhaps the most perfect, purely mythological character in Western literature, in the wake of the events of the 1960s has more than a ring of New Western History about it.

The relationship between the New Western historians and post-Second World War Western literature is not an easy one and needs to be considered from two directions. In the first place there is the need to establish lines of influence, the need to assess the direct impact Western literature in this period had on the revisionist perspective of the New Western History. Secondly, and connectedly, there is the way in which the ideas and focus that constitute New Western History can be discerned in Western literature.

As far as the first path goes, the historians in the New Western camp have had an uneasy relationship with literature, an uneasiness that stems from a number of issues. Forest G. Robinson, in his essay *Clio Bereft of Calliope*, discusses how and why the key New Western historians have or have not dealt with the issue of literature. Patricia Nelson Limerick, he shows, does not like dealing with literature because it forces her, in her words, "to the periphery, away from the daylight zone of political, economic, and social behavior and off to the twilight zone of myth and symbol" (Robinson1998: 68). Her problem with literature is that it is too abstract, that it does not deal with real things. As Robinson points out, "it is telling . . . that Limerick came to the study of history convinced that it gave her unmediated access to real things, real events, real people, and not to their constructions in thought and word" (Robinson 1998: 68). There are to be sure a number of assumptions being made here. Is history any more real than literature? Are not both stories that emerge from certain contexts to answer specific problems or circumstances and face the same problems of language and meaning? Robinson discerns a trend in New Western History, which he designates "the Limerick Maneuver" (Robinson 1998: 69). The term describes the "recurrent strategy" of admitting that "a major precursor has been overlooked or misunderstood" (p. 69). Robinson identifies a number of occasions where Limerick has admitted to "discovering" earlier texts that have an influence on her history, including a reappraisal of myth and symbol in Henry Nash Smith's *The Virgin Land*, the writing of Wallace Stegner, who demonstrated a concern with the issues of minorities in the West several decades before New Western History, and Richard Hofstadter's *The Progressive Historians*, published in 1968 and which included a critique of Turner. This practice as discerned by Robinson suggests another reason why New Western historians are dubious about literature.

There is a wealth of literature dealing with the frontier in terms that the New Western historians would approve of that was published long before Limerick's angst over the title for her conference. Given the New Western historians' willful ignorance, or at best, grudging acceptance of the fact that earlier historians had already been producing work that anticipated their perspective, it is perhaps unsurprising that they would seek to limit the impact of another antecedent which might render the New Western History not so new. Indeed it is possible to identify in writers from as far back as Willa Cather, with her focus on the experience of women in a regionally specific Western landscape, or Hamlin Garland, who made efforts to represent the Indian in a more accurate light, as resonating with the New Western discourse. However, it is perhaps more fruitful to consider writing produced in the aftermath of the Second World War as more properly New Western. As we have seen with film and Old Western History, the war had a tangible impact upon American cultural production.

In this period, literary scholars have noted that writing about the West, as with literature in other genres, became more questioning, self-conscious and self-reflective in the wake of the Second World War. The work of writers like Vardis Fisher (1895), A. B. Guthrie Jr (1901), Frank Waters (1902), Wallace Stegner, and Jack Schaefer (1907) offer insights into the evolution of Western literature and a prefiguring of the concerns of the New Western History. This prefiguring of contexts includes a concern with the environment, a belief in the continuity between past and present, and a focus on region. Thomas Lyons suggests in the writing of this generation there is an "intensity of preoccupation with overcoming myth and establishing a true West" (Milner 1997: 728). As an illustration of this sense that these writers are analyzing the region in more realistic terms, Lyons notes that "several of the first generation of postfrontier interpreters of the West have written long autobiographical novels" (p. 728), the reality of their experiences in the West driving their quest for truth.

However, just as the onset of the 1960s was the crucible that fired the New Western History, so the issues of the decade would prove hugely influential in the tone and texture of a darker incarnation of Western literature, a body of work which used the frontier and its values as a means of challenging the establishment (a similar urge is apparent in Western cinema, as we shall discover). It would do this by focusing on the same elements the New Western

History would claim as their own fresh perspective: race, region, violence, conquest. The Vietnam War, the civil rights movement and a new awareness of the environment were the catalysts for the redefinition and revision of American history and institutions reflected in this literature. So traumatic were the events that inspired these novels, so roundly did they alter American self-concept that writing in this vein refused to acknowledge that there were any rules or boundaries, and it is this urge that perhaps most connects with the spirit of the New Western History.

As the discussion of Western literature in Chapter 4 demonstrates, popular and literary Western fiction had the capacity to speak to audiences and their evolving social and political context, to remain relevant to contemporary America by endlessly replaying the themes of the frontier within a stable generic framework. Western fiction in the post-1960s period, however, gains much of its power, and ensures the genre's relevance, by examining the genre's values and concerns and, often, parodying its techniques. This period also witnessed the emergence of a rich variety of minority voices, among them the work of writers such as Shawn Wong, N. Scott Momaday, Maxine Hong Kingston, Ben Santos, Tomás Rivera, Hisaye Yamamoto, Rudolfo Anaya, John Okada, Richard Vasquez, Simon Ortiz, Leslie Silko, and J. L. Navarro. In keeping with the New Western mission, these writers articulated the hardships and experiences of their cultures in a wider American context. Ishmael Reed's *Yellow Back Radio Broke-Down* is a stunning illustration of the development of both of these patterns.

Ishmael Reed is one of the most important African-American writers of the post-war period. Throughout his work, he challenges dominant cultural assumptions, assumptions which he believes excludes minorities. As the basis for these challenges, Reed uses his personal experience of racism. He acknowledges that this can make his work seem alien and confrontational to some readers:

> I am a member of a class which has been cast to the bottom of the American caste system, and from those depths I write a vision which is still strange, often frightening, "peculiar" and "odd" to some, "ill-considered" and unwelcome to many.

In *Yellow Back Radio Broke-Down* he brings this purpose and perspective to the generic form of the Western, using it in the first place to highlight African-Americans' traditional exclusion from this American narrative and subsequently works to dismantle it. The title of the novel, which at the time of publication was seen as a meaningless, surreal play on words, articulates precisely Reed's purpose. He says,

I based the book on old radio scripts in which the listener constructed sets from his imagination – that's why "radio"; also because it's an oral book, a talking book. People say they read it aloud . . . also "radio" because there's more dialogue than scenery and descriptions. "Yellow Back" because that's what they used to call Old West books about cowboy heroes: they were "yellow covered books and were usually lurid and sensational," so the lurid scenes are in the book because that is what the form calls for. They're not in there to shock. "Broke-Down" is [like] when people say "Break-it-down," they mean to strip something down to its basic components. SO Yellow Back Radio Broke-Down is the dismantling of a genre done in an oral way like radio. (Dick and Singh 1995: 63)

Thus, Reed's novel is a deliberate assault on America using its most famous cultural structure.

Yellow Back Radio Broke-Down is set in a fantastical and disorientating version of the Wild West of popular literature, a landscape which is "weird, irrational, discontinuous." These irrational discontinuities manifest themselves in the novel through Reed's anachronisms like the arrival of Chief Showcase in a helicopter, references to George Gershwin, Mae West and Martha and the Vandellas. Reed's subversion of Western fiction in *Yellow Back Radio Broke-Down* is repeatedly illustrated through his free use of time, characters, and language. The novel ranges from the eighteenth century to the present, combining historical events and cowboy myths with modern technology and cultural debris. His primary characters are deliberately and comically exaggerated racial types: Drag Gibson represents the perverse materialism of the dominant, white culture; Chief Showcase stands as a parody of the Indian's supposed spirituality; and the Loop Garoo Kid articulates the African-American's "different" artistic and spiritual self. Reed's protagonist, the Loop Garoo Kid, wearing black buckskins, is representative of what is distinctive about African-American culture, this sense of difference most obviously embodied in his being an accomplished voodoo houngan. Together with Chief Showcase, the Kid stands up to the forces of political corruption and cultural repression represented by Drag Gibson, a depraved cattle baron, and a version of Turner's "real American personality." Gibson is representative of the dominant culture's obsession with power and property, this obsession depicted in a humorous and troubling manner:

Drag was at his usual hobby, embracing his property. A green mustang had been led out of its stall. It served as a symbol for his streams of fish, his herds, his fruit so large they weighed down the mountains, black gold and diamonds which lay in untapped fields, and his barnyard overflowing with robust and erotic fowl. Holding their Stetsons in their hands the delegation looked on as Drag prepared to kiss his holdings. The ranch hands dragged the animal from his compartment towards the front of the Big Black House where Drag bent over and French kissed the animal between his teeth, licking the slaver from around the horse's gums. (Reed 2000: 19)

His character is further suggested by his tendency to murder his wives. This portrait of a white character is a reversal of the form's traditional narrative structure. In Reed's reconfiguring of the Western, the outsiders are the heroes and traditional American society represents villainy.

Yellow Back Radio Broke-Down uses satire as a means of interrogating America's willingness to suspend civil rights, to exclude certain groups; the novel is not simply concerned with representing contemporary events. Another important feature of the novel is to explore, quite consciously the possibilities of literature. Through the Loop Garoo Kid, Reed makes the case for imagination, freedom of expression and difference as against the repression, violence, and conformity he sees in American society. In taking this stand, the novel exhibits a self-reflexiveness. In a debate with Bo Schmo, a "neo-social realist" who maintains that "all art must be for the end of liberating the masses," the Kid replies,

What's your beef with me Bo Schmo, what if I write circuses? No-one says a novel has to be one thing. It can be anything it wants to be, a vaudeville show, the six o'clock news, the mumblings of wild men saddled by demons. (Reed 2000: 36)

In this sentiment, Reed can be seen to use the form of the Western to challenge exclusion and, simultaneously, he transforms it to comment upon the repressiveness of American society and to re-imagine the form as a celebration of the possibilities and benefits of variation and difference.

One generic element that Reed subverted and which received much attention in this period was the depiction of Western heroism. Many writers of this generation produced Westerns which reconsider the implications of Western heroism, and offer versions of the character that are problematic. This era in the Western's development witnessed the arrival of the anti-hero. In novels such as Max Evans's The Rounders (1960), Robert Flynn's North to Yesterday (1967), Richard Bradford's Red Sky at Morning (1968), Charles Portis's True Grit, (1968) and Edward Abbey's The Monkey Wrench Gang (1975) readers are repeatedly presented with depictions of heroism that compel a reevaluation of such a concept in the wake of the Vietnam War, and its corruption and perversion of such values. Other writers like Thomas Berger in Little Big Man

(1964) and E. L. Doctorow in *Welcome to Hard Times* (1975) and, as the analysis of the novel will show, Cormac McCarthy in *Blood Meridian: or the Evening Redness in the West* (1985) produced novels that go further than simply questioning the values and techniques of the genre and seek to explode the form altogether. This destructive impulse earned these novels the label anti-Westerns.

Neal Campbell suggests that *Blood Meridian* has "a good deal in common with the so-called New Western History." Specifically, he argues, in the way "McCarthy's novel reorganizes the received histories of the West" and "is concerned with the notion of conquest . . . and by the continued consequence of this process" (Campbell 2000b: 218). McCarthy's Western novel employs many of the traditionally mythic tropes of the genre, but his purpose is not to "perpetuate unquestioningly [the] form and its values, but to analyze the hidden history of the West" (Campbell 2000b: 218). To that end, McCarthy's Western embraces the expected tropes of the genre to effectively deliver his revision of it.

Blood Meridian is the story of a 14-year-old boy from Tennessee, simply called the Kid, who runs away from his home and alcoholic father in the 1840s. His journey takes him to New Orleans, Texas and Mexico. In the Kid, even as he is introduced, there "broods already a taste for mindless violence" (McCarthy 1989: 3), a proclivity that meets its match when he joins a gang of Indian scalp hunters. They move across the landscape laying waste to apaches, Mexicans and cowboys alike, without a shred of compassion or humanity. The violence that fills the novel is something that emanates from the landscape, which is itself presented in apocalyptic terms: "they struggled all day across a terra damnata of smoking slag" (McCarthy 1989: 61). In McCarthy's conception, the land that was traditionally the location of possibility and opportunity is a vast nothingness: "the sky is a hole in the heavens, the ground a 'void' or 'caesura'" (Bilton 2002: 103). This nothingness extends to the characters as McCarthy repeatedly describes them as composed of the same mud and dust:

The men, as they rode, turned black in the sun from the blood on their clothes and their faces and then paled slowly in the rising dust until they assumed, once more, the color of the land through which they passed.

Indeed nothingness and "namelessness" (McCarthy 1989: 46) represent central motifs in the novel, McCarthy rejecting the traditional Western's claims to quintessential American values and meanings. In *Blood Meridian*, life itself is repeatedly shown to have no value, the repeated descriptions of horrific, inhuman violence having the effect of desensitizing the reader. As Judge Holden states, "the mystery is that there is no mystery" (McCarthy 1989: 252).

The violence that underpins the reality of Westward expansion lies at the core of the novel and it is McCarthy's purpose not to glorify it at all, something the Western in its traditional form had always done. McCarthy offers passages of startling and disturbing imagery, but no heroism or excitement:

> seizing them up by the hair and passing blades about the skulls of the living and the dead alike and snatching aloft the bloody wigs and hacking and chopping at the naked bodies, ripping off limbs, heads, gutting the strange white torsos and holding up great handfuls of viscera, genitals . . . (McCarthy 1989: 54)

Clearly, McCarthy is seeking to present readers with an alternative version of the Western, an anti-Western, which challenges and ultimately destroys the romantic myths and code of the West. McCarthy presents violence as pervasive in this version of the West. As he writes, "death seemed the most prevalent feature of the landscape" (McCarthy1989: 48). He also rejects the traditional binaries of good guy bad guy, white hat black hat. Rather in the characters of the Kid, the Judge and Glanton, any sense of heroism, morality or redemption is negated. Instead, he offers characters who deal death without a second thought and, more importantly, without reason.

McCarthy's antagonist, Judge Holden, is a terrifying literary creation and a character that can be said to resonate with the perspective of the New Western History. Campbell suggests he is redolent of Turner's frontier type, albeit taken to the furthest extreme. Pushing Turner's frontier characteristics of "that coarseness and strength . . . that practical turn of mind . . . that masterful grip of material things . . . that restless, nervous energy; that dominant individualism, working for good and evil, and with all that buoyancy and exuberance which comes with freedom" (quoted in Campbell 2000b: 221) to the limit, he suggests "these become not the traits of decent democratic society – as Turner had claimed – but the trappings of imperial conquest and individual greed." In this sense, Holden is simultaneously a "vision of an archetypal West(ern) man" (Campbell 2000b: 222) and a monster. This duality is emphasized in the course of the novel as he dances and fiddles with great dexterity and energy, and rapes and murders children of both sexes. McCarthy describes him as "an enormous man . . . he was bald as a stone and had no trace of a beard and he had no brows to his eyes nor lashes to them. He was close on to seven feet in height" (McCarthy 1989: 6). Like the landscape, he is featureless, "almost an incarnation of the dreadful void without" (Bilton 2002: 103). The Judge is engaged in a process of inscribing his own version of history in a book he carries. In the book he records and sometimes collects the flora and fauna and artifacts he comes across and once he has sketched the thing, he destroys it, and sometimes even the sketch itself, in the fire. This displacement of the real for the copy is redolent of New Western History's problem with Turner's frontier thesis. Indeed, Campbell sees in this rewriting and reinterpretation a "parallel to the means by which the West has been written into history as mythology" (Campbell 2000b: 222) The Judge does this because he believes "it is man's job to create the world, not expect it to emerge divinely" (p. 222) In this sense, he is, again, like the hero of Turner's frontier process, a figure "defying all in his determination to succeed in crossing frontiers" (p. 223). When Holden says, "Whatever in creation exists without my knowledge exists without my consent . . . only nature can enslave man and only when the existence of each last entity is routed out and made to stand naked before him will he properly be suzerain of the earth" (McCarthy 1989: 198) he is articulating a kind of individual imperialism that mirrors the conquest of the West.

The book that the Judge keeps provides other interesting resonances with the New Western History. One of the central tenets of the New perspective is to overturn the Old History because it is a story written by the oppressor, the colonizer, the conqueror, and as such does not represent an objective truth, but rather a convenient explanation that glosses over the parts of the history that prove problematic. Campbell suggests that "recorded history is a process of selection and control" (Campbell 2000b: 218): McCarthy is engaged in revealing the extent of the horrors of that project and process by graphically recreating them.

The extent of *Blood Meridian*'s revisionist purpose is further revealed in the fact that McCarthy undertook extensive research in preparation for writing the novel. Like the New Western historians, McCarthy uncovered narratives of the West that give lie to the central precepts of the frontier thesis, manifest destiny and the myth of redemptive violence. Knowing that the world he evokes, the story he recounts is based upon real characters, real events and a real landscape, demonstrates the value of the New Western historian's revisionist perspective.

It has been said that *Blood Meridian* is reminiscent of the West as depicted by Sam Peckinpah, in Westerns such as *The Wild Bunch* (1969) and *Pat Garrett and Billy the Kid* (1973). Indeed the cinematic Western proves incredibly responsive to the reverberations of the 1960s and consequently to the New Western perspective.

CHAPTER EIGHT

The Western and Political Culture, 1960–1992: *Revisions of* Shane

To explore the development of the Western narrative and the cowboy hero in relation to the political culture of the period 1960–92, an analysis of the way in which the Shane narrative evolves is illuminating. *Shane* is remade in the decades following the original release but the question emerges, what kind of *Shane* is produced? What altered forms do the central characters take? What do these new *Shane*'s respond to? By examining the revisions of *Shane* in their historical and cultural context, specifically in the wake of Kennedy's assassination, there emerges a clear difference in tone and purpose from the Westerns being made around them, a difference that resonates with the outlook of the New Western History. The difference that exists between the classic Hollywood Western and these revisions of *Shane* can be articulated in terms of nostalgia and elegiacism. Nostalgic Westerns, Westerns that celebrate ideals from a previous time, no longer spoke to America in the turbulent sixties, and as such that mode of Western in this period is anachronistic. The elegiac Westerns, to which these new "Shanes" are clearly connected, are born from a mourning for the loss of frontier values, the destruction of the genre's vital center, even though the films are a part of that destruction. This dynamic plays out in simple terms: John Wayne is concerned with the former and Clint Eastwood comes to embody the latter. This nostalgia/elegiacism paradigm resonates with a variety of historical and cultural factors in the period after Kennedy's assassination to the presidency of Ronald Reagan.

The cinematic version of *Shane*, contrary to Slotkin's depiction of it as the third link in a chain of similar films, is an original Hollywood Western. Just as its literary source has no direct antecedent, the film, while using existing generic components, emerged fresh and vital, a point of origin. The movie's intention to place a mythical agenda over simple narrative function, and the archetype that is the character Shane, means that the film transcends its generic Western limitations and emerges as an important American cultural artifact. It is so connected to American experience that it is re-imagined, reproduced and re-consumed again and again as the decades pass, and the historical and political context evolves and changes. *Shane*, while being absolutely rooted in the mythology and imagery of the frontier, is a world away from even such exceptional Westerns as *High Noon* and *The Gunfighter*. It does not fit into an easy chronology of the gunfighter mystique and it does not remain locked up in its generic Western confines. In the 1950s it resonated as a model of heroic leadership which would find a connection in John F. Kennedy. And its function as an American meta-narrative, embodying both a historical dimension and a contemporary resonance, is suggested in the re-visions of Shane that punctuate the latter half of the American century. In the 1960s, 1970s, 1980s and 1990s, different "*Shanes*" would reappear, however significantly altered, as a commentary on, a reflection of, and an antidote to the periods that produced/consumed them.

The Kennedy image and style reflected in the character of Shane. The two men embody strength and courage in the face of crisis and as such are almost incorruptible articulations of American heroism. During Kennedy's thousand days in the White House, there were no cinematic attempts to revise Shane. There was not the cultural need to investigate alternative models of leadership or heroism. A brief exploration of the Western in the early 1960s demonstrates that the genre was content to reflect, however fleetingly, contemporary social and political concerns without questioning the figure of the leader.

There are few great Westerns produced during Kennedy's short time in the White House, and the small number of Westerns which can be identified as exceptional in this period are so because they contain, to a greater or lesser extent, political allegory. In relation to one particular series of events, concerning Cuba and Fidel Castro, an examination of Western iconography, of frontier imagery and the depiction of a Shane-type in *The Magnificent Seven* sets it apart from other Westerns.

The Magnificent Seven, made in 1960 and directed by John Sturges, a remake of Akira Kurosawa's *Seven Samurai* (1954), is a vital political allegory, a fact Richard Slotkin recognizes in *Gunfighter Nation*. Slotkin discusses *The Magnificent Seven* in detail, ultimately arguing that the movie anticipates issues and problems surrounding American involvement in Vietnam. While he argues this prophetic reading of the movie well, in so doing, he misses what is perhaps a far more relevant and telling reading of the film's political subtext. *The Magnificent Seven* is much more usefully analyzed as an allegory of the deteriorating situation in Cuba than a foretelling of events in South East Asia.

The movie begins with the Mexican bandit leader, Calvera (Eli Wallach) and his cohorts riding through a Mexican village. That the conflict is set in Mexico is important. Mexico in the popular imagination, as had been fed by the

Western, was in its most frequent incarnation an exotic location of danger, violence and corruption. As such, it represented an easy shorthand for Cuba. Calvera, a version of the colorful primitive rebel, is a paternalist leader. He has come to the village to take corn. The situation has been going on for some time it would seem, but the villagers are beginning to ask questions. Calvera does not leave enough food for the needs of the village. In this latest visit, one person tries to speak up against Calvera and is unceremoniously shot in the street. This episode speaks, perhaps, to the American perception of the contemporary situation in Cuba, of Castro and his regime.

A delegation of villagers is sent on the advice of an old man who lives outside the community to go to the United States to purchase guns, a mission he funds with a gold watch. Like the Cuban exiles washing up in Florida, the delegation arrive at a typical frontier town and enlist the help of Chris (Yul Brynner), "a black-clad Shane" to use Slotkin's phrase. Chris begins to put together a team of elite killers, the seven who will see off the more than forty bandits. The seven are not simply an army to fight the bandits. Rather they aim to educate, to pass on their knowledge to the peasants so they can help themselves. William Manchester's description of the training of Cuban exiles by the CIA in preparation to unseat Castro is instructive:

> when Castro rejected the [Eisenhower] administration's last attempt to reach an understanding . . . the President approved a recommendation that the Cuban exiles be trained for possible uses against Castro . . . [The exiles received] eight weeks of lessons in guerilla warfare – skills, they were told, they would teach to a Cuban liberation army. (Manchester 1974: 863–7)

The Magnificent Seven then becomes a popular rendering of an important contemporary issue: the divisions in Cuba between the people and Castro represented in the town and the gang; Calvera a portrait of Castro; and the seven as the collective of the United States' power, knowledge and influence.

Sergeant Rutledge (1960) and *The Man Who Shot Liberty Valance* (1962), both directed by John Ford, Hollywood's foremost Western mythologizer, are also concerned with the evolving political landscape of the 1960s. *Sergeant Rutledge* is the tale of a black cavalry soldier (Woody Strode) who is wrongly indicted for the rape of a white woman. Through the testimony and cross-examination of colleagues, friends, racists and hostile lawyers, that takes the form of a series of flashbacks, the soldier's actions are brought together into a portrait of a man who is at least as, if not more, noble than some white officers. In a striking scene, Rutledge is provoked into standing up and demanding, "I am a man!" Evidently, the political message is not particularly complex, the reference to the civil rights movement is not subtle, but it does not have to be. Even if it is simply a racial tokenism, its place in a Western is so unusual as to carry with it some impact. Strode makes the point vividly:

> [Sergeant Rutledge] was a classic. It had dignity. John Ford put classic words in my mouth . . . you never seen a Negro come off a mountain like John Wayne before. I had the greatest Glory Hallelujah ride across the Pecos River that any black man ever had on screen. And I did it all myself. I carried the whole black race across the river. (Eyman 1999: 477)

The Man Who Shot Liberty Valance is by far a more politically intricate film. Senator Ransom Stoddard (James Stewart) and his wife return to the town of Shinbone for the funeral of one of the townsfolk. The local press is immediately interested in why such an important political figure would travel so far for the funeral of a cowboy. Stoddard agrees to tell the story of his connection with Tom Doniphon (John Wayne), the dead man. At this point the film moves into flashback. Stoddard is on a stagecoach, having taken up the clarion call of Horace Greeley ("Go West, young man") armed with law books and idealism. While en route, the stage is held up by, he later discovers, Liberty Valance (Lee Marvin). This sets in train a narrative of taunt and provocation. Whilst Stoddard attempts to establish a law practice and educate the town, Valance continues to terrorize it, Stoddard now a focus for his violence. Inevitably this culminates in a showdown which results in Stoddard becoming the eponymous man. The act affords Stoddard the foundation of his political career. However, Stoddard did not shoot Valance, Doniphon did. This debt explains his presence at the funeral, but the newspaper men do not want to run the story: they discard the story with the telling sentiment, "when the legend becomes fact, print the legend."

On one level, certain contemporary issues dealt with in *Sergeant Rutledge* are touched upon again here, albeit in succinct form. In the school room, where Stoddard is teaching an ethnically and generationally diverse group the fundamentals of American democracy, as well as the basics of reading and writing, he asks a question relating to the Declaration of Independence. Pompy, played again by Woody Strode, seemingly the only black actor in Hollywood's West, and a firm Ford favorite, answers haltingly:

> "It begun with the words, 'We hold these truths to be self evident that,' er, that . . . "
> "All men are created equal. That's fine, Pompy."
> "I knew that, Mr. Ranse, but I just plumb forgot."
> "Alright, Pompy. A lot of people forget that part."

Even if it is easy to miss, this is clearly a nod toward the civil rights movement of the period.

But its political dimension can be taken further. James Nadel, in *Containment Culture*, for example, offers *The Man Who Shot Liberty Valance* as an allegory of containment, seeing a similarity in the way in which the narrative repeatedly splits into two versions with the way the policy of containment often contained and expressed conflicting ideals, "that the Western narrative formally and thematically duplicates the containment narrative of U.S. foreign policy: in order to make the world safe for democracy we must resort to antidemocratic measures" (Nadel 1996: 194). If *High Noon* and *Shane* created models of leadership that could be discerned in Eisenhower and Kennedy, then *The Man Who Shot Liberty Valance* posed questions that Americans would come to ask of the nature of heroic leadership, questions such as: on what do we base assumptions about an individual? What happens if the individual becomes too powerful and abuses the power of the position or the trust of the people? How should a miscalculation or error be dealt with?

In construction, *The Man Who Shot Liberty Valance* is similar to *Shane*. Both Shane and Stoddard come to a community and ultimately improve it through a series of violent episodes. The films display the same tensions between old-style farming economy and an encroaching industrial economy. Both characters are concerned with explicit illustrations of American democracy, most obviously the tree stump in *Shane* and Stoddard's teaching of the Declaration of Independence to a cosmopolitan class. It resembles *The Gunfighter* in the larger questions posed about champions and challengers. It fits the imagery of the Cold War in the ever present threat of violence in the form of Liberty Valance. Valance's attempt to gain the region's nomination for congress is significant to this argument. There is a fear of the "alien," articulated as those "south of the picket fence" gaining entrance into "local" politics.

In many ways, *The Man Who Shot Liberty Valance* is a Western that suggests the problems with the presidency in the era immediately following Kennedy, when individual power becomes too great and ultimately lays bare the origins of a situation that would emerge in Nixon's presidency, most visibly in the Watergate affair. More importantly, it signifies an awareness of the dangers in the blind acceptance of the heroic individual while accepting its necessity in the maintenance of a public myth. Further, it examines the media's role in establishing and maintaining the public myth. William McNeill, writing in *Foreign Affairs*, articulates the necessity of maintaining public myths, and in doing so illuminates an interesting aspect of Ford's movie. The immortal concluding line from the film signals the newspaper editor's understanding of the necessity of public myth as a societal adhesive, that "discrediting old myths without finding new ones to replace them erodes the basis for common action that once bound those who believed into a public body, capable of acting together" (McNeill 1982: 2). Stoddard's is a heroic leadership based upon deception, albeit altruistic. In a sense, taking Stoddard and Doniphon, as a doubled hero, the film could be advocating the same principle as the others: that a heroic leader needs to be able to operate in the arenas of intellect and action. *The Man Who Shot Liberty Valance* stands as a bold support of heroic leadership whilst at the same time going a significant way towards deconstructing it. Its message seems to suggest that, regardless of democratic process, a major crisis requires heroic leadership, even if it is just an image of such leadership.

If *The Man Who Shot Liberty Valance* had contained an amount of revision in its "fact/legend" conclusion, Sam Peckinpah's *Ride the High Country* (1962) did the opposite, and in so doing began a trend that was to consider the Western in elegiac terms. Here, the fact of the West outweighs the legend. This theme of the end of the West is one that Peckinpah was to come back to again. Two aging gunmen are employed to escort a shipment of gold from a mining camp into town. Steve Judd (Joel McCrea) sees the job as a way of regaining a measure of his self respect. Gil Westrum (Randolph Scott) intends to steal the gold. They also deliver a girl to the camp who is fleeing a religiously restrictive father to be with her fiancée, but after seeing the brutality of the community and the intention of her fiancée and his brothers to "share" her, they take her back again and are pursued by the warped siblings. On the return journey, Judd foils Westrum's attempt to steal the gold. In the end the two are forced to forget their differences in defense of the gold, the girl and each other. Judd is mortally wounded, but dies hearing Westrum promise to deliver the gold.

On paper, the film seems to fit criticisms of the genre made by Pauline Kael writing in 1967, regarding the function of old Western actors as nostalgia. She sees the Western as nothing more than a repetition, this repetition of formula being the only point:

> the old stars, battling through stories that have lost their ritual meaning are part of a new ritual that does have meaning . . . The fact that they can draw audiences to a genre as empty as the contemporary Western is proof of their power. (Kael 1987: 46)

Certainly the film has for its stars two figures, Joel Mcrea and Randolph Scott, who were only ever identified with Westerns. But this film is in no part akin to the films she is attacking. There is nostalgia here, but among the characters themselves, remembering their lives as they move towards their end and as such it is empty, futile. The West here is not represented nostalgically. It is a dour West, populated by unpleasant characters. The mining community best exemplifies this, in its almost surrealistic, grotesque nightmarishness, all gaudy colors and shrill exuberance. The notion of the family unit on the frontier is subverted, even perverted, into the Hammond brothers who attempt to share the new wife of one of their number. There is no innocent Joey around to remember any of this nostalgically. It is crucial then to differentiate between the nostalgic and elegiac. The first is a celebration, the second is a mourning. John Wayne and friends were working on the former, while the Italian film industry, and Sergio Leone and Clint Eastwood were making ready to formalize the latter.

WHY DOES SHANE COME BACK?

The drive to revise, re-examine or even consciously deconstruct the conventions of the Western in the 1960s was given a major impetus by the murder of John F. Kennedy in Dallas in 1963. If Kennedy's heroic presidency was bound up in the conventions and personality of the *Shane* mythology, the mythology of the exceptional man who will emerge and, through a combination of wisdom, skill and violence, triumph over the threat to security, then in the wake of his assassination there are posed some serious questions for this brand of Western mythology.

Kennedy's assassination further places him within the cycle of the Western. The shooting of the Chief Executive in Dallas has obvious relations in frontier narrative. Kennedy's legend, in a manner similar to that of Wyatt Earp's and William Bonney's, moved away almost immediately from historical fact to legendary hero of the "New Frontier" of the 1960s, primarily through the biographies and memoirs that emerged with incredible speed, in Arthur Schlesinger Jr's, *A Thousand Days* (1965) and Theodore Sorensen's *Kennedy* (1965). If the Western in the Kennedy era concerned itself with nostalgia and a vague awareness of political issues, increasingly after the assassination, traditional patterns began to warp and change. This was in part due to the tenor of the 1960s, and the developing centrality of American involvement in Vietnam. But Kennedy's assassination opened something of a fault line in the Western. And perhaps this is unsurprising: if Kennedy and Shane connect and resonate, what happens when the hero of the "New Frontier" is killed long before the expected conclusion of the narrative?

The assassination, then, represents a significant fault line in American culture, as significant to the Western as the Depression had been in the 1930s. The occasion of this violence was one which traditional Western morality or ideals could not readily cope with. Kennedy, the exceptional stranger, in his three years as president had, in his own way, changed the role of president, as FDR had in the 1930s and 1940s. The heightened consciousness of the Cold War, and his very visible position at its frontline, particularly in relation to Cuba, compounded the *Shane* mystique: this was the threat he had emerged to handle. His murder in Dallas is not only representative of the symbolic killing of Shane, the character, but also the destruction of the innocence of the narrative of *Shane*, the movie. Joey's idealistic dreams of Shane's super-heroic nature, his mythic immortality are devastated. And if *Shane* is a narrative that to some extent explains America to itself, then this loss of innocence is manifest: what can replace it? If Shane could not survive the turbulent 1960s, then who could?

The nature of Kennedy's heroic persona developed quickly after the assassination. Truly an event that reverberated globally, Kennedy became effectively a martyr of political heroism. With his murder the traditional concept of righteous violence that had long been central to frontier mythology was shaken. The good guy had been killed halfway through the movie. The augmented sense of Kennedy as martyr, model of ideal leadership and hero that existed around the event was compounded by the accounts of his presidency in the biographies of Kennedy written by Theodore Sorensen and Arthur Schlesinger Jr, collectively creating the Camelot myth. In the almost immediate publication of such pro-Kennedy accounts, there was no time for his persona to be seriously evaluated, or tarnished. The Western found itself in an entirely alien predicament. The real world could kill off Shane, the hero could be cold-bloodedly murdered, but Hollywood could not. It lacked the cinematic language or generic structures or even the will to portray such bleak visions. And in any event, now was not the time to rub the nation's nose in such a tragedy. As such, the Western, which had been, according to some critics (with Pauline Kael perhaps the loudest voice), in decline since the mid-fifties anyway, became almost immediately anachronistic, documents and artifacts that had little or no relation to the times.

Before the influence of the Italian Western made its impact, in the 1960s the American Western became a largely nostalgic, backward-looking form. Many Westerns were made, but were merely vehicles for old actors who only looked right in such environments. Their intention was not to mourn something gone, but to celebrate its continuation. Pauline Kael argues that in the 1960s:

What makes a "Western" is no longer the wide open spaces, but the presence of men like John Wayne, James Stewart, Henry Fonda, Robert Mitchum, Kirk Douglas and Burt Lancaster, grinning with their big new choppers, sucking their guts up into their chests, and hauling themselves onto horses. That is the essence of their heroism and their legend . . . [audiences] react to the heroes not because they represent the mythological heroes of the Old West, but because they are mythological movie stars. (Kael 1987: 42)

Audiences now turned out for Westerns to see if the old stars could still get on a horse or hold their own in a bar brawl. In their own way, these Westerns fulfilled a measure of the political dimension of the genre by maintaining that link with the safe or safer past, celebrating a time perceived as having gone. Seeing John Wayne or James Stewart going through the motions of frontier heroism was reassuring. However, the films would be resolutely standard in terms of morality and outcome. What emerges as the decade progresses is a dissonance between contemporary issues and concerns, and these essentially traditional frontier morals. From the position of the ideal genre for contemporary commentary, certainly up to the showdown mythology of the Cuban Missile Crisis in 1962, the Western had little to say after the trauma of the assassination of the Chief Executive.

The Western image has an interesting resonance with the presidency of Lyndon Johnson in this regard. Kennedy was able to attach his persona to the frontier hero despite his avowedly East coast character. Johnson, a Texan, would seem to be the ideal articulation of the cowboy president. Indeed he is, but not in any heroic, positive way. Rather his version of cowboy virtues is closer to the anachronistic efforts of Wayne, Stewart, and so on. This can be clearly seen in a number of political cartoons dealing with a variety of issues in his presidency. In many of these cartoons he is depicted as the cowboy, caricatured as an older, paunchier version of the 1960s Wayne. The cowboy image is deployed as the insult that it was originally meant to be. Johnson in this mode is not an American archetype of action, but a figure of naive simplicity, the frontier being used as a metaphor for just how out of touch with the modern world he really is. This distance between Johnson's frontier persona and that of the Kennedy persona, even though that Kennedy was Robert, in the run up to the nomination of the Democrat presidential candidate in 1968, is articulated by Arthur Schlesinger Jr: "[Johnson had] always known that, as in the classic Hollywood Western, there would be the inevitable walkdown through the long silent street at high noon, and Robert Kennedy would be waiting for him" (Schlesinger Jr 1978: 865).

After the assassination of John Kennedy, Robert Kennedy was seen in many quarters to represent the chance to recapture the heroism of the former. As Jon Roper suggests, Johnson was unable to stake a claim to the title of heroic leader:

Kennedy's election had . . . represented a generational shift in American political leadership. The energy associated with his administration was a function of the age of those that joined him on the New Frontier. Lyndon Johnson was the antithesis of the telegenic ironic existentialist, who captivated the imagination of American liberals and who then, in the tragedy of his early death, left them with the powerful myth of a promise unfulfilled. (Roper 2000: 86)

That is not to say that Johnson did not provide leadership at all. Indeed he was elected in 1964 in one of the largest victories in American history. But his leadership was based upon holding a fragile American nation together by appearing to be a paternalist leader, safe and inclusive. John Hellmann offers this version of Johnson:

> Older and far less open to new perspectives [than Kennedy], Johnson could not feel, much less connect with, the subterranean force of the huge post-World War II "babyboom" generation that was moving through adolescence. However adept Johnson seemed at carrying through Kennedy's domestic political program, however decisive he appeared in foreign affairs, Johnson was incapable of carrying on Kennedy's role as a cultural model and leader. (Hellman 1999: 71)

As his administration went on, and Vietnam escalated, Johnson fell foul of the "credibility gap." The fat cowboy or redneck that is the cartoon version of LBJ is a cutting metaphor of the distance between JFK's heroism and LBJ's wish to claim it. Jules Feiffer in his introduction to *LBJ Lampooned: Cartoon Criticism of Lyndon B. Johnson* (1968) makes this explicit:

> Style only became a problem to Johnson after he won as a peace candidate and promptly went to war. And the problem was not one of style so much as one of identity. Before the policy of escalation [in Vietnam] we didn't know who the President really was. We have since found out. We have come to see him as not vital but violent, not clever but devious, not shrewd but cynical, not political but hypocritical, not populist but paranoiac. He is less John Wayne in the White House (as popular mythology would have it) than he is Victor Jory. Or to put the movie metaphor in its proper context: if Richard Nixon reminds us of the man who sells whiskey to the Indians, Lyndon Johnson reminds us of the man who has sold the whiskey to Nixon. (Feiffer in Rosenblum and Antin 1968: 100)

The oppositions of qualities that Feiffer discerns in the Johnson style are almost a plan for Western villainy, boiling down ultimately to a two-facedness. Johnson is not Wayne then, a benign anachronism, but Jory, one of the Western's villains, and a B-grade villain at that. Clearly, Johnson failed to connect with frontier qualities in any positive sense.

The credibility of the heroism that was destroyed by the assassination of Kennedy, as well as the increasing awareness of the realities of the Vietnam conflict that was preventing Johnson from any heroic claim, had significant impact upon the career of John Wayne. In this period, the public's relationship with the Western was dislocated and contradictory; it appealed to something, yet was irrelevant. The 1960s saw flux in Wayne's and the American Western's popularity. Westerns, and Wayne, still, on the whole, made money, but the country was changing. However, the Western form and Wayne did not seem to have any idea how to change with it. Hollywood was becoming increasingly liberal, a result of Kennedy's presidency and the rise of the civil rights movement. The Republican Barry Goldwater was comprehensively beaten by Lyndon Johnson in the 1964 election. Wayne's role in the emerging new era was uncertain. Gary Wills' description of Wayne as an "impressive anachronism" is an ideal description for the Western itself in the period from 1963 to the arrival in the United States of the Sergio Leone, European-produced Western *A Fistful of Dollars* in 1967. In this period Wayne made three Westerns (*McLintlock!* was released in December, 1963, but given its production began before the assassination, its traditional comic Western status illuminates nothing but Wayne's accepted persona). These offer some interesting perspectives on the state of the genre in the period after Kennedy's death and before the arrival on American shores of the so-called Spaghetti Western. At this time, Wayne's profile was high for reasons other than his movies.

This period saw Wayne's health diminish, which is important in explaining the shifts in his popularity. He was diagnosed with lung cancer in late 1964, at the time when he was preparing himself for *The Sons of Katie Elder*, due to shoot for Henry Hathaway in November. Wayne, still a national icon, as reviews and box-office receipts on his previous Western, *McLintlock!*, demonstrated, was concerned about what to tell the press. That the truth of his situation was not revealed goes some way to illustrating his place within the national psyche. Wayne's agent, Charlie Feldman, believed that his client's image – the virile, active Westerner – would not survive an announcement that he was a victim of cancer. So the press statement explained that Wayne's visit to hospital was to correct an old ankle injury sustained on a previous film. The surgery was performed on 17 September 1964. Although it was successful, his recovery was hard. He left hospital on 7 October:

> He did not want to put on his toupee, so he wore a cloth hat with the brim turned down. A sport coat and cotton shirt buttoned all the way to the top camouflaged some of his thirty-pound weight loss. He was hunchbacked because of the chest surgery . . . he did not have the tell-tale limp of somebody who had undergone ankle surgery. (Roberts and Olsen 1995: 511)

This image was a world away from the one Wayne had created in the movies. Very soon, gossip columnists were questioning the ankle story and reporters were asking him if he had in fact undergone major surgery. For the moment he maintained the lies. But Wayne's health was the big topic in Hollywood in autumn 1964. Speculation about his time in hospital and the possibility of a bribed orderly revealing the truth led Wayne in December 1964 to acknowledge the facts:

> I wanted to tell [the truth] right from the start but . . . my advisers all thought it would destroy my image, but there's a lot of good image in John Wayne licking cancer – and that's what the doctors tell me . . . I had the Big C, but I've beaten the son of a bitch. Maybe I can give some poor bastard a little hope by being honest. I want people to know cancer can be licked . . . I feel great now. On January 4th, I'll . . . start The Sons of Katie Elder. It's a typical John Wayne Western, so you know I have to be in good health. (Roberts and Olsen 1995: 511)

Although he had been able to turn his illness into another traditional Wayne victory, the cancer had also shown him to be simply another man. The illness, and the reporting of the illness, would necessarily form part of the background in the appreciation of his films from now on. In his first Western after the surgery, such signs are not difficult to trace.

The Sons of Katie Elder, directed by Henry Hathaway, does indeed conform to the typical Wayne template. His character is a mature version of the Ringo Kid, the good-bad man of *Stagecoach*. For most of the picture he occupies the moral high ground with a gang, comprised of his brothers, who cover a range of social types: the young upstart, the shopkeeper, the gambler, and Wayne himself in the role of the gunslinger. The narrative follows the traditional pattern of the good guys' ultimate victory, although it is perhaps a little more violent than is usual for a Wayne Western. But there is one major difference, and that is the star himself. Wayne no longer sits so tall in the saddle. His walk is no longer as graceful. He becomes breathless in some scenes when delivering his lines. Where the film is attempting to provide Wayne with another archetypal, immovable Western hero, Wayne comes over as a figure jarringly in decline. An incident during the shooting of the picture highlights not only his condition, but also Wayne's awareness of its possible effects upon his public:

> when Gene Sysco, a photographer for the Globe, took a picture of Wayne breathing air out of an oxygen tank after a difficult scene . . . Duke exploded in rage, throwing a can at him, and screaming, "You goddamned sonofabitch! Give me that fucking film!" (Roberts and Olsen 1995: 518)

Joan Didion, in 'John Wayne: a love song,' written as *The Sons of Katie Elder* was being shot, offers this portrait of him:

There was Wayne, working too soon, finishing the picture with a bad cold and a racking cough, so tired by late afternoon that he kept an oxygen inhalator on the set . . . "That guy," he muttered of a reporter who had incurred his displeasure. "I admit I'm balding. I admit I got a tire around my middle. What man fifty-seven doesn't? Big news. Anyway, that guy." (Didion 1993: 37)

As she goes on to say, "he was no longer the Ringo Kid." The film premiered at the end of August, 1965. Although his post-operation television appearances may have prepared audiences to some extent for this new look, the Wayne on display here is very different from the one to which audiences were accustomed. Roberts and Olsen suggest that *The Sons of Katie Elder* appealed to a nation yearning for the security of a safer past. Certainly this could account for the film's success. Yet it is difficult to believe that audiences left the theatre feeling terribly reassured. Even the national monument that is John Wayne is having trouble surviving the 1960s. From Didion again: "[he reduced] those outlaw cells to the level of any other outlaws, but even so we all sensed that this would be the one unpredictable confrontation, the one shoot-out Wayne could lose" (Didion 1993: 32).

The Western which followed *The Sons of Katie Elder* was *El Dorado*, directed by Howard Hawks. The film, released in 1966, is essentially a reworking of the 1959 Wayne-Hawks Western, *Rio Bravo*, with Robert Mitchum in the Dean Martin part, James Caan in the Ricky Nelson part and Walter Brennan playing Walter Brennan. John Belton has suggested that *El Dorado* is a sunset Western, an elegiac Western in the mould of *Ride the High Country* (Buscombe 1992: 261–2). Certainly, the film presents both Mitchum and Wayne as ageing Western heroes. Mitchum is the sheriff, a drunkard and a joke in the town. Wayne is a gunslinger who, as a result of a rifle shot early in the film, is prone to intermittent paralyses down one side, and significantly this will recur just prior to the final shoot-out. Yet ultimately, the film is not a lament for a time and a code that is dying, but a celebration of their continuation. This is not an elegiac Western at all, but a devoutly nostalgic one. Where Joel Mcrea was left to die alone, Wayne and Mitchum walk up the main street triumphant, their wounds and crutches only augmenting their exceptional abilities. Wayne, although suffering from paralyses is still able to outgun and outsmart Nelse, the hired gunman. Such a heroic ethic was a far cry from the experience of a nation embroiled in a conflict such as Vietnam. This lack of sensitivity would be illustrated much more graphically in *The Green Berets* in 1969.

As if to prove that *El Dorado* was not for Wayne a Western describing the end of a time, his next movie was a wholesale return to his films of the late 1950s, a comic caper Western, *War Wagon*, released in 1967. Again, Wayne is head of a gang who plans the robbery of an iron stagecoach full of gold taken from his land, land that was wrongfully taken from him. Such a narrative, combined with the fact that Wayne was looking much stronger physically, signaled that the Wayne national monument was not going to change just yet, even if the Western form itself was about to.

This forms some of the context into which Leone's Spaghetti Western, *A Fistful of Dollars*, would arrive. The American Western seemed to lose any sense of drive in the mid-sixties, unable to offer very much other than nostalgia and ready re-runs of Western stars' finest moments, although now with incumbent creaking and stiffness.

The Spaghetti Westerns brought the form back to America, reinvented the genre so it could again be politically, socially and culturally relevant. And it is in analyzing *A Fistful of Dollars* that this action can be traced. Such nostalgic Westerns as the three Wayne made in the mid-sixties held little or no contemporary commentary, few responses to or reflections of the pressing questions of the day. Indeed, it is impossible to imagine *Shane* reappearing as successfully without the revision of the Spaghetti Western. If the Western was to be again relevant as it had been in the 1950s, what was required was a redefinition of the landscape, language and character of the genre to allow it once more a political voice. This process has a precedent in the 1930s when the Western, unable to cope with the dire reality of the Depression, transformed into the gangster movie. When the Western returned, it returned invigorated having learned the lessons of the gangster genre, having lost an element of its innocence. For the Western in the 1960s however, such re-definition was not to come from Hollywood. The savior of the American Western was the European film-industry, and, in particular, Italian film.

LEONE, EASTWOOD AND THE SPAGHETTI WESTERN

The Italian or Spaghetti Westerns, originally applied as a derogatory term, present problems for the study of what is usually regarded as *the* American genre. They can be easily dismissed because they were not made in America; they can be dismissed because they are more an exercise in style than Western film-making; they can be dismissed because of the problems they cause theoretical models. In the preface to what is the best overall history and analysis of the genre, *Spaghetti Westerns*, Christopher Frayling suggests: "The recent full length studies of the American Western (by Cawelti, Nachbar and Wright) have tended to neglect Italian Westerns – and, on occasion, have even included actively misleading statements about them" (Frayling 1981: xiii). However, apart from a short appendix, he does not consider in any real depth the effect these films had upon Hollywood. Paul Smith, in his 1993 book *Clint*

Eastwood: a Cultural Production, offers a more useful approach to the Spaghetti's impact, an impact that is absolutely fundamental to any discussion of the American Western in the late 1960s and into the 1970s: "whatever their merits as movies [the Dollars Trilogy] constitute an undoubtedly important, almost unique moment in the history of Hollywood cinema" (Smith 1993: 1).

The arrival of the Italian Western in 1967 offered a new lexicon for the makers of American Westerns, reinvigorating its appeal and voice, stretching the boundaries of the genre, discarding impotent structures and creating vital new ones in equal measure. So armed with this fresh sense of purpose, this new cinematic language, a younger generation of film-makers began to use the Western form as commentary upon such cataclysmic events as the war in Vietnam. Crucially, the significance of the Spaghetti Western is also seen in the emergence of Clint Eastwood, the force behind the repeated revisioning of *Shane* as actor and director. Eastwood's film-making world view lies with Leone to such an extent that *Unforgiven*, Eastwood's masterpiece, is in part dedicated to him.

CINECITTÀ STUDIOS: HOLLYWOOD COMES TO ROME

The connection between the American and Italian film industries is grounded in the Cinecittà Studios in Rome. During the 1950s, the facility came to be known as "Hollywood on the Tiber" when American film-makers arrived taking advantage of Italy's low cost facilities and labor. During this period, such peplum or sword-and-sandal epics as *Quo Vadis* (1951) and *Ben Hur* (1959) were produced. This relationship is vital in the origins of the Spaghetti Westerns. American films had dominated Italian cinemas since the end of the war, but by 1960, this domination was reinforced by the arrival of American film crews. The cheap overheads that Italy offered meant that the lavish and thus expensive biblical epics, that were much in demand at this time, guaranteed an American presence in Italy until the genre's popularity faded in the 1960s and the bottom fell out of the Italian film economy. There was an element of exploitation in Hollywood's use of the Italian film facilities, but this was offset, at least early on, by the argument that the American film crews brought money and resources, and as such, their presence was a part of the Marshall plan, designed to help European countries return to economic stability after the Second World War. Predominantly, this involved American productions hiring Italian crews. Once demand fell away for these films, however, America left. Understandably, this caused anger among the Italians. And there is something of this anger acting as a central factor in the creation and tone of the Spaghettis. The Italian film industry was left in dire financial straits when

Hollywood pulled out, and the film-makers who had acted as second unit or assistant directors found it increasingly difficult to keep working. But in this American-Italian relationship, there is a vital aspect of the genesis of the Italian Westerns. Many Italian film-makers, and specifically Sergio Leone, cut their teeth as assistant directors on these American productions. And a brief biographical sketch of Leone's career at this time pinpoints his movement towards the Western: "I was more in love with the idea of America than anyone you could imagine; I had read everything I could on the conquest of the West" (Frayling 2000: 68).

During his time at Cinecittà, Leone worked with some of the greatest American directors: Orson Welles, Raoul Walsh, Robert Wise, William Wyler, Fred Zinneman and Robert Aldrich. Some of these were the directors of a collection of the finest American Westerns. In the excellent biography of Leone, *Something to do with Death* (2000), Frayling describes how excited Leone was at his proximity to these figures, how he wanted to learn from these men, and specifically how he wanted to talk to them about the Westerns they had made: "I had to watch all these Hollywood cineastes, like Walsh and Wyler, sacrifice themselves to the taste of the moment by making peplums" (Frayling 2000: 68). One occasion in particular is indicative of Leone's excitement and frustration. When filming *Helen of Troy* (1955) with Raoul Walsh, Leone remembers:

> Walsh had been a master of the Western. I admired his work very much and I wanted to take full advantage of my time with him . . . alas! Whenever I brought up the subject, he always replied, "The Western is finished." (Frayling 2000: 68)

Even though, as Frayling demonstrates, these meetings were less illuminating than Leone hoped, it cannot be denied that this contact with Hollywood forms a significant element of his film education. It was working on these peplums, these huge epics, with casts, literally, of thousands that he learned how to manage and stage action. But the disappointment in working with these men, especially Aldrich, also helps explain his devoutly revisionist stance in dealing with the staples of so American a genre. The personal disenchantment felt by Leone at the decline of the Western, which is in its own way almost a mourning, is manifest in his Western movies and it would be this disenchantment that would be re-interpreted by American audiences. As Frayling explains, "[Leone] had outgrown the American cinematic heroes of his youth, as well as learning from them" (Frayling 2000: 117).

Paul Smith connects the idea of American exploitation of the Italian film industry in accounting for the disenchantment of Leone's films.

In this context where the hegemony of American interests had been consistently powerful over the years since World War II, and where the workers in the Italian industry had always had their work constrained by the models of American production, it is scarcely surprising that in their adoption of the Western – perhaps the quintessential American genre – Italian filmmakers effected changes that can be read as a certain kind of resistance to their masters. (Smith 1993: 3)

It is interesting to examine Smith's survey of the Spaghettis. He sees in them a tirade against a culture that had all but colonized Italy, and that Leone's "deliberate transformations" in the Westerns he made were acts of defiance: revision as resistance. In this sense, the Spaghettis are for Smith a challenge to the hegemony of the American film industry, an attempt at almost reverse colonization, a coup de genre:

When the Spaghetti Westerns were released in the United States, critics . . . were exceptionally disparaging, by and large thinking of them as "cold blooded attempts at sterile emulation." Yet . . . the project of emulation might not accurately describe what filmmakers were doing. Rather, the particular kinds of operation done on the American Western by the Spaghettis might be best grasped as the response – or, more strongly, the riposte – to colonizing models on the part of what can effectively be called a subaltern culture. (Smith 1993: 4)

This political reading of Leone's purpose seems at odds with the portrait of the man set down by Frayling. Rather than attempting to take revenge on Hollywood by hijacking the Western, and destroying it through a cheapness of production values, or an inauthenticity of locale, character or style, or parody, Leone seems to be actively trying to resuscitate a genre that since his childhood he has loved, but has long since lost its direction. One point, however, is well made: the Spaghettis are not inept copies but, to repeat Smith's phrase, "deliberate transformations." Undoubtedly Leone has his own style and agenda, and as Frayling demonstrates in *Spaghetti Westerns*, he employs structures, themes and imagery that Hollywood does not, quite possibly cannot use (although once Leone has done it, others follow very quickly). Leone himself has said that he sees the Spaghetti as a "critical cinema," but he is more concerned with getting back to the truth of the Western, the mythology pared down, action rather than dialogue, than with sending a message to Hollywood. Significantly, then, when Leone remembers *Shane* as "particularly important during the gestation of the script [for *A Fistful of Dollars*]" (Frayling 2000: 127), the first re-vision of *Shane* comes into focus. As Frayling points out therefore:

Leone has said that Shane was the major influence on his early Westerns, and it is easy to see why: . . . the central theme of a "stranger" who rides into the neighborhood from nowhere, helps the family, and "moves on" to nowhere having done good by evil means . . . [has] obvious connections to Leone's style and intentions. (Frayling 1981: 152–3)

A *Fistful of Dollars* was originally conceived as a Westernization of the Akira Kurosawa samurai movie, *Yojimbo* (1961). Similarities between the films are common: situation, character, even the formal construction of some shots. It was suggested in Italian reviews of *Yojimbo* that Kurosawa got the idea for his movie from the Dashiell Hammett novel, *Red Harvest* (1929). The novel depicts the first outing of Hammett's recurring character, the Continental Op, attempting to clean up the Western mining city of Personville, although it is pronounced "Poisonville" by its inhabitants. However, Kurosawa has also said he is a great fan of American cinema, especially Westerns, and it seems inconceivable that *Yojimbo* does not borrow much from George Stevens' *Shane*, Hammett's story becoming perhaps a smoke-screen to fuzz exactly how close the two movies are. Frayling writes:

Kurosawa . . . had conceded that *Yojimbo* was originally born, in part, out of a love for the Hollywood Western, and particularly for *Shane*: an incredibly popular film in Japan and an unusually self-conscious piece of myth-making. (Frayling 2000: 122)

Such efforts to fuzz the origins of A *Fistful of Dollars* were being undertaken by Leone almost as the film was being finished. His producers had not secured the rights to remake *Yojimbo*, and Kurosawa understandably wanted to be paid some kind of royalty. As an attempt to find a bargaining chip, Goldoni's A *Servant of Two Masters* was invoked as a source, and while Leone still had to pay up (he gave up distribution rights in Asia), the reference diffused the sense of plagiarism.

This copyright wrangle was instrumental in keeping A *Fistful of Dollars* from American screens for three years. The film was shot in 1964, and Eastwood hoped it would demonstrate a side of his abilities that playing the "ramrod" Rowdy Yates in television's *Rawhide* had not allowed him. However, it would not arrive on American screens until 1967. Paul Smith is wary of attributing this delay purely to the legal proceedings over ownership. He suggests that the film was just too much for the American film industry to take. American reviews, witnessing the European success, were disparaging of the film, and such bad word of mouth would necessarily make it difficult to attract a distributor. Smith cites American xenophobia and specifically an American hegemony over the Western genre – how could something as quintessentially American possibly be replicated by Europeans? For Smith, the transformation of the genre led to a muted fear of the film – it was too different – and the American film establishment did not want to give it any credence (something audiences would do regardless once the film arrived).

When it did appear in 1967, *A Fistful of Dollars* became the point of origin for the redefinition of the American Western. The film was instrumental in giving an allegorical voice back to the Western – timely because of American involvement in the war in Vietnam. It is vital to note that this is not because it was deliberately acting as an allegory itself. Regardless of Smith's assertion that Leone was acting politically in its creation (even if he was, it was a message that would be largely lost on an American audience), Leone conceived of and created a film that is purely stylistic, mythical. Rather, the release in 1967 meant that it attached itself to certain prevailing conditions and situations. The power of the film is symbolized in the lack of any critical framework for many critics to comment from. Christopher Frayling bluntly points out that on their international release *A Fistful of Dollars*, along with the other two Westerns in the Dollars trilogy (*For a Few Dollars More* and *The Good, the Bad and the Ugly*), were universally panned by the critics. However, audiences treated them differently. In Joe or more famously, the Man with No Name, there appeared a character that made sense to the times: not moral or emotional, not altruistic but self-centered, not heroic but adept at violence. Given the perception, as articulated by Feiffer, that there was a cowboy in the White House escalating the war in South East Asia and students on the streets protesting the war, the older generation of heroes seemed increasingly out of touch with the current situation. Eastwood's No Name was in many ways a Shane that a disenchanted nation could believe in. Even the trailer used in the United States signals the intent of the film's distributors to connect *A Fistful of Dollars* with *Shane*. By systematically running through No Name's attire (the gun, the poncho, the cheroot), the teaser establishes a sense of difference in much the same way as Shane's buckskins mark his. The trailer shows his arriving, the Shane-like existential moment, as well as demonstrating subtly the nature of the mark of Cain, by having him walk under a tree with a noose (although the shoot-outs are trailered also). It is suggested that he is "The most dangerous man alive," akin to the comment that is made about Shane in both the novel and the movie. However his difference, his newness is also noted in the comment that this "is the first motion picture of its kind" and that it represents "a whole new style of adventure."

And indeed, right from the opening titles, the film jars the viewer with its difference. The rotoscoped figures riding horses and being gunned down in vivid reds and yellows against the trilling soundtrack of Ennio Morricone's infamous score marks the film with a contemporary tone that the Western usually eschews. The credit sequence is bleached out by a glaring white light, which in turn becomes the sun beating down upon No Name. The featureless landscape is recognizable yet alien. Coming from nowhere, from the vast, empty desert, rides this man, dressed in an unusual costume that is more usually equated with Mexican peasants than Western heroes, especially the poncho. In place of a horse he rides a mule. All of this reinforces early on Leone's stylistic and imagistic difference.

His arrival is almost the same as Shane's, except that it is he who watches the child, the youngster being too pre-occupied with family problems to notice him. Like Shane, he has stopped looking for water. As he reaches the well at the edge of the town of San Miguel, he watches a child emerge from one building, cautiously approach, and then enter, via a window, a white clay building opposite, oblivious to the gaze of No Name. Almost immediately, he is ejected, clearly distressed, and is being beaten and kicked by a large Mexican. The stranger does not intervene on behalf of the child, but watches. The Mexican shoots the ground at the child's feet. His father comes to protect him, but he too is set upon by the fat bandit. The boy's father gathers him up and takes him inside their house. Since the boy was thrown out, a woman, the boy's mother, has been watching from the window. She and No Name exchange a glance, making a connection that will be played out later in the film. At witnessing this kind of event in a traditional Western, the cowboy hero would make a stand, choose a side or at least draw his gun in protection of the clearly innocent child. This family unit immediately connects A Fistful of Dollars with Shane – this perverse separation supplanting the domestic stability of the Starretts. And the family unit will feature prominently as No Name's only act of altruism in the entire film. Evidently this is an environment that needs to be made safe, the original impetus for Shane's staying on at the Starrett homestead. But the rider has made no decision yet. He rides on, passing a barren tree with a noose dangling from it, a clear intimation of the mark of Cain, of the capacity for violence that this man carries. He talks to the town bell ringer who explains the arrangement between the opposing "families." His arrival at the town is as opportune as Shane's, just in time to reap rewards by seeing off both factions:

Why are you here? To see the Rojas? No, not the Rojas. Is it the Baxters maybe? No, maybe not even the Baxters. You want to get rich? Well, for that you have come to the right place. If you use your head. That's because everyone here has become very rich or else they are dead. What do you want to buy? Some guns? Liquor? You don't buy you sell. You sell lead in exchange for gold. You will get rich here or you will get killed.

In this rant, the bell ringer maps out vaguely the conflict in the town between bandits, the Rojas, and smugglers, the Baxters, a conflict that exists entirely on the wrong side of the law, in counterpoint to that of the ranchers and homesteaders in *Shane*. At this point, No Name makes his existential decision to stay. Like *The Gunfighter*'s Jimmy Ringo, his actions are not based in altruism: the abuse of the family did not affect his decision to stay it would seem, but the promise of personal profit does.

The action described here makes up a little over the first five minutes of the film's running time, but already, *Shane* has been evoked and perverted, and more generally, the traditional Western has been warped and made strange. On arriving in the center of town, No Name is harassed by Baxter's men, and ultimately his mule is run off, but he does not respond in the expected manner. He takes the abuse, very much like Shane in his first encounter with Chris in the saloon. The saloon in San Miguel, a stock Western feature, is again made strange. No-one goes there, the place is grey and unkempt. The saloon keeper is still the person with the information, and it acts as an observation post, but it is not the social center of the town. Indeed, apart from the Baxters on one side and the Rojas on the other there are few townspeople at all. But it is in the middle of the two factions that No Name sees the profit. Once more, *Shane* resonates, or at least a distortion of it.

Like Shane, No Name has no past. The original script suggested a back story for him, but it was cut from the final draft. Only two references to any sense of a life remain. The first comes early on, after he has killed the four men who chased off his mule, and thus ingratiated himself with the Rojas, who in return give him a room. Even as he is unpacking he overhears them having a heated conversation about him and the danger he may represent. One of those involved, having been talked around, comes to his room to welcome him, but No Name is re-packing his things. The bandit asks where he is going, and explains that this place is home for all the men in the Rojas employ. He replies, "I never found home that great." The other, more illuminating reference comes when he frees Marisol from Ramon, the leader of the Rojas, and sends her, Julio her husband, and her son Jesus across the border with the money he has just made. It is the one moment of selfless courage in the film, the one Shane-like moment. Marisol asks why he does this for them. He responds, "Why? I knew someone like you once, there was no-one there to help." Such vagueness is an integral part of the Shane character, and Leone has imported it wholesale. Another important element of Shane is his closeness to death, to violence, a characteristic that No Name shares. Asked if he does not admire peace, he responds: "It's hard to like something you know nothing about." This is indeed another character with the mark of Cain, a man who carries killing and death with him. Shane though at least flirts with the idea of becoming a farmer, of shedding his previous life. No Name knows there is no point. Shane has been commended by critics and film-makers, significantly Leone among them, for its realism, usually seen in terms of Wilson's murder of Torrey. But if *Shane* is violently realistic, then *A Fistful of Dollars* must be hyper-realistic. Shane and Joe bleed during the bar brawl in glorious Technicolor, but Marian has them cleaned up easily. No Name is not so lucky. He is horrifically beaten in return for liberating the family, and the effects are grotesque. His face is battered to a pulp, one eye is so badly bruised it is shut, his hand is crushed under the fat Mexican's heel. Perhaps even more violent than that are the scenes that follow the beating. No Name escapes and hides in a coffin, but the Rojas believe that the Baxters have taken him in. They proceed to set fire to the house. As the Baxters emerge from the burning building, coughing, vulnerable, they are massacred. The last person riddled with bullets is the matriarch of the gang. The sight of a woman being so callously killed is shocking, and certainly would not appear in a traditional American Western.

No Name recovers from his beating in a mine and plans his revenge on Ramon. His plan involves making a breastplate of thick iron. The showdown takes place on the streets of the town. Ramon and his gang are torturing the saloon keeper regarding the whereabouts of No Name. There is an explosion and a cloud of dust. As the cloud settles, No Name appears, spectral. This ghost-like representation of the hero is something that Eastwood will revisit in several of his Westerns, and all of the *Shane* remakes, perhaps demonstrating the sheer difference of the character, and its displacement from a fixed time and place, a version of something that has passed. For the Rojas, No Name is supernatural. In an earlier conversation, Ramon bragged that when a man with a pistol meets a man with a rifle, the former will be killed. He also says that to kill a man you must shoot the heart. But the breastplate protects No Name. Ramon shoots No Name five times, and each time he gets up. He reveals the breastplate, all perfect shots for the heart, and, in a manner similar to the killing of the four men earlier, he dispatches all of the Rojas bar Ramon. He challenges him to a test of skill based upon his brag – which one can reload their weapon first. No Name wins and kills him. He gathers his things and leaves. The saloon keeper asks if he wants to stay, the Mexican government will be arriving soon, but he declines: "the Mexican government on one side and maybe the American government on the other, and me smack in the middle? Too dangerous." His leaving is similar to Shane's except no-one shouts after him. His decision is not based upon a separateness like Shane's, a recognition that there is no living with a killing. In Joe's world, killing is all there is. Rather there is no money in San Miguel, no further reason to stay. Significantly, No Name is leaving behind a different legacy. Where Shane leaves behind a community that can now grow as a result of his intervention, No Name has finished off a community that was bleak and desolate in the first place.

In many ways, then, the power of this first Western in Leone's Dollars trilogy lies in its reconstruction of the Shane myth for the post-Kennedy, or more precisely post-assassination or even Vietnam, generation. A generation increasingly well-versed in the reversal of expectations found they could relate to something in *A Fistful of Dollars*:

> [Leone's Dollars Trilogy] . . . effect[s] a huge change in what audiences will watch under the heading "Western." The most remarkable thing about their popularity in America . . . is that at the same time as they counter generic expectations, refuse the [genre's] "moral messages" . . . and in general stand as a kind of resistance to and questioning of this crucial Hollywood genre. Indeed, it would not be an exaggeration to say that they equally question the integrity and the consistency of the imaginary that American culture has chronically constructed around the Western and its concomitant ideologies. (Smith 1993: 13)

The seismic shifts occurring in American life that had resulted in a wide-spread questioning of previously accepted truths is mirrored in Leone's film. Pauline Kael suggests that the Spaghetti Westerns "stripped the Western form of its cultural burden of morality. They discarded its civility along with its hypocrisy" (Kael 1994: 541). And the effects of these shifts can be measured in the changes in this new incarnation of *Shane*. Peter Biskind describes this process:

> The pasta pictures were the cultural Muzak for the post-Kennedy era: the Man With No Name became the big screen version of JFK, who forced Khrushchev to back down over the Berlin Wall and the Cuban Missile Crisis, launched the Bay of Pigs, and cultivated the Green Berets . . . Eastwood's films ushered in a new era of cinematic violence. Some 50 people are killed in *A Fistful of Dollars*. The line between the hero and the heavy was becoming blurred. With the war in Vietnam heating up, there was no time for niceties. (Kapsis and Coblentz 1999: 200)

Leone is extremely aware of American Westerns and in his other work he references them voraciously. If *Shane* is the driving force behind *A Fistful of Dollars*, Robert Aldrich's *Vera Cruz* is the narrative forerunner of the sequel, *For A Few Dollars More*. Leone's masterpiece, *Once Upon a Time in the West*, demonstrates most clearly the referential element of his vision.

A Fistful of Dollars offered Americans a Shane they could believe in again, the one fragment of altruism enough to make him a hero in a world of moral relativism. But of equal importance, the Spaghettis saw the introduction of Eastwood as a next generation cowboy. Where Wayne no longer had anything to say, Eastwood stepped in and spoke to a new generation. That he had started his Western career as Rowdy Yates, an absolutely straight laced hero, is essential to understanding his new persona. Both Eastwood and Leone saw a way of taking the expectations of the character and perverting them. In a strange world, No Name is undeniably American. And this sense of an American connection with the Spaghetti style is reinforced in the two Dollars sequels where the stars become more recognizably American (Lee Van Cleef, who had starred in many Westerns, significantly as one of Miller's gang in *High Noon*, appeared in *For a Few Dollars More*, and Van Cleef and Eli Wallach, who had played Calvera in *The Magnificent Seven*, appeared in *The Good, the Bad and the Ugly*). Eastwood would then make his appearance in his first Hollywood Western after returning from Europe, with *Hang 'em High* (1967).

Although not a revision of Shane in itself, *Hang 'em High* represents the first American Western to attempt to combine traditional frontier narrative patterns (the film's concern with the nature of law and justice has antecedents in such films as *The Ox-Bow Incident* and *Warlock*) with the violence and stylization of the Spaghetti. As such, the movie is a crucial antecedent to the revisions of Shane that would follow. In the film Eastwood plays Jed Cooper, a lawman turned farmer, who at the opening of the film is driving a herd across a river. In these scenes, Eastwood seems to be deliberately invoking his television incarnation, that of the honest hard-working good guy, even doing Rowdy Yates' job. The audience knows he is a good guy because he carries a helpless calf that has collapsed in the river. Presently a group of men ride towards him. The men have formed a posse to catch the murderer of the man Cooper has recently bought the cattle from. He shows them a receipt, but the signature is not that of the original owner. Immediately they prepare to hang him and, once he is strung up, leave him to die. A marshal finds him in time, cuts him down and takes him to Fort Grant, the legal center of Oklahoma State, where he will be judged. At Fort Grant, the real killer is found and Judge Fenton sets Cooper free. However he warns Cooper he will not tolerate any revenge outside the law. In this way he hires Cooper as a marshal. The remainder of the film sees Cooper attempt to bring to justice the mob who tried to lynch him.

Hang 'em High is not a strong example of either an American Western or a Spaghetti. However, it is a pivotal movie in that it is consciously bringing together elements of the two styles. In the credit sequence the lettering is a vivid red, and the title zooms towards the audience, displaying an unusual exuberance. If the credits hint at the borrowing of Spaghetti style, the film score is more obviously colonized. The soundtrack, by Dominic Frontiere, mixes a traditional Western score with emphatic phrasing, trilling harmonicas and jangly guitars, blatantly imbuing the whole with a quality akin to Ennio Morricone's music, to produce a curious hybrid. Formally then, the film is importing some of the Spaghetti qualities. But this borrowing is continued in the film's narrative and character of Cooper.

In the transition from farmer to lawman that occurs through his attempted lynching, Cooper moves from a Rowdy Yates-type to a No Name-type, frowning, squinting and, as a result of the attempted lynching, speaking in the trademark hoarse whisper. However, Eastwood seems uneasy about going the whole way: some of No Names props and characteristics are apparent, cigars, neat one-liners (before killing Reno, one of the lynch mob who does not recognize him, Cooper tells him, "when you hang a man you better look at him"), close-ups on squinting eyes, but Eastwood is mindful of the law, and wears throughout the movie a resolutely white hat.

The tenor of the violence in the film is most obviously something taken from the Spaghettis. Violence is an intrinsic part of the genre, but the stylization of it on display here is something different. As he is being lynched, he struggles and some of the mob tries to subdue him with a beating. Once cut down, the facial wounds and bruising look not dissimilar to those he receives at the hands of the Rojas in *A Fistful of Dollars*, even including the closed right eye. Later in the movie, Cooper is bringing Miller, another of the mob, in for trial. Miller works his bindings loose and attacks the marshal. The fight takes place in a desert, the sand is a pure white. Miller grinds Cooper's face in the sand and the punches to the head and the subsequent blood make for some stark images. Later again, the remaining members of the mob attempt to kill the marshal by shooting him in the back. The construction of this sequence is startling, a succession of staccato images. But, more importantly, the last of the Spaghetti features which emerge in this movie becomes apparent as Cooper recovers from the attack. He does so in a brothel. When the Judge comes to visit, the Madam says, "I have never seen a man who has more right to be dead." As in the scene in *A Fistful of Dollars* where Ramon cannot kill No Name, this almost supernatural aspect of the new style hero has emerged into the American Western.

Hang 'em High is also an important film insofar as it is the first film to be produced by Eastwood's company, Malpaso. And it is Eastwood's control over his career that his company affords which allows him to make personal and unusual, as well as straight box-office blockbusters, for the next thirty-five years.

A Fistful of Dollars and *Hang 'em High* can be seen to almost immediately redraw the boundaries of the Western. Film-makers like Sam Peckinpah, Don Siegal, Ralph Nelson, and most importantly Eastwood himself, develop and extend such stylistic action and violence and formal structures in the American

Western of the late sixties and into the seventies at a time when the contemporary social and political situation was becoming increasing dark and fraught.

HIGH PLAINS DRIFTER (1973)

In his 1986 work, *American Myth and the Legacy of Vietnam*, John Hellmann sets out to examine the effects of American involvement in South East Asia upon dominant national myths. His work considers a wide variety of cultural artifacts but they are all scrutinized with the same hypothesis:

> Vietnam is an experience that has severely called into question American myth. Americans entered Vietnam with certain expectations that a story, a distinctly American story, would unfold. When the story of America in Vietnam turned into something unexpected, the true nature of the larger story of America itself became the subject of intense cultural dispute. On the deepest level, the legacy of Vietnam is the disruption of our story, of our explanation of the past and vision of the future. (Hellman 1986: x)

In Hellman's analysis, America's frontier heritage has been perverted in the wake of Kennedy's assassination. The New Frontiersman, who had so energized the nation with "a symbolic . . . deeply psychological and cultural leadership" who had conveyed "an impatient idealism and yet a detached 'cool,' a desire to serve coupled with a reaching for greatness, a frontier vigor and yet a sophisticated 'class'" in his death has, as Hellman quotes John Aldridge, "left a 'cancerous emptiness' creating 'psychological pressures that have driven us to commit the atrocity of Vietnam." The pursuit of lost or damaged frontier ideals in a "sick contemporary American society" (Hellman 1986: 71–81) resulted in Vietnam. However, such perversion does not mean the end of the frontier myth or hero, rather it precipitates the adaptation of such mythology to a new cultural terrain.

It is in this notion of disruption to the "distinctly American story," of which *Shane* is a prime example, that there emerges the force of revision that is apparent in *High Plains Drifter*. If *A Fistful of Dollars'* popularity amongst Americans suggested that something was going wrong with this most American of stories, then *High Plains Drifter* is a direct evocation of the society's connection with the rituals of the frontier. *Shane* is in many ways a pure American myth and as such is one of the most visible casualties of the Vietnam War.

In the period between the release of *Hang 'em High*, in 1967, and *High Plains Drifter*, in 1973, Eastwood made nine films. These films show him experimenting with different genres: two war movies (*Where Eagles Dare* and *Kelly's*

Heroes), a musical (*Paint Your Wagon*), a psychological thriller (*Play Misty For Me*, his directorial debut), a gothic horror tale (*The Beguiled*) and the police thriller (*Coogan's Bluff* and *Dirty Harry*) as well as the Western (*Two Mules For Sister Sara*, *Joe Kidd*). Indeed, the Western is still the most prominent genre in his oeuvre, and even when the film is not explicitly a Western, cowboy/frontier elements can be discerned (*Coogan's Bluff* and *Dirty Harry* can be read as modern Westerns). Although Eastwood made his first film as star and director with *Play Misty For Me*, he would not direct himself in a Western until *High Plains Drifter*. Don Siegal directed the majority of the films in this period of his career, and along with Leone, Siegal becomes a significant influence upon Eastwood's style as a filmmaker.

The style that the Spaghetti had brought to the American Western was by the 1970s thoroughly digested. In films like *The Wild Bunch*, *Little Big Man*, *Soldier Blue*, *The Ballad of Cable Hogue*, *Butch Cassidy and the Sundance Kid*, *Monte Walsh* (from Schaefer's novel), *A Man Called Horse* and *Ulzana's Raid* can be seen the liberating effects of the Italian Western upon the American original, to the extent that parody became a valid approach, good examples being *Cat Ballou* and *Blazing Saddles*. These films all reflected at some level a concern with contemporary situations. *A Fistful of Dollars* started out with *Shane* as a narrative model in the hands of an Italian film-maker and was subsequently reconsidered in America as a corollary of how far things in general had gone horribly wrong. Eastwood's *High Plains Drifter* is an infinitely more knowing revision of the pure myth of *Shane*, and this self-awareness extends beyond revising the structures of the myth to actively reflecting the domestic realities of the Vietnam conflict.

The Western had been reflecting similar themes from around the end of the decade. *The Wild Bunch* and, more graphically, *Soldier Blue* re-enact the violence, and futility of violence, in their narratives of massacre and misguided sense of honor and right. The latter is by far the clearest rendering of Vietnam on celluloid outside of the war genre. The film is ostensibly concerned with the depiction of a native American massacre, a loose conglomeration of the massacres at Wounded Knee and Sand Creek, but watched by an audience made graphically aware of the situation in Vietnam by the television media, and especially in view of the incidents and subsequent legal proceedings surrounding the destruction of the village of My Lai in 1970, the contemporary reference comes into focus. *High Plains Drifter* is less about the actualities of specific events, and more about representing the tenor of the war domestically, with the unique caveat: how would Shane operate as a product of this time?

There are two aspects to Eastwood's initial conception of *High Plains Drifter*: how it acted as a response to the times, and how it related to the Western genre as a whole. Eastwood commissioned Ernest Tidyman to write the film's screenplay. Tidyman was an experienced action writer, whose screenwriting credits included *The French Connection* and *Shaft*, both released in 1971, and both films very much of their time. In the latter, the detective John Shaft is a Vietnam veteran, adding an important layer to Tidyman's connection with the period. Daniel O'Brien in *Clint Eastwood: Film-maker* (1996), and John Lenihan in *Showdown* (1980), suggest that Eastwood and Tidyman drew an element of their inspiration for the treatment of the story from the real-life incident, in April 1964, of Kitty Genovese, a resident of New York who was violently killed while her neighbors looked on from their windows. The knife attack lasted over thirty minutes, the assailant returning and stabbing Genovese again and again. Her screams would have attracted attention, indeed, there were reported to be around forty witnesses, but no-one intervened. From this event, O'Brien suggests Eastwood, "wanted to make a statement about public apathy and group responsibility" (O'Brien 1996: 118). This gives *High Plains Drifter* a more deliberate, more immediate connection to the contemporary culture of America in the 1970s. In any event, from the outset, Eastwood saw the story as a morality play and thus by definition, the film has a message beyond its form. In an interview given to Michael Henry, Eastwood extends this sense that *High Plains Drifter* is relating to the tenor of the times:

Henry: High Plains Drifter is a bizarre allegory that shatters all the rules of the classic Western.
Eastwood: I decided to do it on the basis of a treatment of only nine pages. It's the only time that's happened to me. The starting point was: "What would have happened if the sheriff of *High Noon* had been killed? What would have happened afterwards?" In the treatment by Ernest Tidyman, the sheriff's brother came back to avenge the sheriff and the villagers were as contemptible and selfish as in *High Noon*. But I opted eventually for an appreciably different approach: you would never know whether the brother in question is a diabolic being or a kind of archangel. It's up to the audience to draw their conclusions . . .
You like characters who form part of the system, or at least appear to form part of it, but don't play by the rules of the game it has established and end up by revealing its corruption . . .
I'm aware that that type of character attracts me. Why? Maybe because I've always hated corruption within the system, no matter what it is. In this respect, *High Plains Drifter* goes further than *High Noon*. When the hero helped them get organized, the townspeople believe they can control him, manipulate him. As soon as he leaves, they fall back into the error of their ways and their failure is obvious, their disgrace is unpardonable . . . (Kapsis and Coblentz 1999: 99–100)

These comments illuminate much of Eastwood's political and stylistic intent. Fred Zinneman had intended *High Noon* as an attack upon the ever growing silent majority, and Eastwood is certainly furthering this mission to an apocalyptic degree and in so doing setting himself at odds with the rhetoric of Nixon's silent majority. In this sense, he is "taking sides" with those protesting the corruption surrounding Nixon and Vietnam. To some degree, by linking *High Plains Drifter* to *High Noon*, Eastwood is demonstrating the way in which the latter is a closed narrative. Whatever the outcome of the Kane and Miller showdown, the narrative has nowhere to go. The next chapter can only be told via a *Shane*-style narrative. It is curious that, although *High Plains Drifter* is linked by many critics to *A Fistful of Dollars* and the Leone style (something Eastwood suggests is not the case), *Shane* is never mentioned in relation to the creation of *High Plains Drifter*. Indeed, the only occasion the two are mentioned together is in an interview with Christopher Frayling where Eastwood is attempting to distance the film from his work with Leone:

Frayling: A lot of the technical lessons of the Italian films seem to me to have been carried over into your first Western as director . . . the sound effects, the heavy framing, the way in which your hero is presented . . .
Eastwood: Yeah. I don't really associate *High Plains Drifter* as closely with those films as maybe some do – other than the same actor and this mysterious drifting character who comes in, which is like the character in *A Fistful of Dollars*. But then that's sort of the classic Western – that's been done so many times before – with *Shane* . . . (Kapsis and Coblentz 1999: 132)

High Noon may give *High Plains Drifter* a starting point, but that is where the similarities end. From the very first frame to the very last, *High Plains Drifter* is an incarnation of *Shane*.

The pre-title sequence begins with a shimmering white desert scene. Almost magically a hazy figure materializes in the distance, a spectral stranger upon a white horse. There is an immediate sense of the supernatural in his truly appearing from nowhere. This is further enhanced by a series of piercing notes, almost like a ghostly shriek, that accompanies the stranger's movement across the landscape. This approach to the town of Lago, a sparse wooden-framed community on the edge of a lake, is articulated in a manner which references the arrival of Shane in Stevens' movie. Through a collection of mid- and long-shots, the Drifter is established as one with the environment, elemental. He passes through the mountains, across the plains and eventually comes to the edge of town. At this point, another aspect of the character is suggested in a familiar fashion. To enter town, the Drifter must pass through the graveyard. The camera is angled up, offering the view from one of the graves as he passes through: this is another character that has upon him the Mark of Cain.

As the stranger enters the town, he is watched by everyone, but there is a reference, albeit perverted, to the childhood innocence of Joey's gaze in the dwarf, Mordecai. Eastwood consciously establishes Mordecai as the nearest thing to a child in the whole town. He is insulted by the townsfolk, who call him a runt, and he is given menial tasks to perform. However, in the figure of Mordecai, Eastwood perhaps comes closer to Schaefer's original conception of his narrator, Bob Starrett, than Stevens did. Mordecai is able to be both a version of the innocent "child" while plainly being a grown man. In general terms, this lack of children is another unsettling aspect of the movie, suggesting little in the way of a future for the community. The town of Lago is peopled by a collection of corrupt adults.

Unlike Shane's approach to the Starrett homestead, the Drifter's approach does not seem accidental. This is no existential decision the Drifter makes upon entering Lago, although he will later claim that it is. He heads for the saloon, for a bottle and a beer. The men in there stare and three of them attempt to provoke him. The three, it transpires, are hired guns, brought in to protect the town, or more precisely the mining company that forms the center of the town's economy. Upon leaving the saloon, the Drifter makes for the other traditional frontier establishment, the barber shop, where he asks for a shave and a bath. However, even before the blade has touched his chin, the three gunmen are provoking him again. This time, the Drifter shoots the three dead, with three bullets. This establishes the character as a specialist in violence, akin to a gunfighter, a skill the town will come to want. It also reiterates the Cain element of his character – that to attempt to harm him will result in the visitation of a terrible violence. His shave and bath disrupted, the Drifter leaves, seemingly heading for the hotel. On the way, the wife of one of the mining company partners, Callie, deliberately bumps into him and begins to abuse him. He attempts to walk away, but she will not stop the insults. His solution is telling: he drags her into the barn and rapes her, although Eastwood is keen to suggest, in line with traditional male fantasy, that she wanted this, and receives a good deal of pleasure from the incident. This scene is another reference to Shane, one which allows the inference of the different contemporary context. The chaste glances and unspoken attraction between Marian and Shane is here reduced to an animal sexuality that is violently manifested. Any sense of the cowboy's chivalric code has no place in this incarnation of the West. This scene is important too in the way it develops the relationship between the Drifter and Mordecai. Although the midget has already demonstrated a fascination with the stranger, in the saloon and in being the first on the scene after the killings in the barber shop, it is cemented in his voyeurism. He watches the two from a crack in the barn, which given his function as child, provides a disturbing image. Where Joey's respect for Shane came from a quiet strength, an exceptionalism, Mordecai's respect for the Drifter is based in the same sense of his difference, but it is his violent actions which create a sense of awe, adding another level of subversion of the original myth.

Upon his arrival at the hotel, where he declines to register his name, a key element of his character's purpose is introduced. As he sleeps, the audience is shown his dream. In it, a figure is being whipped by three men in the town's main street at night. The sound of the whip has already been signaled as having some significance for the stranger: a whip crack, directed at a horse drawing a cart, startled him into a kind of operational readiness upon his arrival in town. In the dream, the townsfolk look on, but do not intervene. The figure, the town marshal Jim Duncan, asks for help, but the people recede further into the night. With almost his last breath, the bloodied marshal whispers hoarsely, "Damn you all to hell." Given the Drifter's later actions, this sentiment is pivotal.

The following morning, the Drifter heads again to the barber's shop to claim the bath he had already paid for. While bathing, the current sheriff explains that there will be no charge made against him for the killing of the three hired guns. This is a prelude to the town's decision to hire the Drifter as a gunfighter to protect them from a gang who they fear will return to Lago for revenge. This gang was originally hired as protection, and they did a good job. However, they began to take over, so the townspeople framed them and had them jailed. Now they are to be released. When he is asked to take the job, the Drifter replies, "I'm not a gunfighter." But the townspeople are persistent, and they offer him anything he wants if he will stay on and see off the threat of Stacy Bridges and his cohorts. Upon seeing the Bridges gang, the audience is made aware that these are the men that whipped the late marshal to death, and in so doing, the Drifter's purpose comes into ever sharper focus. Like Shane, he is placing himself between two factions, as a sacrifice, knowing that violence will befall whoever tries to challenge him. Unlike *Shane*, however, there are no good guys here. Both sides are equally as guilty and corrupt as the other.

Mirroring a scene in *A Fistful of Dollars*, the Drifter is given over to one genuine moment of altruism, albeit on a small scale. Having been offered the run of the town, and unlimited credit, the Drifter begins shopping. In the town store, a family of Native Americans is looking at blankets. The storekeeper tells them to keep off the merchandise. Almost inevitably, the first actions of the Drifter are to give the old man a large pile of blankets and the children a jar of sweets each. Although not so grand a gesture as releasing Marisol and returning her to her family, the scene nevertheless establishes an important aspect of the character of the Drifter. However, from such good deeds, he begins to milk his privileges. He takes material things such as hand-stitched cowboy boots, a saddle, a huge handful of cigars. He arms the town with rifles, thereby establishing the "City of Lago Volunteers" and then orders a drink for everyone, all of this at no cost, and all of this already to the chagrin of the business community. But his most important act is to make Mordecai sheriff and mayor of Lago, again subverting the Shane/Joey relationship. Mordecai responds like an excited child. Whereas Shane tries to teach Joey how to use a gun morally and with some sort of ethic, the Drifter simply gives Mordecai such power without any sense of responsibility. The way he acts in these roles inevitably stirs the hostility of the townsfolk.

The Drifter begins to mobilize the town. In a sense he acts like a military advisor and sets up a series of exercises to improve the town's ability to defend itself, not unlike the scenes in *The Magnificent Seven* where the peasants are trained by Chris and friends. Perhaps this is closer to the type of analysis Slotkin made of *The Magnificent Seven*: these scenes acting as a parody of the initial American involvement in Vietnam, the movement from advising to action. Just as these efforts are begun, Eastwood shows Bridges and his gang killing a group of innocent men for their horses. Once they are mobile, there begins something of a slow burning showdown motif. This construction echoes that of *Shane* in so far as it seems that the Drifter will place himself between the community and the gang. But his purpose is darker than that, and the sense is that somehow he has deliberately engineered this chain of events to culminate in all the guilty parties being in the same place at the same time. The character of the Drifter almost systematically alerts the audience to his difference from Shane after Eastwood has made apparent the initial similarities. If Shane is "a good man with a gun," then the Drifter is not. As his control over Lago escalates, he demands that the tenants of the hotel are cast out, because, as Mordecai explains, "he likes his space." Disagreeing with the Drifter's actions, the town's priest explains the error of his actions, "brother, this is not right." His response is simple, "I'm not your brother." If the Drifter is an angel, this disaffiliation demonstrates he is not one sent from the priest's camp. This version of him is further compounded when, in a church meeting, the owner of the hotel is complaining that the town has given the Drifter too much power: "It couldn't be worse if the devil himself and ridden right into Lago." With these thoughts that perhaps the Drifter does not have the town's best interests at heart, a group of men try to attack him in his bed. Again, his Cain qualities manifest themselves and those who attempted to kill him are themselves killed without the Drifter receiving so much as a scratch. During the attack, part of the hotel is destroyed by dynamite, leaving only the proprietor's room intact. This facilitates another adulterous affair. But unlike the purely sexual assignation between the Drifter and Callie, his connection with Sarah Belding, wife of the hotel proprietor, Lewis, signals another connection with Shane. Paul Smith, citing the family unit as an important construct in the Western generally describes that which is found in *High Plains Drifter* in these terms: "[a] quite perverse family – avenging and enigmatic father, intuitive and stolidly sympathetic mother and the little man as son, with the 'other woman' hysterically on the periphery" (Smith 1993: 41–2).

This perversion of the family unit is a crucial element of adapting *Shane* to the Vietnam era. Indeed, it is significant that Sarah becomes a contemporary voice, and it is through this character that the Vietnam connection is most strongly forged. In the first place, she sees through the Drifter's claim of accidentally riding into Lago:

> Drifter: Well I was just passing stopping by for a bottle of whiskey and a nice hot bath.
> Sarah: If you say so.

After they have spent the night, and the Drifter makes to leave, she calls after him:

> Sarah: Be careful . . . You're a man who makes people afraid and that's a dangerous thing.
> Drifter: Well it's what people know about themselves inside that makes them afraid.

Clearly this is a reference to the guilt, the loss of innocence, the scapegoating of the Vietnam period. It also speaks of an America that has realized it is corrupt, reacting to events such as the Manson murders in 1969 and the political corruption of the Nixon administration (after all the murder of the sheriff was a political one, an attempt to protect the mine which he had discovered was on government land and was about to inform the authorities). The Drifter's philosophical line seems to be clumsy in the generic spirit of the movie, he is not given to uttering sentences this long, but read in this contemporary context, that clumsiness becomes a purposefulness. Sarah, it has been revealed in an earlier dream sequences, is the only person who made an attempt to intervene in Duncan's death, to stop the violence. She is prevented by her husband. The quiet resentment created that night presents itself in a conversation she has with Lewis, which acts as a further window upon the film's message.

Her husband has returned to the hotel after she has spent the night with the Drifter. He tells her she has to come to a community meeting. She refuses stressing a dislocation from the community of Lago:

> Sarah: They make me sick. Hiding behind words like faith, peace and trust.
> Lewis: Good words. Damn good words.
> Sarah: But we hid a murder behind them.

Once again, the words speak to the era surrounding the movie. These words are quintessential American words, values that lie at the heart of the American way. They signal good intentions, but Sarah sees through them. Again this seems to be a comment upon the initial aims of American involvement, the public face of government policy, and the increasingly ugly face of the reality of the killing. In W. D. Ehrhart's memoir *Passing Time*, there is a similar passage dealing with words and the actions that are hidden behind them:

> I'd borrowed a television set that warm spring night in May. Nixon was going to address the nation. Undoubtedly he would use the speech to try to justify whatever it was he was planning to do to stop the [NVA's April 1972] offensive . . . I was alone in my room . . . when Nixon appeared.
>
> "Hey, you, Ehrhart," he sneered, his jowls shaking. "I just mined Haiphong. This time I'm going to make those gook fuckers squeal like stuck pigs, and you can't stop me. Put that in your little hash pipe and get high on it, you bleeding-heart pinko Commie creep. Why don't you move to Russia? Who needs you, anyway?"
>
> He prattled on and on in the euphemistic language of politicians and diplomats, alternately smiling or shaking his finger as if on cue. But the gist of what he said was that he had tried everything he could think of to get the North Vietnamese to do exactly what he wanted them to do so that the United States wouldn't appear so much like the colossal helpless fool it was, but since the North Vietnamese wouldn't play ball by his rules, he had been forced to take his ball and blow them up with it. There it was. Maybe most other people watching the speech that night didn't realize what was happening, but I did. (Ehrhart 1995b: 227–8)

Ehrhart, who saw action in Vietnam as a Marine and became subsequently an anti-war activist, writer and poet, can be taken as representative of a broad section of American society in the 1970s, and as such, Sarah's views can be interpreted as a version, albeit simplified, of the views of Ehrhart and those who share his cause. In an interview, Ehrhart makes explicit the general sense of the distance between "fine" words and actuality:

> Nixon . . . was elected to end the war in Vietnam, and he quite specifically said "I have a plan" when he was campaigning. "I have a plan, I have a secret plan, I can't tell you what the plan is because then that will balls up the surprise and the wily North Vietnamese will thwart me, but I have got this plan and if you just elect me I'll end the war" and at that point the American people wished the war to end. Not for the most part any high reasons of thinking it was immoral or anything like that, it was just their kids kept

coming home in body bags and the government couldn't give them a good reason why, and they wanted the nightmare to stop, and their own self image was getting badly pummeled . . . Americans . . . just wanted it to go away. And Nixon instead of doing what he had been elected to do and what he promised to do, he in fact prolonged the war in the most Machiavellian ways. (Unpublished interview with McVeigh 1998)

The sense of a duplicitous elite is mirrored in *High Plains Drifter*. As the conversation between Sarah and Lewis continues, the audience discovers the reason behind the murder of Duncan, the fact that he would have turned the mine over to the authorities, and ruined the town. Sarah's husband defends the actions of the community:

Lewis: Now sometimes we have to do what's necessary to do for the good of everybody. That's the price of progress.
Sarah: And what's the price of a human life?
Lewis: Ah! Your damn conscience. It's sure taken a helluva while to bother you.

In a sense, her closeness to the Drifter seems to have given her the strength to see the truth. She had already known the killing was wrong, but now, she is willing to contradict her husband and the intentions of the town, the key figures of authority. She tells her husband she is leaving. The arrogance of the sentiment expressed by Lewis, as a man of power, a man with a voice in the town's hierarchy, resonates with the split in American life that ran along similar lines, splitting those with a conscience from those expanding and escalating the war in South East Asia. It could be argued that Sarah and Lewis represent a 1970s version of Marian and Joe Starrett, the corruption of Joe and the relative purity of Marian a useful indicator of the moral climate of the decade.

As the town buries the men who would attack the Drifter, he is writing over the town sign. He then instructs the men to paint every building in town blood red. One of the men says in surprise, "but that'll make the place look like hell." The Drifter moves back toward town. As he moves the camera pans with him, revealing in the foreground the sign that at the beginning said "Lago," has been overwritten in a red scrawl, "HELL." This is the clearest indication of the Drifter's supernatural persona. Duncan's damning last words have been brought to fruition through him.

At the climax of the film, Eastwood revises another aspect of *Shane*. Here, as the moment of violent confrontation approaches, the Drifter mounts his horse and seemingly leaves town. The men are in position as practiced, but he is not staying on to see the thing through. Mordecai asks him who will give the signal. Like a father figure passing on his power, he tells him to do it. In contrast to the similar moment in *Shane*, Shane has to physically incapacitate Starrett to meet the climactic clash. But the Drifter was never interested in saving the town of Lago, as Shane was the community of homesteaders. He has positioned himself between two factions who are essentially the same, both as guilty of the murder of Duncan as the other. His leaving, knowing full well that the resistance will crumble, allows him to return and deal with both parties as one.

Bridges and his gang brush aside the cowardly community and take control. In the saloon that night, the town burning already, they begin to take their revenge upon the townsfolk for the wrongs they feel were done to them. As compensation they want the contents of the mining company safe and if the community complies, they will leave. Bridges tells one of the gang to ready the horses. As he moves towards the door, a whip cracks and wraps itself around his neck. He is dragged into the street and whipped to death by the Drifter, silhouetted against the burning town, an Old Testament figure of vengeance. Inside, the people do not move as the events of the night of Duncan's murder are replayed. Bridges and the remaining member of his gang go outside. The latter is hung by the whip. The Drifter taunts Bridges with the voice of Duncan, "help me," further connecting the actions of the Drifter with Duncan's revenge. Bridges is shot in a draw. As he dies, he asks, "Who are you?" but like every other time this question is asked, he receives no answer. In another replay of a similar scene in *Shane*, after killing Bridges, the Drifter is standing in the open. Lewis Belding takes aim at him from the side of a building. As he is about to fire, a shot rings out. Belding drops to the ground and behind him is Mordecai holding a seemingly outsize revolver. Just as Joey saves Shane's life by preventing him from being shot in the back after the main threat of Wilson has been neutralized, so the midget saves the Drifter.

The following morning, the Drifter rides through town, now a black, smoking, charred wasteland. The flames and the aftermath call to mind another Vietnam connection, the military rhetoric of Major Chester L. Brown's infamous line, as quoted in Neil Sheehan's *A Bright Shining Lie* (1989), "it became necessary to destroy the town to save it," first uttered in relation to the destruction of the village of Ben Tre (Sheehan 1990: 719). The futility that the phrase evokes resonates with the Drifter's actions. The town of Lago is saved in so far as the external threat has been neutralized, and, internally, the ringleaders of the murder are dead: in any sense, the evil has been purged. But this is a community with nowhere to go. It has been saved, but at what cost? As he reaches the cemetery on the outskirts of town, Mordecai is working on a gravestone. He says to the Drifter, "I never did know your name." The Drifter replies, "Yes you do." At that the Drifter continues on, and the camera reveals the name on the grave: Jim Duncan. The opening shot is repeated. A long-shot of a shimmering, white desert scene. The Drifter rides to the horizon, and then disappears with a spectral quality.

High Plains Drifter used the purity of the *Shane* myth to expose the perversity of the contemporary situation. By offering a vision of the "anti-Shane," the film depicts a society where the values through which it was created have been rendered meaningless, and a society that is given over to moral relativism in its sense of right and wrong. Indeed this difference was noted in some striking quarters. A couple of years after its release, John Wayne wrote to Eastwood regarding a script treatment that the latter had sent as a possible joint project. Wayne was not too interested, but while declining he took the chance to attack *High Plains Drifter*. Although Eastwood has never released the text of the letter, he has in interviews talked about the tenor of its content. Wayne wrote, "that isn't what the West was all about. That isn't the American people who settled this country." Peter Biskind offers Eastwood recalling that his "Westerns were more akin to Elizabethan revenge tragedy than to John Ford." He goes on to quote Eastwood: "I was never John Wayne's heir." In an interview quoted by Patrick McGilligan, Eastwood explains *High Plains Drifter*'s function:

It's just an allegory, and it wasn't intended to be the West that's been told hundreds of times over by many players, about pioneers and covered wagons and conflict with the various Indian nations. *High Plains Drifter* was a speculation on what happens when they go ahead and kill the sheriff and somebody comes back and calls the town's conscience to bear. There's always retribution for your deeds. (McGilligan 1999: 268)

The dynamic here between the two stars is illustrative of a larger generational and ideological split. And this split neatly sums up the way the traditional, pure mythology of *Shane* has been subverted to produce something darker, more reflective of its time in *High Plains Drifter*. Wayne cannot see his West reflected in Eastwood's because his values, the innocence of his persona, have been tainted by the war in South East Asia. However, the damage sustained by the Western and the brand of frontier heroism that Wayne personified would be healed in the years after Nixon's resignation. This healing mission, initially undertaken by Gerald Ford and Jimmy Carter, found its fullest meaning in the presidency of Ronald Reagan.

It is indicative of the openness of the *Shane* narrative that the same character can be invoked in times of change, times of violence, but also times of healing, as in Eastwood's *Pale Rider*, the third revision, the "born-again Shane."

PALE RIDER (1985)

If *A Fistful of Dollars* and *High Plains Drifter* are only given a passing reference to *Shane* in critical material, *Pale Rider* is recognized as practically a remake. Michael Coyne dismisses it on these grounds, calling *Pale Rider*, "no more than second-hand dross" (Coyne 1998: 187). To dismiss it in such colloquial terms damages Coyne's critical credibility: he is discounting an important film. Daniel O'Brien describes it as "basically a supernatural-allegorical retelling of George Stevens' *Shane*" and demonstrates Eastwood using the Western genre again "as a vehicle for a statement or two" (O'Brien 1996: 159). Patrick McGilligan similarly describes *Pale Rider* as "a modern-sensibility *Shane*, an artistic Western, with [Eastwood] himself as an archetypal stranger similar to the character, who defended the homesteaders in the 1953 screen classic" (McGilligan 1999: 374). That this is not the first time Eastwood has revised *Shane* is not recognized by his critics. Nevertheless, even the most lackluster critic can see *Shane* throughout the movie. Rex Reed, writing in the *New York Post* in 1985, sees this connection between the films as a flaw: "*Pale Rider* owes such a nostalgic debt to George Stevens' *Shane* that the similarities, scene by scene, become almost a parody."

Yet Eastwood is clearly doing more than simply copying a classic Western. In a pre-release interview, Eastwood offered his reasons for re-making *Shane* in such an explicit manner: "Basically, I wanted to have contemporary concerns expressed within . . . the classical tradition" (Schickel 1996: 403). It makes perfect sense that after a period of healing, of dealing with the ghosts of Vietnam and the subsequent divisions in American society that the two earlier re-visions of *Shane* deal with, *Shane* should be remade here without any real subversion or darkness. In that sense, *Pale Rider* becomes an articulation of the intention, the mission, of Reagan's presidency. In an administration that had attempted to return to former ideals and better times, what better proof of success than reproducing a text of such innocence, clear cut morality and pure mythology which ten years earlier could not be made without horrific violence and perversion, cynicism and irony? Its success can be further seen in its consumption, in its finding an audience.

Pale Rider and Reagan's presidency intersect at a variety of points. In general, given the almost terminal decline of the Western in this period, that *Shane* should reappear at all is a fact of Reagan's movie star presidency. Paul Smith suggests:

> More than loosely associated with the Hollywood industry, and indeed with Westerns particularly, Reagan in many of his public remarks and often in his physical trappings and demeanor made overt allusion to this American tradition. (Smith 1993: 46)

The characteristics of the altered Shane of *Pale Rider* seem predicated upon Reagan's own persona. Although not immediately apparent upon his entrance, the Rider is actually a preacher. This vision of a man of action, a force of healing wrapped up in the imagery of a preacher, has resonance with Reagan's rhetoric and style. The fact of the assassination attempt by John Hinckley and crucially Reagan's survival given the proximity of the bullet to his heart, suggests something of the supernatural qualities that have been an element of *Shane* from the outset, but these are heightened in his newest incarnation, the Preacher. The symbolic effect of Reagan's survival is to reverse the effects of Kennedy's death: Shane can return, not as a narrative of elegy or mourning but as nostalgia, a celebration of the return of more traditional frontier morality. In this sense then, Reagan's revisionist mission means elegiacism gives way to nostalgia. A more explicit connection that is drawn by Edward Gallafent in *Clint Eastwood: Actor and Star* (1994), relates to the effects of Reagan's policies on the environment: "*Pale Rider* can be seen in this context as a narrative expressing current anxieties that exploitation of the natural world was leading to irrevocable damage" (Gallafent 1994: 137).

The Western in the 1980s was in very bad shape. As the 1970s moved on, the number of important Westerns dwindled. Indeed, Eastwood's *The Outlaw Josey Wales* can be said to be the last great Western of the decade, critically and commercially. Dealing as it does with redemption, creation of new community after trauma (in this case the Civil War, but clearly resonating with a post-Vietnam audience), *The Outlaw Josey Wales* is a Western that speaks to the contemporary culture and demonstrates a measure of the healing process that America was involved in. And this perspective could account for its success. The optimism that emerges at the conclusion of *The Outlaw Josey Wales* contrasts with the more pessimistic "end of the West" movies around it. So prominent was this type of Western narrative that Richard Schickel suggests, "people wondered if a movie could again live comfortably in an earlier Western era" (Schickel 1996: 406). If the Western's profile was in danger before 1980, and it was, even taking into account the phenomenal success of George Lucas' space Western, *Star Wars*, in 1977 (seemingly understanding Schickel's point by setting the tale "A long time ago, in a galaxy far, far away"), after the turn of the decade it became a downright liability. A large measure of the genre's problems can be laid at the door of Michael Cimino's 1980 Western, *Heaven's Gate*, one of the greatest box office disasters of all time. And although it has received something of a critical rebirth in recent years, it is generally accepted that Cimino's film killed the Western. And yet, in 1984, Eastwood announced his intention to star in and direct another Western. To some extent, with Eastwood as the cowboy hero, the production of a Western was a different matter. Having said that, he was still asked why he wanted to produce another Western, given the current situation:

one of the earliest films in America was a Western: The Great Train Robbery. If you consider film as an art form, as some people do, then the Western would be a truly American art form, much as jazz is. In the sixties, American Westerns were stale, probably because the great directors – Anthony Mann, Raoul Walsh, John Ford – were no longer working a lot. Then the Italian Westerns came along, and we did very well with those; they died of natural causes. Now I think its time to analyze the classic Western. You can still talk about sweat and hard work, about the spirit, about love for the land and ecology. And I think you can say all these things in the Western, in the classic mythological form. (Kapsis and Coblentz 1999: 127)

So why remake *Shane*? Because it speaks to and of something in the contemporary culture. In another interview, Eastwood offers a reason for making another Western that is reminiscent of Schaefer:

Henry: It's to be hoped that Pale Rider will contribute to the resurrection of the genre, but isn't it a gamble to film a Western today?
Eastwood: I don't know if the genre has really disappeared. There's a whole generation, the younger generation, that only knows Westerns from seeing them on television. And I notice that audience ratings for High Plains Drifter and The Outlaw Josey Wales continue to be excellent. When someone asks me, "Why a Western today?" I'm tempted to answer, "why not? My last Western went over very well." It's not possible that The Outlaw Josey Wales could be the last Western to have been a commercial success. Anyway, aren't the Star Wars movies Westerns transposed into space? (Kapsis and Coblentz 1999: 113)

In much the same way as Schaefer considers himself a serious writer who happens to produce Westerns, Eastwood is a renowned director who happens to be best known for frontier narratives and both men are able to create versions of the genre that extend it and surprise audiences. As such Eastwood does not expect *Pale Rider* to sell simply because it is a Western, as would have been the case in the forties and fifties. Rather, he is using the Western to reflect the surrounding American political and social scene. This scene, and the movie's success, are neatly summed up in a review of the film in *Progressive*, in September 1985: "Pale Rider . . . persuade [s] us that we have never lost the simple straightforward values of the mythic old West. Look here, these films declaim, America is America again."

Once again, the title sequence runs over panoramic shots of a breathtaking landscape. However, this time, instead of tracking the arrival of the stranger figure, the camera follows a gang of men on horseback, riding hard. They are heading towards a small community of gold prospectors. The scenes of their thunderous movement is interspersed with glimpses of life in the camp, the dynamism of the posse juxtaposed with the calm of mundane chores, children playing and men working. They arrive and set to terrorizing the community, destroying lodgings and possessions. These are the men of LaHood, a Ryker-type, who controls this industry in the region and wants their claims to further his own interests. This conflict is a replay of *Shane*'s, gold prospectors instead of farmers, but the power struggle underpinning it remains the same. LaHood arrived in the region many years before and began prospecting. His methods are practically industrial, stripping away the landscape with hydraulic water cannons to reveal the resources. Like a locust, he sacks an area and moves on. Carbon Canyon, the area in which the community is working is the last rich lode in the region and as such is a prized prospect. Like the Starretts though, the community have nothing but the most basic means to work. Just as Ryker wanted the homesteaders off "his" land so he could keep more cattle, LaHood wants rid of the prospectors. The classic conflict in *Shane*, which was abstracted and perverted in *A Fistful of Dollars* and *High Plains Drifter* into a questioning of violence and corruption, returns in the 1980s with a distinct environmentally friendly spin.

The film, like *Shane*, is very clear cut in its morality. A pivotal early illustration emerges in the opening attack upon the community. The raiders, clearly the bad guys, prove it beyond doubt by killing a dog, a good measure of Hollywood heartlessness. The dog belongs to Megan, a 14-year-old girl who functions as the Joey character. After the men have left, she buries the dog in the nearby woods. As she places the makeshift cross over the mound she says a prayer, a version of Psalm 23:

The Lord is my shepherd, I shall not want . . . but I do want.

He leadeth me beside still waters. He restoreth my soul . . . but he killed my dog.

Yea, though I walk through the valley of the shadow of death, I shall fear no evil . . . but I am afraid.

For thou art with me, thy rod and thy staff they comfort me . . . I need a miracle.

Thy loving kindness and mercy shall follow me all the days of my life . . . if you exist.

And I shall dwell in the House of the Lord forever . . . But I'd like to get more of this life first. If you don't help us we're gonna die. Please. Just one miracle. Amen.

As Megan is saying her piece, the scene dissolves to a magnificent sky scene, moody and brilliant. As she reached the part about the miracle, the Pale Rider can be seen. In a sense, the expected title sequence of shots tracking the stranger's approach are played here. Like the Drifter and unlike Shane, the rider's arrival into the lives of the community is not an accident. This prayer signals a major difference between *Shane* and *Pale Rider*. Where Shane emerges at the right time to aid the community of homesteaders, Megan asks for help, for a miracle. In his depiction – the title coming from Revelations: "And I looked, and behold a pale horse: and his name that sat on him was Death, and Hell followed with him" (6:8) – Eastwood has yet again forged a supernatural persona, a benign version of the Drifter.

After the raid, Barret, the Joe Starrett of this version of Shane, rides into town, named LaHood, to collect supplies needed to rebuild the camp. In town, he is provoked and attacked by LaHood's men. One of the men notices a figure on a pale horse on the edge of town. He looks away for a moment and when he looks back, the man is gone. He prepares to set light to Barret's buggy, containing the supplies. From off screen, the match is extinguished with a bucket of water. The Rider proceeds to see off the half dozen or so men with a hickory pick-axe handle. The townsfolk, watching from windows marvel at the display, and the audience once again recognizes the Mark of Cain. They also see Shane re-emerging. No Name and the Drifter immediately use the gun in their first confrontations. Shane and the Rider do not. Like Shane, the Rider's revolvers will not appear until much later. The Rider walks away without a word and Barret follows him, offering him food and lodgings by way of a thank you. Once inside the Barret home, yet more *Shane* connections appear. The family is once again crucial. The nuclear family, a symbol of stability and traditional values, is here presented in a very contemporary fashion. Barret and Sarah (connecting the Marian figure from *High Plains Drifter*) are not married, yet live together. Sarah has been a one-parent family since her husband ran off. Into this comes the Rider. Where in *Shane*, the relationship between him and Marian was one of intense but unspoken attraction, and in *High Plains Drifter* there is an element of coercion, here that relationship is fairly open, consensual and, ultimately, consummated. Sarah's daughter, Megan, takes over the role of narrator. Turning Joey into a teenage girl gives the film a large element of its revision. When Joey tells Shane he loves him, it is a statement of respect, a belief in Shane as a role model and an endorsement of the pure frontier values he represents. Here, such sentiments are replayed, but in a highly sexualized tenor. She even goes so far as to ask the Rider to marry her when she is fifteen, the age at which her mother was married. In this way, she seeks to learn from the Rider in the same way as Joey does from Shane but the child-like innocence of the boy's gaze is lost amidst an adult interest in sex. In one sense, what is displayed is perhaps a comment upon the effects of the sixties, that family values and traditional sensibility has suffered because of the decade of free love and rebellion. However, another reading of this would suggest that this concern with family offers a version of America that is in chaos, a place where traditional roles, whether they be gender roles or heroic models, are no longer stable. The simple mythology of the Western is now more complex, the mythology is no longer as universal, innocence is no longer a given. And in many ways, this seems to be the key to understanding *Pale Rider*: *Shane* is remade in an attempt to recreate the mythology as a show of solidarity, that the problems of the previous decade have been overcome and that consensus is again possible. While the film recognizes significant changes in the cultural and social landscape into which it enters, reflects and is consumed, ultimately it wants to reinstate frontier values into the American experience.

Not since *High Noon's* Will Kane, has a Western been so redolent of a serving president. *Pale Rider* is able to reflect several aspects of the presidency of Ronald Reagan. In an interview given to Tim Cahill in 1985, Eastwood is asked about his connection to the president:

> *I've read that you occasionally speak with Reagan on the phone.*
> Well, I don't know where that came from. I think some secretary or someone mentioned it. I've talked to him a couple of times, but they make it sound like I'm some great adviser. (Kapsis and Coblentz 1991: 127)

Reagan was inclined to refer to contemporary movies in his rhetoric and the famous Dirty Harry line, "make my day" was certainly part of his lexicon. However there are more substantial links. Two key elements of the Rider immediately alert the audience to the connection. Shortly after the Rider has accepted a room from Barret, he is washing, his shirt off. Barret enters his room and notices marks on his back: unmistakably healed bullet wounds, six in total, in a circular pattern. This relates to Shane insofar as it suggests the scars of conflict and survival that marks his existence. It reflects in Reagan an early incident of his presidency: the attempted assassination by John Hinckley. Hinckley, imitating the plot of Martin Scorsese's *Taxi Driver*, cast himself as Travis Bickle, the gun freak, Vietnam veteran psychopath, who tried to win the woman he loved by assassinating a political leader. From this event, *Pale Rider* can be seen as a response to the turbulence of the 1960s, a turbulence wrapped up in JFK's murder, his death signifying the death of the new frontier hero, and a period of mourning in the Western. But Hinckley fails, Reagan survives the trauma, symbolically recreating the terrain in which the good guys win, and this goodness can be celebrated. Haynes Johnson suggests: "[his survival] conveyed a sense to the public that Reagan possessed larger-than-life qualities

. . . Reagan's survival alone was proof enough that the country's luck had turned for the better" (quoted in Roper 2000: 139). Jon Roper, analyzing the cultural implications of this event reveals an important point:

> The attempt to assassinate Ronald Reagan, symbolically the most significant event of his presidency, fused memories of the death of Kennedy with the image of an assassin inspired by a movie that portrayed a contemporary popular perception of one cultural consequence of the Vietnam War – the unstable veteran taking revenge upon American society. Reagan survived and in so doing transcended that narrative. And he achieved the mythic status and political authority to mould the contemporary mood. (Roper 2000: 140)

If surviving the assassin's bullets represents one connection between Reagan and *Pale Rider*, there is another. Prior to his emergence from his room for dinner, the family are arguing about who or what the Rider might be:

Susan: Is he a gunman?
Barret: I half hope he is. I'd sure as hell chip in an ounce of dust for a little protection.
Susan: From a hired killer?

The Rider enters the room and shocks them all into silence: he is wearing a dog collar. As a preacher, his goodness is a given, removing the ambiguity of the Drifter. But by presenting him as a preacher figure, another Reagan allusion is produced. Several critics view Reagan's style and rhetoric as that of "an evangelical preacher." Jon Roper again notes:

> Among the faithful of the Republican Party, Reagan sometimes appeared as an evangelical preacher . . . In his acceptance speech at the Republican National Convention in August 1980, he confessed that "more than anything else, I want my candidacy to unify our country; to renew American spirit and sense of purpose" and had ended his speech with an appeal to "begin our crusade joined together in a moment of prayer." (Roper 2000: 142)

And it is in these terms that the third revision of *Shane* can be seen to reflect upon and resonate contextually with the presidency of Ronald Reagan.

Barret explains the conflict between the prospectors and LaHood in the same terms as Starrett and Ryker. LaHood is an older settler. Barret and the community came legally to work the canyon but LaHood feels he has some right over their claims. His methods of mining, using water pressure that erodes the landscape, is as wasteful as Ryker's wish to allow cattle to graze on the open range. The conflict has shifted from the agricultural to the industrial, another element of the revision. One of the key sequences in *Shane* is the united removal of the tree stump. This scene is replayed in *Pale Rider*, only instead of a stump, the Preacher and Barret set to work on a boulder that the latter believes conceals a nugget. In any event, a similar sense of man against nature is evoked. The Preacher sets to work, Barret joins in and the community watches. Like Shane, the Preacher becomes a unifying force. This is strengthened when LaHood's son, Josh and a heavy named Club come to tell the Preacher to leave. Club, played by Richard Kiel (Jaws from the Bond films), moves to attack the Preacher, after first striking the rock and splitting it in two. Quickly and easily, the Preacher disables him with a mallet to the groin. In this scene, the community "sees through" him – one character, seeing him work, mutters, "Preacher, my ass!"

This sentiment is repeated later when LaHood returns from a business trip and is met by his son who explains, "a stranger came through. Kinda pulled them together." LaHood is angered by this. He feels that he had almost succeeded in destroying their morale: "When I left those tinpans had all but given up, their spirit was nearly broken and a man without spirit is whipped. But a preacher, he could give them faith."

Just as Barret believed, there is a sizeable gold nugget within the rock. The Preacher suggests going into town to celebrate and pay off some debt. As soon as they arrive, the Preacher is asked to speak to LaHood in his office. LaHood tries to buy the Preacher, he offers to build him a church. He turns him down, at which point LaHood flies into a tirade against the prospectors in a manner similar to Ryker. He thinks of himself as an empire builder and the miners as squatters, who are holding back progress. In this scene, the Preacher takes up the Cain position, positioned between the two factions. LaHood says he will resort to bringing in hired guns, a "marshal" Stockburn and his deputies, a move similar to Ryker bringing in Wilson. He is able to negotiate a $1000 offer to buy each of the prospector's claims. When this is put to the community the same divisions as those in *Shane* emerge – some want to take it and move on. However, Barret, like Starrett, effectively persuades the community to stay and fight, arguing that money is not the reason for their efforts, but their way of life is, articulated in the image of putting down roots. However, it is clear that a large element of his success relies upon the Preacher being on their side and leading the fight. Given that this is the case, when the community realize the following day that the Preacher has gone, it becomes understandably nervous, this anxiety increasing when, realizing his offer has been refused, LaHood dams up the creek they were panning.

But the Preacher has not disappeared. Rather, he has gone to an unspecified town. His purpose is similar to the moment in *Shane* when, after he attempted to live as a farmer, Shane realizes to save the community he must return to his true self and puts his buckskins and gun belt on. The Preacher retrieves a safety deposit box from a bank. Inside are two revolvers and a gun belt. He exchanges them for his collar, his persona shifting to the figure of violence required to save the community.

Upon discovering the Preacher gone, Megan is upset and takes off on a horse. She winds up at LaHood's mining operation. LaHood's son attempts a clumsy seduction, which quickly degenerates into attempted rape. The other men come to watch, suggesting the violence of a gang rape. However, Club, having been "touched" by the Preacher, emerges from his tent, to stop the wrongdoing. Like Chris in *Shane*, "something kinda came over him." The Preacher appears and rescues Megan, shooting Josh through the hand in doing so. There is something of the violence of the Vietnam era wrapped up the image of rape, as well as a reference to the morality of the Drifter, and as such it is significant that it is no longer tolerated. The rape imagery in the film is manifest, in human and environmental terms, and resonates with a sense of guilt over American involvement in Vietnam. The implications of events like My Lai and the policy of defoliation are wrapped up in this imagery.

One of the pivotal scenes in *Shane*, where Wilson kills Torrey on the main street, is replayed in *Pale Rider*. Conway strikes a huge nugget and goes to town to celebrate with his two simple sons. He gets very drunk and takes to the street, yelling insults at the windows of LaHood's office. Stockburn and his deputies emerge. Like Wilson, Stockburn provokes Conway, shooting at his feet to make him dance. The deputies open fire, riddling him with bullets. A violent scene in the original, here it is imbued with explosions of blood at each impact, reflecting the heightened threshold for violence embodied in the United States in the wake of Vietnam. Stockburn tells Conway's sons to tell the Preacher to meet him tomorrow in town.

Just prior to this killing, LaHood and Stockburn are listening to Conway and discussing the Preacher. LaHood describes him and asks if Stockburn knows of someone who may match the description. Stockburn does, and LaHood asks if it could be the Preacher. Stockburn replies, "No, the man I'm thinking of is dead." This connects the Rider to the Drifter, figures of vengeance, ghosts, two sides of the same coin.

Once the community learns of Conway's murder, understandably there begins an element of fear and panic. The Preacher attempts to calm them down:

Preacher: You voted to stick together, that's just what you should do. [Conway] made a mistake. He went into town alone. A man alone is easy prey. Only by standing together are you going to be able to beat the LaHood's of the world. No matter what happens tomorrow, don't you forget that.

This quote is significant. If Reagan's presidency was one that attempted to heal America after Vietnam, attempted to overcome the "Vietnam syndrome," then this passage suggests a similar intent. Reagan's revisionist mission seems bound up in recreating a consensus, in the same terms as the Preacher describes.

As the Preacher readies himself to go to town and face Stockburn and his men, Barret tells him he is going as well. The Preacher says no, but Barret is insistent. "Suit yourself," he says, and the two head off. They stop first at LaHood's mining operation and destroy it with dynamite. Josh attempts to shoot the Preacher in the back, but he is saved by Club, who knocks the gun away. The Preacher dupes Barret, and runs his horse off:

Preacher: You're a good man, Barret. Take care of Sarah and the girl.
Barret: So long, Preacher.

Back at the camp, Megan has missed the Preacher but wants to say good-bye and heads, like Joey did, for town. In town, the showdown runs in line with the *Shane* narrative. In no time, the Preacher has killed all of LaHood's henchmen and Stockburn's marshals. Stockburn and the Preacher face off against each other on the main street. In many ways, this reflects *High Plains Drifter* in that the Preacher seems to have known that Stockburn would arrive and as such his efforts are not entirely altruistic. He has saved the community, but he has also exacted some personal revenge. As he approaches Stockburn, the latter experiences a horrific moment of recognition. He repeats, "You . . . you." The Preacher draws quickest and fires six shots, significantly in the same pattern as those on the Preacher's back. As Ryker tried to kill Shane, LaHood takes aim on the Preacher. Barret, who has walked to town, kills him. The Preacher leaves. Megan arrives but he has already gone. She shouts after him:

Megan: Preacher, Preacher . . . We love you, Preacher. I love you. Thank you. Good bye.

There is no request for him to come back. The town is safe and the community has been saved. The end credits roll over the Preacher moving into the distance of a magnificent landscape. In its denouement, *Pale Rider* has returned to the Western an altered nostalgia. The sadness that Megan feels at the departure of the Preacher is the same as Joey's at watching Shane ascend the mountain pass. However, unlike *Shane*, there is no sense here of the continuation of a story outside of the movie and in this regard, *Pale Rider* sees the Shane narrative as conceived by Eastwood, closed. His work is done. This sense of closure is compounded in its reflection of the stages of frontier settlement as described by Turner:

> It begins with the Indian and the hunter; it goes on to tell of the disintegration of savagery by the entrance of the trader, the pathfinder of civilization; we read the annals of the pastoral stage in ranch life; the exploitation of the soil by the raising of unrotated crops or corn and wheat in sparsely settled farming communities; the intensive culture of the denser farm settlement; and finally the manufacturing organization with city and factory systems. (Turner 1996: 11)

Where *Shane* left behind a fledgling community in the farming stages of settlement in Wyoming, the Preacher leaves behind a Californian community approaching industrialization, as demonstrated by LaHood's mining technique. The community the Preacher protects is clearly moving towards the latter stage of frontier settlement, *Pale Rider*'s narrative closure reflected in the sense of frontier closure.

Shane is not revised in any comprehensive way after *Pale Rider*. The Western, which finds a fresh resonance in the figure of Reagan, makes less sense as the 1980s become the 1990s. Bill Clinton's rhetoric of building bridges to the twenty-first century is decidedly forward looking, and as such negates the relevance of the frontier as an American value. The Western does enjoy a limited revival in the 1990s, and it does so in something of the New Western History's spirit of revision and deconstruction. These Westerns deal with single issues in a Western setting: race (*Posse*, 1993), gender (*Bad Girls*, 1994; *The Quick and the Dead*, 1995; *The Ballad of Little Jo*, 1993; *Painted Angels*, 1998) or historical reality (*Wyatt Earp*, 1994; *Tombstone*, 1993). However, there is one great Western of the nineties that offers some further insights into *Shane* and American political culture: Clint Eastwood's 1992 release, *Unforgiven*.

UNFORGIVEN (1992)

By examining *The Gunfighter*, *High Noon* and *Shane* it is obvious that there is far more going on in these movies that simple generic progression. *The Gunfighter* emerges from traditional generic components, not only of the

Western, but the gangster movies, as the ultimate articulation of the gun-fighter character – the man with a past, fighting to survive his legend, but ultimately unable to transcend the narrative of closure, signified in the inevitable conclusion that he must "pay" for his infamy. *High Noon* is a much different Western, though one still concerned with the closed narrative. As a cultural artifact it is rooted in the Eisenhower style, Will Kane emerging as a version of Ike on celluloid. The film is fundamentally political, containing readings of such contemporary events as McCarthyism and the activities of HUAC, the war in Korea and the anxiety of entrance into the Atomic Age. It presents the central character as a model of heroic leadership that resonates with Eisenhower, the established hero, whose heroism resided in past deeds and subsequently constituted his mandate. But such perspective means there is nowhere for the character, like the president, to go. When Kane drops the star in the dust, he moves out of town to live with, significantly, his pacifist wife. The narrative closes.

Shane presents a radically different version of the Western. Here is the existential hero, the hero who establishes himself in the role. The character of Shane resonates in the culture and finds common ground with Kennedy. In the wake of Kennedy's assassination, the Western generally, but *Shane* in particular, is subverted, the innocent values lost, along with the possibility of heroic leadership and all of this compounded by American involvement in Vietnam. As such, the Western enters a period split along the lines of nostalgia and elegiacism, a remembrance and celebration of frontier values and a mourning of their passing. The *Shane*-Westerns fall into the second category. This period of mourning ends with Reagan, who is able to revise and rehabilitate notions of the heroic leader (by surviving assassination) and turns the Vietnam War into a noble cause. The films *A Fistful of Dollars*, *High Plains Drifter* and *Pale Rider* form the landscape of this flux in the *Shane*-Western. When the Preacher rides off at the conclusion of *Pale Rider*, it feels like an ending. This sense of closure is more widely compounded by the genre's fragmentation, its movement towards a self-conscious revisionism and decon-struction. This development in the genre is especially vivid in the postmodern Western, *Unforgiven*.

Pale Rider presents the closure of the *Shane*-style narrative. That is not to say that Shane will not return, and as we shall see in the next chapter, the presidency of George W. Bush, a conservative Texan, and events early in the twenty-first century have created something of a resurgence of Western and frontier values in the American mainstream. It can be said though that Clint Eastwood will not be the driving force behind any future revision of *Shane*, and *Unforgiven* (1992), his next Western after *Pale Rider* offers multiple reasons for this. The film's central character of William Munny, while not an explicit revision of Shane, does present some interesting connections and references to the hero of Stevens' 1953 Western.

Unforgiven is a film that deconstructs, quite consciously, the American Western. It takes features of the instantly recognizable stock of Western character types and situations with the intention of revising and subverting generic expectations. And given that *Shane* is such an archetype of this genre, it too is deconstructed.

Eastwood is keenly aware of the elegiac/nostalgic paradigm of the post-Kennedy Western. The avowedly revisionist stance of the movie gives it a sense of elegiacism. The mourning of the loss of frontier mythology that underlies the movie represents an unquestionably knowing revision of the genre. This revision is undertaken in several ways: in the figure of the Schofield Kid; W.W. Beauchamp, the biographer; the final shootout. *Unforgiven* feels like an epitaph for the Western genre itself. Eastwood deconstructs many of the genre's key elements, exposing the mythology, the genre's fictions. In this sense it is elegiac. The audience is mourning at an autopsy. However, Eastwood finally turns *Unforgiven* towards nostalgia. This dynamic between the two styles that had been a feature of the Western over the last thirty or so years, can be seen in the self-conscious construct of the biographer looking for facts, while simultaneously, he is the writer searching for the legend of the West for dime novels. Time and again, he is faced with both elements of the paradigm: the nostalgic vision of the West and its elegiac counterpoint.

An initial point of reference for *Unforgiven*'s deconstruction of Shane is his arrival: traditionally, the character comes from nowhere, has no history, and no name. Eastwood is at pains to provide a full background story for his character, William Munny. A prologue tells of his vicious and intemperate disposition, it tells of his wife, now dead, who "changed" him. The audience is shown a failing pig farmer who when questioned about the deeds in his past repeats the phrase, "I ain't like that no more." Munny is persuaded to chase a whore's bounty in the town of Big Whiskey, Wyoming. Although there are three men in the company, Munny rides into town alone, replaying the moment of arrival for the townsfolk. One of the fundamental constructs of the Shane character is his moral difference, regardless of which side of the equation he may reside, a High Plains Drifter or a Pale Rider. Yet, in *Unforgiven*, it is very difficult to distinguish anybody from anybody else, good or bad. The traditional Western genre is based upon a rigid moral code, whether heroic or anti-heroic. In *Unforgiven*, the audience is presented with a selection of men, none of whom, seemingly, have much to set them apart from the others. William Munny is a Wild West legend, infamous for the violent exploits of his youth. Despite his constant efforts to rationalize and legitimize such infamy, whether a one off or not, Munny is returning to killing. Ned Logan was his partner in the "Old Days," and is lured into the killing of the cowboys for the bounty. Little Bill Daggett is a sheriff who uses his authority and power in despotic fashion; his power is kept absolute through the local ordinances, one of which obliges any person entering Big Whiskey "to surrender all side arms to the proper authorities." Indeed, the contravention of the ordinance leads to the beating of both English Bob and Munny on separate occasions. Daggett is perhaps, ultimately, the most conventional of all the characters in the film, nostalgically evoked as a traditional bad guy. However, he is from the same mould as English Bob and Munny in terms of having a dark past. The difference is that he has the sheriff's star, which becomes a license for his repeated acts of violence. Daggett and English Bob are contemporaries, figures from a shared past, demonstrated when the sheriff corrects Bob's story for the biographer.

The four central characters are all so similar in terms of background, history and reputation that the nature of their difference becomes blurred. The whole issue of morality becomes one large grey area, as opposed to the black and white morality of the traditional mythology. This is best illustrated in the scene in the gully where Munny has shot in the stomach one of the two cowboys blamed for slashing the prostitute Delilah.

Davey: I'm dying boys.
Schofield: Well you shouldn't have cut up no woman, you asshole.
Davey: Jesus, I'm so thirsty. Slim. Slim, gimme some water please? Please Slim? I'm bleedin' Slim. Gimme some water, please?
Munny: Give him a drink of water, godammit!
Davey: Gimme a drink of water please, Slim?
Munny: Will you give him a drink of water for Christ's sake! We ain't gonna shoot.
Slim: You ain't gonna shoot?
Munny: No!
Slim: Hold on, Davey boy. Here I come now.

This deconstructs the traditional line that exists between a bad guy and a good guy. In this scene, it is difficult to identify who the bad guys are. The cowboy who is shot, although he had initially held Delilah down, once he realized what was happening, had attempted to stop his friend from slashing her. Indeed, he even tried to apologize for the attack in the best way he could, by offering Delilah a pony, though the offer was rejected. His murder is motivated purely by fiscal gain; Munny, Logan and the Kid have no personal reason to kill him. They rationalize the killing by building up in their heads a horrific picture of the cut-up woman, embellishing it each time it's retold, and so make the killing morally defensible, in much the same way as Daggett uses the town ordinances and the tin star as a defense for his own psychotic behavior.

It is impossible to decide categorically who is good and who is bad. Curiously, this does not render *Unforgiven* morally barren, as *A Fistful of Dollars* and *High Plains Drifter* are. *Unforgiven* is arguably the most moral Western ever produced. It depicts violence and its effects without the glamorous heroism of most nostalgic Westerns. Invariably, a fist-fight might give the traditional hero a bloody nose or a split lip, but he will live to fight another day. *Unforgiven* deconstructs Hollywood's notion of violence by creating a world where an act of violence has repercussions throughout the narrative. Violence begets violence, and the narrative progresses from one act of violence to another. Whereas, in a conventional Hollywood Western, there is an exhilaration in the depiction of violence, there is no such thrill in the acts of violence in *Unforgiven*. Rather, they are sickening in their sudden viciousness.

Violence perpetuates violence; it does not solve the problems of the society as traditional Westerns with a central Shane/Cain figure seemed to believe. The violence begins in the first scene with the disfigurement of Delilah, the act that sets the narrative in motion. It ends with the slaughter of Daggett and his deputies in Skinny's saloon. In between, Munny and English Bob are beaten half to death by Daggett. The two cowboys are killed. Logan is tortured and murdered by Daggett. Violence is portrayed as a continuous cycle. The only positive aspect in the whole cycle of violence is the Schofield Kid's breaking out from it when confronted with its reality. This is another element of the deconstruction of Shane, or more precisely, Joey. The Kid is fascinated by stories of the "Old Days" in a way reminiscent of Joey's hero worship of Shane. He even invents such stories around himself: he talks of killing two men. The Kid's gaze, though, is flawed: he is desperately short-sighted, both physically and psychologically. The Kid is eager to kill the second, guilty, cowboy, believing the myth of exhilarating violence. However, his encounter with violence almost breaks him psychologically, and, as a result, he admits that his bragging about the men he killed was either untrue or exaggeration. There is a romantic idealism in the mythology that the Kid wants to be a part of and to live up to. He is so enthralled in the whole mythology of the West that he ignores the actual truth. Munny and Logan negate the past by not recollecting it when the Kid asks about the "Old Days" but still the Kid persists in believing the myths. The Kid repeatedly asks Munny about different incidents that have been recounted to him by his

Uncle, undoubtedly with some element of embellishment. At the same time, he seems to attempt to add his own stories to the mythology. The Kid wanted to become a part of the whole cycle of mythology but, as soon as he experiences it at close quarters, he realizes the reality is nothing like the myth.

> The Kid: Was that what it was like in the old days, Will? Everybody ridin' out and shootin'? Smoke all over the place, people yelling, bullets whizzin' by?
> Munny: I guess so.
> The Kid: Shit. I thought they was goin' to get us. I was even scared, a little. Just for a minute. Were you ever scared in the old days?
> Munny: I can't remember. I was drunk most of the time.
> The Kid: I shot that fucker three times! He's takin' a shit, he went for his pistol and I blazed away. First shot I got him right in the chest. Say, Will.
> Munny: Yeah.
> The Kid: That was the first one.
> Munny: The first one what?
> The Kid: The first one I ever killed.
> Munny: Yeah? . . . Well you sure killed the hell outta that fellah today.
> The Kid: Hell yeah. [breaking down] I killed the hell outta him, didn't I? Three shots and he was dead as shit.
> Munny: Take a drink, Kid.
> The Kid: Jesus Christ. [breaks down] It don't seem real – how he can never breathe again, never – How he's dead. The other one too, all on account of pullin' a trigger.
> Munny: It's a hell of a thing killin' a man. You take away all he's got and all he's ever gonna have.
> The Kid: Yeah, well I guess they had it comin'.
> Munny: We all have it comin', Kid.

His break from the cycle is completed in the symbolic act of giving up the Schofield pistol, the icon that would have given him the name by which legend would have "remembered" his exploits. The stark realities from which the myth grew affects the Kid as it does the audience into re-examining the grounds for their fascination with screen violence and Western mythology. Ironically, at the point the Kid realizes the truth Munny is sucked back into the cycle.

The Schofield Kid is one of the characters Eastwood uses as an explicit tool to demythologize the West, the West that is wrapped up in the archetypal narrative of Shane. The Kid, young and completely devoid of any sense of his own mortality, reflects the viewers' acceptance of violence as a part of the cinematic myth without it ever being able to affect them. The audience can relate the enthusiasm of the Kid to their own enthusiasm for the myths of the West and the thrill of a Hollywood gunfight. Consequently, as the Kid is shocked into giving up the thought of violence as a way of life when confronted with its reality, the audience is similarly forced to re-think their own perception of violence.

Just as Eastwood uses the Schofield Kid as a tool to deconstruct the romanticized notion of violence in the myth of the West, two other characters are used in similar fashion to deconstruct other aspects of the myth. English Bob could be considered the personification of the myth in general. He exists in the narrative only long enough for him to be symbolically deconstructed by Little Bill Daggett. As would be expected from a mythical figure, he has the reputation of a Western legend:

> Man on train: Might be that this dude here is English Bob. He's the one that works for the railroad shootin' Chinamen. Might be he's waitin' for some crazy cowboy to touch his pistol so he can shoot him down.

To this English Bob, eccentrically, responds with a challenge of a pheasant shoot from one of the carriages on the train whereupon he displays his undeniable marksmanship. Once he reaches Big Whiskey, he arrogantly denies he is carrying a side arm when he is asked to surrender it under the conditions of the town ordinance, even though it is perfectly, indeed deliberately, visible. English Bob is a character who has begun to believe his own legend as it appears in fiction. However, this persona begins to visibly crack once he recognizes Daggett, a figure from his past who he thought was dead. From this pairing, Eastwood, similarly, expects the myth of the West to crack under the audience's juxtapositioning of it and history. The explosion of violence is only part of the deconstruction of English Bob. The crucial phase of his deconstruction occurs in the jail-house when Daggett corrects one of the stories from Bob's biography, in contradiction to the version recounted to Beauchamp:

> Daggett: I was at the Blue Bottle saloon in Wichita the night that English Bob killed Korky Cochran and I didn't see you there, nor no woman, nor two guns shooters nor none of this . . . First off Korky never carried two guns, though he should have . . . Folks did call him two guns but that wasn't because he was sportin' two pistols. That was because he had a dick that was so long it was longer than the barrel on the Walker Colt he carried. And the only insultin' he ever did was to stick that thing of his

into this French lady that English Bob here was kinda sweet on . . . You see the night that Korky walkin' into the Blue Bottle, before he knows what's happening Bob here takes a shot at him and he misses 'cos he's so damn drunk. Now that bullet whizzin' by panicked old Korky and he did the wrong thing. He went for his gun in such a hurry he shot his own damn toe off. Meantime Bob here, he's aimin' real good and he squeezes off another but he misses 'cos he's still so damned drunk . . . now the Duck of Death is as good as dead 'cos Korky does it right. He aims real careful, no hurry and BAM the Walker Colt blew up in his hand . . . You see if Korky had of had two guns instead of just a big dick he would have been there right to the end to defend himself . . . Old Bob wasn't gonna wait for old Korky to grow a new hand, no he just walked up there real slow, 'cos he was drunk and shot him right through the liver.

The "Duke of Death," the grand title of Bob's biography, is reduced to the "Duck of Death" and the deconstruction is complete. It is not clear whether Daggett's version of events is any more factual than Bob's, but ultimately this does not matter. Eastwood has used the story to illustrate the ways in which stories are told and re-told and changed in the process, until they become unrecognizable, untrue or mythology. In addition, it allows the biographer to attach himself to another character, and thus commencing a whole new series of stories. Daggett completely demythologizes Bob. As Bob is expelled from Big Whiskey he has lost his perfect, aristocratic accent in place of a "cockney" one which he subsequently uses to vitriolic effect, cursing the entire town, a huge contrast with the well chosen words of his earlier "monarchy versus republic" speeches.

W. W. Beauchamp, the biographer, or rather dime novelist, who arrives in Big Whiskey with Bob, presents possibly Eastwood's most knowing deconstructive device. Beauchamp and the Kid are in some ways similar. They both confuse Western mythology with Western history. One produces as the other consumes. When Beauchamp is introduced to Daggett he recognizes him through a story:

Beauchamp: Daggett? Daggett from Newton Hayes, from Abilene!

Initially, Beauchamp is writing Bob's biography, until Daggett deconstructs it. Beauchamp offers this defense in the face of Daggett's version of events:

Beauchamp: You see, er, it's generally considered desirable in the publishing business to take a certain liberty when depicting the cover scene . . .

Daggett: Well, Mr. Beauchamp, this book here, the writings not much different than the picture.

Beauchamp: Well, I can assure you, Mr. Daggett, that the events that are described in there are taken from the accounts of eye witnesses.

Daggett: You mean like the Duck himself?

Beauchamp: The, the Duke.

Daggett: The Duck I says.

Ironically, Beauchamp then begins to write Daggett's biography, but again, what he actually records is more fiction, more mythology. The story he recounts for Beauchamp smacks of the same kind of poetic license or exaggeration Bob gave him. Indeed, it would seem that Daggett too has begun to believe his own legend. When, finally, Munny is about to kill Daggett, he says:

Daggett: I don't deserve this . . . to die this way.

Munny: Deserves got nothing to do with it.

As Daggett is killed, Beauchamp approaches Munny, and the whole process of myth-making seems about ready to start over. However, Munny tells him in no uncertain terms that he is not interested, effectively closing the narrative:

Beauchamp: Who'd you kill first? When confronted by superior numbers, an experienced gunfighter will always fire on the best shot first.

Munny: Is that so.

Beauchamp: Yeah. Little Bill told me that. You probably killed him first didn't you?

Munny: I was lucky in the order but I've always been lucky when it comes to killing folks.

Beauchamp: Who was next? It was Clyde right? You must have killed Clyde . . . well could have been Deputy Hendy . . .

Munny: All I can tell you is who's gonna be last.

By doing this Munny is, symbolically, breaking the cycle of myth creation, even though, of the three characters Beauchamp talks to, Munny is the only one about whom the stories are categorically true. The final shoot-out is in many ways incongruous with the elegiacism that underlies the movie. It is the only violent act that in some way thrills the audience; by the time Munny enters the saloon, the audience is willing the action and violence to commence. The ongoing brutality of Daggett and his subsequent murder of Logan allow Munny a kind of moral high ground from which he can legitimately avenge his partner's death and put an end to Daggett, who, by this time has become a discernible bad guy.

> Daggett: Well, sir, you are a cowardly son of a bitch. You just shot an unarmed man.
> Munny: Well he should have armed himself if he's gonna decorate his saloon with my friend.

Eastwood the film-maker here demonstrates his awareness of the nostalgia/ elegiac paradigm. And given the postmodern nature of the film, they can co-exist, both now assimilated into the Western. As Munny leaves the saloon, he has become exactly that which he has been denying throughout the film, and thus is elevated to the level of Western legend/hero. It seems to suggest that Eastwood is resigned to the fact that a complete deconstruction of the myth is impossible, at the very least, impractical. Instead, he offers the audience a game; he offers a "realistic" picture of what lies beneath the mythology, without actually destroying it.

Munny's progression from negating any similarities between "William Munny . . . killer of women and children" and pig-farmer to the efficient, truly mythical killer of the final reel is not unexpected. His determination and pedantry in repeating that he "ain't like that no more" is always too determined for the audience to completely accept. In William Munny, Eastwood has found a character that represents his screen persona up to this point. Eastwood is conscious of his role as a film-maker in the desensitization of violence. Munny illustrates metaphorically the stress this has put on him. In Eastwood's other Westerns, he has dealt with the supernatural, the spiritual or ghosts, all riffs on the original incarnation of Shane, most notably in *High Plains Drifter* and *Pale Rider*. In *Unforgiven*, while not playing anything as ambiguous as a ghost, by the end, Munny has become almost a supernatural force. His gnarled features and recent scars, the result of his beating from Daggett, give the character the look of death, a death mask; his face represents a lifetime of killing. The list of types he has killed has an Old Testament resonance. Munny could be considered the tool by which Eastwood deconstructs his own screen persona, one significantly wrapped up in the character of Shane. His portrayal of William Munny is almost as that of a canvas, every line evidence of the effect that a life time of violence has had for both Munny/Eastwood and Shane.

Unforgiven contains multitudes, and as such it attempts to speak to and of many different perspectives. *Unforgiven* is in this sense *the* postmodern Western, the Western that attests to the fragmentation of the genre, the nostalgic and the elegiac in the same space as evidence. Ultimately, *Unforgiven* is a closed narrative. Eastwood makes sure of this by repeating the prologue caption at the end, with the addition that Munny went off to become a dry goods salesman in San Francisco. The audience knows where he came from, and now knows where he goes to. Yet *Unforgiven* does not represent the end of the Western. Indeed, a new century, launched by a shocking event, has brought the Western back into focus in a way that it had not been since the Cold War.

CHAPTER NINE

Wanted Dead or Alive: 9/11 and the American Western

Unforgiven is an introspective Western, more concerned with interrogating and deconstructing the genre, its structures, values and assumptions, than with representing anxiety, conflict or pressing social issues as the Western had done in the era of the Cold War. This concern lies at the heart of the film's claims to postmodernity. Indeed, the 1990s in many ways resonates with the implications of postmodernism. The presidency of Bill Clinton, for example, is often associated with the term, for a number of reasons. One element of postmodernism is the centrality of mass media, of information overload, something that resonates with a presidency spent in the glare of sensational media coverage. His politics have been seen as fluid, meaning some commentators suggested he could be considered to "be both left and right." As *Time International Magazine* editorialized in 1996, "He is the first postmodern President, the first to turn 'anything goes' into a political creed."

This sense that there are no fixed points of reference is an element of the postmodern too. In the 1990s this concept took on a troubling dimension for the United States. America, as I've suggested throughout, is a nation that understands the world and its place in it in adversarial terms: it understands its values by defining and testing them against an "other," whether it be the colonial overlords that informed the writing of the Constitution, the Indians on Turner's meeting point between savagery and civilization, the inhuman and fanatical Japanese of the Second World War or Kennan's Communists after it. But the Cold War was over and the 1990s represented a significantly quiet time for war in America. Even the 1991 Gulf War was postmodern in the sense that it was a virtual war. It was a war that existed in images transmitted via CNN, and even then those images were so heavily censored that they could in no way be considered real. When Jean Baudrillard suggested that the "Gulf War did not take place" he is suggesting the war was so one-sided that, while the Iraqis fought a traditional war, for America the war did not happen.

The Gulf War was the first war to feature the technological advances and innovations associated with the Revolution in Military Affairs (RMA) that had been underway in the American military establishment since the Vietnam War. At the core of the RMA was a wish to remove the human from the war zone, to see future wars fought between machines, with the human component acting as an information node, controlling the action from far away. This kind of technological reliance has no better illustration than the constant television images of missiles with mounted cameras recording their last moments before they slam into their target.

This post-Cold War period, devoid of any particular threat after the collapse of the Soviet Union, saw an American culture reaching out for the certainties of an enemy against which to test itself and its exceptionalism. The lack of an enemy in the real world was partially solved by popular cinema, in films like X-Files: the Movie (1998), Armageddon (1998), Godzilla (1998), Deep Impact (1998), Independence Day (1996), Mars Attacks! (1996), Volcano (1997), Dante's Peak (1997), End of Days (1999), and Strange Days (1995). These films replayed narratives which pitted the spirit and values of America against natural disaster, aliens, millennialist angst or a corrupt government, acting as the villains for the good guys to overcome. The implications of the post-Cold War situation were reflected upon and discussed in the epochal work of social scientist Francis Fukyama's articulation of "The End of History" in which he suggests that democracy, the rule of law, and the market economy have emerged victorious over every ideological model, and specifically Communism. Elsewhere in this period, other thinkers are exploring possible future enemies. Perhaps most renowned was Samuel Huntingdon, a Harvard history professor, who posited in a 1993 Foreign Affairs article a coming "clash of civilizations." Such was the interest in the piece that it received more discussion and correspondence than anything Foreign Affairs had published since the Second World War. The article discussed the conditions under which future conflicts may operate, which he suggests would not be at the level of nation-states, vying for political supremacy. Rather civilizations, systems of history, religion, tradition, would be the location for future war.

Identifying and, more importantly, being prepared for the next enemy was of concern for the Project for the Next American Century (PNAC), a right-wing think tank whose main goal is to strategize the maintenance of the American global dominance that had marked the twentieth century into the twenty-first. They envision full spectrum dominance, militarily and economically, in the global arena as well as in space and cyberspace. In September 2000, PNAC published a 90-page report entitled, Rebuilding America's Defenses: Strategy, Forces and Resources for a New Century. The document clearly articulated the need for a new enemy, in the form of an event or crisis that would serve to focus the nation on the mission. The historical example they use is evocative: "Further, the process of transformation, even if it brings revolutionary change, is likely to be a long one, absent some catastrophic and catalyzing event – like a new Pearl Harbor" (PNAC 2000, 51).

With such aims in mind, it is perhaps unsurprising that the new Republican administration in 2001 would propose the biggest increase in defense spending since the Cold War, an increase of $33 billion which would take the Pentagon's budget to $344 billion. On 4 September 2001, Ben Cohen, of Ben & Jerry's ice-cream fame posted a spoof job advertisement on the internet, which was subsequently picked up by the nation's newspapers. It read:

> ENEMY WANTED. Serious enemy needed to justify Pentagon budget increase. Defense contractors desperate. Interested enemies send letter and photo or video (threatening, ok) to Enemy Search Committee, Priorities Campaign, 1350 Broadway, NY, NY, 10018.

His aim was to draw attention to the absurdity of such military expenditure in a time of peace. However, within a week the proposed increases would come to seem justified. As Ashton B. Carter states, "On September 11 2001, the post-Cold War security bubble finally burst" (Carter 2001/2002: 5).

President Bush's response to the events of 11 September and America's reaction to his leadership, demonstrate the ongoing and central importance of Western mythology in America. Just as the Western had been evoked in previous moments of war, crisis and anxiety, so it would be again in the wake of 11 September and the advent of the War of Terror. Bush used the language, values and imagery of the frontier in the rhetoric he employed to respond to the crisis. Such rhetoric served on the one hand to mobilize the country for the coming wars, in Afghanistan and more generally, on terror, and to offer a sense of familiar security to the national psyche. Bush used the quintessential American meta-narrative of the West to explain his stance and garner support for the bombing of Afghanistan. As Silberstein observes, "As the War on Terrorism was formulated, familiar images and themes contributed to the consolidation of support [for the prosecution] of a war on Afghanistan" (Silberstein 2002: xii).

The Western meta-narrative was, for the most part, a readily accepted and accessible script, which, as it had been in the era of the Cold War, was metaphorically marshaled to explain Bush's post-9/11 security and military strategies. Even as the European press lamented his folksy response to the atrocities, Americans demonstrated no such disapproval. As Rob Watson asserted at the time,

> Though often strange sounding to foreign ears, the president's cowboy style directness . . . goes down well with many Americans. His description of

Osama Bin Laden as wanted dead or alive, and his promise to smoke out his followers, is seen as good old-fashioned plain speaking here.

That President Bush should conceptualize security issues in this way is not surprising. His world view, in terms of family background and political career in Texas, meant that he identified with the values of the Western. In addition, this world view was shaped by the Cold War era, in relation to his father's presidency and also because of the cold warriors which constituted his cabinet.

It might almost be with a sense of relief, then, that on 20 September President Bush declared, "we are a country awakened to danger . . . We have found our mission and our moment." The "axis of evil" that he identified in the State of the Union Address, 29 January, had provided the enemy America so needed.

In effect, Bush used the Western meta-narrative to re-affirm America's sense of identity and purpose within the contexts of the international arena. Bush employed key Western symbols, among them, the heroic cowboy, the founding ideals of the American nation and the existence of an "other" as the enemy, as a means of mobilizing the United States, and its allies, for war. In so doing, Bush is replicating the choice made by Kennedy and his advisors to use the frontier as a "metaphor . . . descriptive of the way in which they hoped to use power . . . [as] a complexly resonant symbol, a vivid and memorable set of hero-tales . . . a model of successful and morally justifying action on the stage of historical conflict" (Slotkin 1992: 3).

In the first instance, the heroic virtues associated with the archetypal cowboy underpin Bush's articulation of the Western meta-narrative. Time and again in speeches delivered in the wake of 9/11, Bush depicts himself as the courageous cowboy who must inspire, guide and protect America during this time of unparalleled crisis. Silberstein analyzes the ways in which this image was created and maintained through the president's deliberate use of a series of rhetorical actions. Primarily, Bush delivers his speeches in a determined and resolute tone, using active grammar. This rhetorical action places him at the forefront of a given situation and encourages the American public to trust presidential decisions (Silberstein 2002: 1, 7). For example, on 11 September, Bush stated, "I have spoken to the Vice President, to the Governor of New York, to the Director of the FBI, and I have ordered that the full resources of the federal government go to help the victims and their families . . ." In this statement Bush establishes his authority as commander in chief, as would the cowboy guaranteeing the safety of the community in the Western. The success of this strategy is apparent in the broad acceptance of Bush in the role of commander in chief, despite questions regarding his character and the manner in which he attained the White House in 2000. Americans did look to him for security and leadership during this time of crisis.

In establishing his authority, real and rhetorical, Bush implies that he embodies the virtues associated with the figure of the cowboy and proceeds then to equate these values with the objectives of the "War on Terrorism." The cowboy's ethos is traditionally based upon certain assumptions. As Hellman asserts, cowboys possess "a conceptualization of the world as a battleground between the forces of light and darkness . . . [They have] a belief in the special virtues of America" (Hellman 1986: 44). Through his invocation of the Western narrative, Bush seeks to present himself as a leader possessing these traits.

While his use of the values of the West as political rhetoric operates on an individual level, they also work at a national level. Bush depicts the United States as the harbinger of justice, the superior state in military and moral terms, within the anarchical, international arena. For example, whilst discussing the formation of the Coalition against Terrorism, Bush stated, "I want justice . . . There's an old poster out West . . . that said, 'Wanted Dead or Alive' . . . We are putting together a coalition. We will do what it takes to find the terrorists . . . The United States is proud to lead the coalition." In this statement Bush suggests an image common to the Western movie. America in this conception is portrayed as the heroic leader of a Western posse, made up of its allies in the international community.

Bush further mobilizes the American public for war through continual reference to a common enemy, represented by Al Qaeda. He articulates America's opposition to the "other" in an attempt to unify the nation behind his strategies. The concept of the "other" is an essential component in the definition of any nation's construction of identity. The idea of the "other" has repeatedly facilitated the development of the American nation throughout its history. The "other" in the guise of the Native American is obviously a central Western trope. Bush utilizes versions of otherness to depict Al Qaeda. In a statement delivered on 12 September, Bush said, "This is an enemy who has no regard for human life. This is an enemy who preys on innocent and unsuspecting people, and then runs for cover. But it won't be able to run forever." This construction of the enemy resonates with the kind of imagery equated with Indians. It mirrors the Old Western portrayal of the Indian as a faceless and savage enemy who seeks to deny American's their Manifest Destiny. In this way, Bush portrays Al Qaeda as a similarly savage, faceless, ideologically primitive enemy. Americans, in contrast, are viewed as a civilized and progressive people. This juxtaposition in Bush's rhetoric points quite clearly to a central theme of the American West: savagery versus civilization. More specifically, it connects the current conflict to the historical conflict between Indians and white settlers. Throughout the early stages of the War against Terrorism, Bush actively promoted the savagery/civilization dialectic. During a speech to the Joint Session of Congress on 20 September, Bush declared, "You are either with us or you are with the terrorists. This is civilization's fight." The use of such language suggests that violence can be morally justified because the enemy is inferior. As America knows, the successful defeat of an enemy, or primitive people, facilitates a revitalization of faith in its moral principles and the virtues of its national character. And in that way we come full circle, back to Turner. In his evocation of the Turnerian paradigm of savagery versus civilization as a means of comprehending the nature of 9/11, Bush is effectively projecting American values, such as democracy and freedom, onto the rest of the world.

Bush's metaphorical use of the Western meta-narrative proved to be a highly successful rhetorical strategy then during the initial months of the War against Terrorism. He successfully packaged the themes of the archetypal heroic cowboy, the ideals of the American nation, and the existence of a primitive enemy to unite the American people behind his post-9/11 leadership and security strategy. The measure of his success can be seen in approval ratings which, throughout the year following 9/11, reached between 85 and 90 per cent. Assessing the nature of Bush's popularity, Watson observed that "Bush . . . captured the hearts and minds of the American people, something few would have thought possible when he first entered the White House."

POST-9/11 WESTERNS

In the wake of 9/11, and Bush's effective use of Western mythology as a script through which to frame his administration's reaction to the attacks, it is not surprising that a number of Westerns emerged. Indeed, in the years since the events of 2001, the Western has had something of a renaissance, critically and commercially. Among the earliest were Ron Howard's *The Missing* (2003), an adaptation of Thomas Eidson's *The Last Ride* (1995), and Disney's *Hidalgo* (2004) and *Home on the Range* (2004) (though it actually went into development in early 2001).

Of greater significance to the implications of 9/11 are John Lee Hancock's *The Alamo* (2004) and Kevin Costner's *Open Range* (2003). The appearance of a new version of *The Alamo* is by itself worthy of note. When John Wayne produced his version in 1960, it was done so to revive a nation that he believed had grown lazy as a result of the age of affluence. Wayne stated of the urge to make the film,

> We want to recreate a moment in history which will show to this living generation of Americans what their country really stands for, and to put in front of their eyes the bloody truth of what some of their forebears went through to win what they had to have or die – liberty and freedom.

Hancock's film is clearly designed to associate these values with the fallout of 9/11. In one direction the film represents a yearning for a time when war was simpler, when armies would mass and battles would be decisive. However, a more explicit aim of the film emerged at the announcement of its development. In May 2002 as Disney signaled its intention to produce a new version of *The Alamo*, Michael Eisner, head of the studio claimed the film would "capture the post-September 11 surge in patriotism." However, after a troubled production and long reshoots, it missed that surge and the brand of triumphalism that the film represents missed its audience.

Open Range is a much more interesting and textured film. Based on the 1990 novel *The Open Range Men*, by Lauran Paine, the film tells the story of a group of "free-grazers" who come into conflict with a greedy Irish land baron. In its tone, pace and sense of purpose it resembles the more realistic, revisionist look and feel of *Unforgiven*. The story inverts the *Shane* premise so that it is the cattlemen who fight to defend their free-spirited individuality, against the ranch owner who wishes to selfishly fence in the open range, a timely inversion given the debate about freedom and the erosion of civil liberties that followed in the wake of 9/11. Another undercurrent in the movie resonates with the transition from post-Cold War to post-9/11 America. Charlie Waite is a character who has a dark, violent past, which began when he kills the abusive man who held the mortgage on his family's farm and escalated when he became an irregular during the Civil War. However, since he met up with Boss Spearman, he has experienced a period of calm, but Baxter's attempts to limit their personal freedom force him to take up the gun again. In this way *Open Range* mirrors the sense that America has to embrace the possibility of violence to defend that which it cherishes.

The vitality of the Western is also apparent on the small screen. Prior to 9/11, the last successful television Western was the 1989 adaptation of Larry McMurtry's Pulitzer Prize-winning *Lonesome Dove*, which attracted astonishing audiences and garnered seven Emmy awards. Two television Westerns appeared in the aftermath of 9/11. *Firefly* (2002–3), ostensibly science fiction, mixes Western and lost cause elements in its recounting of the adventures of a band of smugglers who find themselves on the wrong side of both a civil war and consequently a faceless, bureaucratic industrialized empire. Although it was cancelled half way through its first season, *Firefly* had such a huge cult following that it spawned a feature film, *Serenity* (2005), which played successfully with the conventions of both science fiction and the Western. HBO's *Deadwood* (2004–onward) presents the infamous prospecting town in all of its gritty, violent, foul-mouthed glory. The show weaves fictions around the historical figures of Wild Bill Hickock, Calamity Jane and Al Swearengen, who is destined to be one of the most memorable television characters in one of television's most striking shows.

More recently, two Westerns have captured the attention of critics and audiences alike and illustrate the Western as a reinvigorated cinematic form. Ang Lee's *Brokeback Mountain* (2005), based on the short story from Annie Proulx's 1999 collection of short stories set in Wyoming, *Close Range*, details the love between two cowboys that develops while they tend sheep one summer in the 1960s. Their intermittent but passionate relationship spans two decades and is movingly and sensitively depicted. One of the most interesting aspects of the film is the way in which it invites a reappraisal of similar male pairings in other Westerns. However, the "gay Western" label is one that Lee refutes. As far as he is concerned it is not "gay" but rather a great American love story, and he suggests "it has very little to do with the western" though it is almost traditional in its narrative of love and struggle against a Western landscape. Although it won the Golden Lion at the Venice Film Festival and was nominated for, amongst others, the Academy Award for Best Picture at the 2006 ceremony (losing out to *Crash*, 2005, may represent something of a belated backlash against its taboo-breaking subject matter), the film did spark controversy, understandably, in the American heartlands, but to find that a Western can still be a vehicle for such a fresh, intelligent perspective is heartening.

Three Burials of Melquiades Estrada (2005), directed by and starring Tommy Lee Jones, from Guillermo Arriaga's beautifully constructed script, has reso-nances of other border-Westerns like Sam Peckinpah's *Bring me the Head of Alfredo Garcia* (1974) and John Sayles' *Lone Star* (1996) and even the Border Trilogy of Cormac McCarthy. A picaresque tale of revenge and redemption, the narrative revolves around the shooting of the eponymous character by a border patrolman and the subsequent effort of Jones' character, a friend of the dead man, to fulfill Estrada's final wishes and to bring the patrolman to account for his actions. Jones' contemporary Western works on a number of levels; it is a tale of friendship and honor, that is both funny and grotesque, but its great strength is the insight it offers into two incredibly different cultures that continually cross into each other.

And this new wave of Western production shows no sign of abating. At the beginning of the twenty-first century, more precisely in the aftermath of 11 September, the Western has once again returned politically and culturally to the forefront of the American imagination. While production is necessarily on a different scale, the range and intention of the Western is as fresh and vital now as it was in the golden age of the 1940s and 1950s. This vitality stems from the form's resonance with the political culture of the United States. And it is because of this that the American Western will continue to shape, reflect and challenge the course of American development in the years to come.

Bibliography

Abbey, E. (1982), *The Monkey Wrench Gang*, London: Picador.

Adams, S. (1961), *First Hand Report: the Story of the Eisenhower Administration*, New York: Harper & Brothers Publishers.

Albertson, D. (ed.) (1963), *Eisenhower as President*, New York: Hill & Wang.

Allmendinger, B. (1998), *Ten Most Wanted: the New Western Literature*, London: Routledge.

Anderson, L. (1999), *About John Ford*, London: Plexus.

Anonymous (1946), 'Crossroads: Einstein portrait', *Time*, 1 July, in *Time Multimedia Almanac: a Journey Through Seven Decades of Time*.

Anonymous (1996), *Primary Colors: a Novel of Politics*, London: Chatto & Windus.

Aquila, R. (ed.) (1996), *Wanted Dead or Alive: the American West in Popular Culture*, Chicago: University of Illinois Press.

Bach, S. (1996), *Final Cut: Dreams and Disaster in the Making of Heaven's Gate*, London: Pimlico.

Bailey, T. A. (1980), *The Pugnacious Presidents: White House Warriors on Parade*, New York: Macmillan.

Balio, T. (ed.) (1977), *The American Film Industry*, Madison: University of Wisconsin Press.

Barber, J. D. (1992), *The Presidential Character: Predicting Performance in the White House*, 4th edn, New Jersey: Prentice Hall.

Baxter, J. (1999), *George Lucas: a Biography*, London: HarperCollins.

Bazin, A. (1971), 'What is cinema?', in Hugh Gray (ed.), *What is Cinema?*, Berkeley: University of California Press, vol. 2.

Bergman, A. (1972), *We're In the Money: Depression America and its Films*, New York: Harper & Row.

Bible, The, Authorized King James Version with Apocrypha, (1998), Oxford: Oxford University Press.

Billington, R. A. (1960), *Westward Expansion*, New York: Macmillan.

Billington, R. A. (1973), *Fredrick Jackson Turner: Historian, Scholar, Teacher*, New York: Oxford University Press.

Bilton, A. (2002), *An Introduction to Contemporary American Fiction*, Edinburgh: Edinburgh University Press.

Biskind, P. (1999), 'Any which way he can', in R. E. Kapsis and K. Coblentz (eds), *Clint Eastwood Interviews*, Jackson: University Press of Mississippi.

Blum, J. M. (1991), *Years of Discord: American Politics and Society, 1961–1974*, New York: Norton.

Bobbitt, P. (2003), *The Shield of Achilles: War, Peace and the Course of History*, London: Penguin.

Booker, C. (1992), *The Neophiliacs: the Revolution in English Life in the Fifties and Sixties*, London: Pimlico.

Brookeman, C. (1984), *American Culture and Society since the 1930s*, London: Macmillan.

Brownlow, K. (1979), *The War, the West and the Wilderness*, London: Secker & Warburg.

Burdick, E. and H. Wheeler (1962), *Fail-Safe*, New York: McGraw-Hill.

Buscombe, E. (ed.) (1992), *The BFI Companion to the Western*, London: Andre Deutsch.

Buscombe, E. and R. E. Pearson (eds) (1998), *Back In the Saddle Again: New Essays on the Western*, London: BFI Publishing.

Cahill, T. (1985), 'Clint Eastwood: *The Rolling Stone* Interview', in R. E. Kapsis and K. Coblentz (eds), *Clint Eastwood Interviews*, Jackson: University Press of Mississippi.

Cameron, I. and D. Pye (eds) (1996), *The Movie Book of the Western*, London: Cassell.

Campbell, J. (1993), *The Hero with a Thousand Faces*, London: HarperCollins.

Campbell, N. (2000a), *The Cultures of the American New West*, Edinburgh: Edinburgh University Press.

Campbell, N. (2000b), 'Liberty beyond its proper bounds: Cormac McCarthy's history of the West in *Blood Meridian*', in R. Wallach (ed.), *Myth, Legend, Dust: Critical Responses to Cormac McCarthy*, Manchester: Manchester University Press.

Carter, A. B. (2001/2002), 'The architecture of government in the face of terrorism', *International Security*, Winter 2001/2002, 26: 3.

Carter, J. (1982), *Keeping Faith: Memoirs of a President*, London: Collins.

Carter, R. A. (2000), *Buffalo Bill Cody: the Man Behind the Legend*, New York: John Wiley & Sons.

Cather, W. (2003), *O Pioneers!*, Lincoln: University of Nebraska Press.

Caute, D. (1978), *The Great Fear: the Anti-Communist Purge Under Truman and Eisenhower*, New York: Simon & Schuster.

Cawelti, J. G. (1970), *The Six-Gun Mystique*, Ohio: Bowling Green University Popular Press.

Cawelti, J. G. (1976), *Adventure, Mystery and Romance*, Chicago: University of Chicago Press.

Cawelti, J. G. (1978), 'Chinatown and generic transformation in recent American films', in Mast and Cohen (eds.), *Film Theory and Criticism*, Oxford: Oxford University Press.

Cawelti, J. G. (1999), *The Six-Gun Mystique Sequel*, Ohio: Bowling Green University Popular Press.

Childs, M. (1959), *Eisenhower: Captive Hero*, London: Hammond, Hammond & Company.

Cody, W. F. (1994), *The Life of Buffalo Bill*, London: Senate.

Colton, R. C. (1959), *The Civil War in the Western Territories*, Norman: University of Oklahoma Press.

Cook, D. A. (1990), *A History of Narrative Film*, New York: Norton.

Countryman, E. and E. von Heussen-Countryman (1999), *BFI Film Classics: Shane*, London: BFI Publishing.

Coyne, M. (1998), *The Crowded Prairie: American National Identity in the American Western*, London: I. B. Tauris.

Crane, S. (1984), *Prose and Poetry*, New York: The Library of America.

Cripps, T. (1997), *Hollywood's High Noon: Moviemaking & Society before Television*, Baltimore: Johns Hopkins University Press.

Cronon, W., G. Miles and J. Gitlin (eds) (1993), *Under An Open Sky: Rethinking America's Western Past*, New York: Norton.

Cullen, J. (1995), *The Civil War in Popular Culture: a Reusable Past*, Washington, DC: Smithsonian Institute Press.

Cunningham, J. M. (1947) *The Tin Star* [reprinted in Work, J. C. (ed.) (1996), *Gunfight!: Thirteen Western Stories*, Lincoln: University of Nebraska Press].

Dary, D. (1989), *Cowboy Culture: a Saga of Five Centuries*, Lawrence: University Press of Kansas.

Davies, P. and B. Neve (eds) (1981), *Cinema, Politics and Society in America*, Manchester: Manchester University Press.

Debo, A. (1993), *Geronimo: The Man His Time His Place*, London: Pimlico.

De Toth, A. (1994), *Fragments: Portraits from the Inside*, London: Faber & Faber.

Dick, B. and A. Singh (1995), *Conversations with Ishmael Reed*, Jackson: University Press of Mississippi.

Didion, J. (1993), *Slouching Towards Bethlehem*, London: HarperCollins.

Diggins, J. P. (1989), *The Proud Decades: America in War and Peace, 1941–1960*, New York: Norton.

Divine, R. A. (1981), *Eisenhower and the Cold War*, Oxford: Oxford University Press.

Donald, A. D. (ed.) (1966), *John F. Kennedy and the New Frontier*, New York: Hill & Wang.

Donovan, R. (1956), *Eisenhower: The Inside Story*, New York: Harper & Brothers.

Drummond, P. (1997), *BFI Film Classics: High Noon*, London: BFI Publishing.

Easton, R. (1970), *Max Brand: the Big "Westerner"*, Norman: University of Oklahoma Press.

Ehrhart, W. D. (1995a), *Busted: a Vietnam Veteran in Nixon's America*, Amherst: University of Massachusetts Press.

Ehrhart, W. D. (1995b), *Passing Time: Memoir of a Vietnam Veteran Against the War*, Amherst: University of Massachusetts Press.

Ehrhart, W. D. (1995c), *Vietnam-Perkasie: a Combat Marine Memoir*, Amherst: University of Massachusetts Press.

Eisenhower, D. D. (1963), *Mandate for Change 1953–1956*, New York: Doubleday & Company Inc.

Eisenhower, D. D. (1965), *Waging Peace, 1956–1961*, New York: Doubleday & Company Inc.

Engelhardt, T. (1995), *The End of Victory Culture*, New York: HarperCollins.

Erisman, Fred (1974), 'Growing up with the American West: fiction of Jack Schaefer', *Journal of Popular Culture*, III: 3, Bowling Green State University.

Etulain, R. W. (1996), *Re-Imaging the Modern American West: a Century of Fiction, History and Art*, Tucson: University of Arizona Press.

Eyman, Scott (1999), *Print the Legend: The Life and Times of John Ford*, New York: Simon and Schuster.

Fagen, H. (ed.) (1998), *Duke: We're Glad We Knew You*, New Jersey: Citadel Press.

Fenin, G. N. and W. K. Everson (1973), *The Western: From Silents to the Seventies*, New York: Grossman.

Fiedler, L. A. (1972), *The Return of the Vanishing American*, London, Paladin.

Fleming, D. (ed.) (1969), *The Intellectual Migration*, Cambridge, MA: Harvard University Press.

Forbes, B. D. and J. H. Mahan (eds) (2000), *Religion and Popular Culture in America*, Berkeley: University of California Press.

Ford, G. (1979), *A Time to Heal: the Autobiography of Gerald R. Ford*, London: W. H. Allen.

Frayling, C. (1981), *Spaghetti Westerns: Cowboys and Europeans from Karl May to Sergio Leone*, London: Routledge & Kegan Paul.

Frayling, C. (1985), 'Eastwood on Eastwood', in R. E. Kapsis and K. Coblentz (eds) (1999), *Clint Eastwood Interviews*, Jackson: University Press of Mississippi.

Frayling, C. (2000), *Sergio Leone: Something to do with Death*, London: Faber & Faber.

French, P. (2005), *Westerns: Aspects of a Movie Genre and Westerns Revisited*, Manchester: Carcanet.

Frohock, W. M. (1971), *The Novel of Violence in America*, Dallas: Southern Methodist University Press.

Frost, R. (1969), *Selected Poems*, London: Penguin.

Fukayama, F. (1993), *The End of History and the Last Man*, London: Penguin.

Fussell, E. (1965), *Frontier: American Literature and the American West*, New Jersey: Princeton University Press.

Gallafent, E. (1994), *Clint Eastwood: Actor and Director*, London: Studio Vista.

Gardiner, Dorothy and Katherine Sorley Walker (eds) (1962), *Raymond Chandler Speaking*, London: Hamish Hamilton.

Ginsberg, A. (1989) [1955–6], *Howl*, in Geoffrey Moore (ed.), *Penguin Book of American Verse*, London: Penguin.

Ginsberg, A. (1989) [1955–6], *A Supermarket in California*, in Geoffrey Moore (ed.), *Penguin Book of American Verse*, London: Penguin.

Golden, F. (1999), 'Albert Einstein: person of the century', *Time*, 31 December 1999.

Goldman, Eric F. (1960), 'Good-by to the 'fifties – and good riddance', *Harper's Magazine*, 220 (1316), January: 27–9.

Goodman, W. (1969), *The Committee: the Extraordinary Career of the House Committee on Un-American Activities*, London: Secker & Warburg.

Graham, M. (2004), *The Cambridge Companion to the African American Novel*, Cambridge: Cambridge University Press.

Graulich, M. and S. Tatum (2003), *Reading* The Virginian *in the New West*, Lincoln: University of Nebraska Press.

Greenstein, F. I. (ed.) (1988), *Leadership in the Modern Presidency*, Cambridge, MA: Harvard University Press.

Gressley, G. M. (ed.) (1997), *Old West/New West*, Norman: University of Oklahoma Press.

Grey, Z. (1994), *Riders of the Purple Sage: the Authorized Text*, Lincoln: University of Nebraska Press.

Guerif, F. (1986), *Clint Eastwood: From Rawhide to Pale Rider – the man and his films*, London: St. Martin's Press.

Guillemin, G. (2004), *The Pastoral Vision of Cormac McCarthy*, Texas: Texas A & M University Press.

Guthrie Jr, A. B. (1947), *The Big Sky*, Boston: Houghton Mifflin Company.

Guthrie Jr, A. B. (1949), *The Way West*, Boston: Houghton Mifflin Company.

Hall, R. A. (2001), *Performing the American Frontier: 1870–1906*, Cambridge: Cambridge University Press.

Hardy, P. (1995), *The Western*, London: Aurum.

Haslam, G. (1975), *Jack Schaefer*, Western Writers Series no.20, Boise: Boise State University Press.

Hayes, H. (ed.) (1969), *Smiling through the Apocalypse*, New York: McCall Publishing Group.

Hellmann, J. (1986), *American Myth and the Legacy of Vietnam*, New York: Columbia University Press.

Hellmann, J. (1999), *The Kennedy Obsessions: the American Myth of JFK*, New York: Columbia University Press.

Henriksen, M. A. (1997), *Dr. Strangelove's America*, Berkeley: University of California Press.

Henry, M. (1984), 'Interview with Clint Eastwood', in R. E. Kapsis and K. Coblentz (eds) (1999), *Clint Eastwood Interviews*, Jackson: University Press of Mississippi.

Hoganson, K. L. (1998), *Fighting for American Manhood: How Gender Politics Provoked the Spanish-American and Philippine-American Wars*, New Haven: Yale University Press.

Hollingdale, R. J. (ed. & trans.) (1977), *A Nietzsche Reader*, London: Penguin.

Holloway, D. (2002), *The Late Modernism of Cormac McCarthy*, Westport: Greenwood Press.

Hughes, E. J. (1963), *The Ordeal of Power: a Political Memoir of the Eisenhower Years*, London: Macmillan.

Hull, D. S. (1969), *Film in the Third Reich*, Berkeley: University of California Press.

Huntington, S. P. (2002), *The Clash of Civilizations and the Remaking of World Order*, London: The Free Press.

Jacobs, L. (1968), *The Rise of American Film*, New York: Teachers College Press.

Johnson, D. (1995), *Indian Country*, Lincoln: University of Nebraska Press.

Johnson, L. B. (1971), *The Vantage Point: Perspectives of the Presidency 1963–1969*, New York: Holt, Rinehart & Winston.

Jowett, G. (1976), *Film–The Democratic Art*, Boston: Focal Press.

Kael, P. (1983), *5001 Nights at the Movies: A Guide from A–Z*, London: Hamish Hamilton.

Kael, P. (1987), *Kiss Kiss Bang Bang*, London: Arrow.

Kael, P. (1994), *For Keeps: 30 Years at the Movies*, New York: Penguin.

Kaplan, A. and D. E. Pease (eds) (1993), *Cultures of United States Imperialism*, Durham: Duke University Press.

Kapsis, R. E. and K. Coblentz (eds) (1999), *Clint Eastwood Interviews*, Jackson: University Press of Mississippi.

Karnow, S. (1991), *Vietnam: a History*, London: Pimlico.

Katz, W. L. (1987), *The Black West*, Seattle: Open Hand.

Kearns, D. (1976), *Lyndon Johnson and the American Dream*, London: Andre Deutsch.

Kennan, G. (1987), 'The sources of Soviet conduct', reprinted in *Foreign Affairs*, vol. 65, no. 4: Containment 40 Years Later.

Kennedy, J. F. (1964a), *Profiles in Courage: Memorial Edition*, New York: Harper & Row.

Kennedy, J. F. (1964b), *The Burden and the Glory*, London: Hamish Hamilton.

Kennedy, R. F. (1969), *Thirteen Days: a Memoir of the Cuban Missile Crisis*, New York: Norton.

Kern, S. (1983), *The Culture of Time and Space, 1880–1918*, Cambridge, MA: Harvard University Press.

Kilpatrick, J. (1999), *Celluloid Indians: Native Americans in Film*, Lincoln: University of Nebraska Press.

Kinnard, D. (1990), *Ike 1890–1990: a Pictorial History*, New York: Brassey's.

Kitses, J. (2004), *Horizons West: Directing The Western from John Ford to Clint Eastwood*, London: British Film Institute.

Kitses, J. and G. Rickman (eds) (1999), *The Western Reader*, New York: Limelight Editions.

Kittredge, W. (ed.) (1997), *The Portable Western Reader*, New York: Penguin.

Kolodny, A. (1975), *The Lay of the Land: Metaphor as Experience and History in American Life and Letters*, Chapel Hill: The University of North Carolina Press.

Kowalewski, M. (1996), *Reading the West: New Essays on the Literature of the American West*, Cambridge: Cambridge University Press.

Lee, H. (1997), *Willa Cather: a Life Saved Up*, London: Virago Press.

Lenihan, J. H. (1980), *Showdown: Confronting Modern America in the Western Film*, Chicago: University of Illinois Press.

Lennon, J. M. (ed.) (1988), *Conversations with Norman Mailer*, Jackson: University Press of Mississippi.

Limerick, P. N. (1988), *The Legacy of Conquest: the Unbroken Past of the American West*, New York: Norton.

Limerick, P. N., C. A. Milner II and C. E. Rankin (1991), *Trails: Toward A New Western History*, Lawrence: University Press of Kansas.

Louvre, A. and J. Walsh (eds) (1988), *Tell Me Lies About Vietnam*, Milton Keynes: Open University Press.

Lubell, S. (1977), 'Personalities vs. issues', in Sidney Kraus (ed.), *The Great Debates: Kennedy vs. Nixon, 1960*, Bloomington: Indiana University Press.

Lyon, T. J. (ed.) (1987), *The Literary History of the American West*, Fort Worth: Texas Christian University Press.

Mailer, N. (1948), *The Naked and the Dead*, New York: Rinehart.

Mailer, N. (1964), 'Superman comes to the Supermarket', in *The Presidential Papers*, New York: Bantam.

Mailer, N. (1971), *The Essential Mailer*, London: Hodder & Stoughton.

Mailer, N. (1985), *Pieces and Pontifications: A Decade of Essays and Interviews*, London: New English Library.

Mailer, N. (1991), *Harlot's Ghost*, New York: Random House.

Mailer, N. (1994), *Advertisements for Myself*, London: Flamingo.

Mailer, N. (1998), *The Time of Our Time*, London: Little, Brown.

Manchester, W. (1974), *The Glory and the Dream: a Narrative History of America, 1932–1972*, Boston: Little, Brown.

May, E. R. and P. D. Zelikow (eds) (1997), *The Kennedy Tapes: Inside the White House During the Cuban Missile Crisis*, Cambridge, MA: Harvard University Press.

McBride, J. (ed.) (1996), *Hawks on Hawks*, London: Faber & Faber.

McCarthy, C. (1989), *Blood Meridian or The Evening Redness in the West*, London: Picador.

McCarthy, C. (1993), *All the Pretty Horses*, London: Picador.

McCarthy, C. (1995), *The Crossing*, London: Picador.

McCarthy, C. (1999), *Cities of the Plain*, London: Picador.

McCarthy, C. (2005), *No Country for Old Men*, London: Picador.

McGee, P. (1997), *Ishmael Reed and the Ends of Race*, London: Macmillan.

McGee, P. (2007), *From Shane to Kill Bill: Rethinking the Western*, Oxford: Blackwell.

McGilligan, P. (1999), *Clint: The Life and Legend*, London: HarperCollins.

McMurtry, L. (2005), *The Colonel and Little Missie: Buffalo Bill, Annie Oakley, and the Beginnings of Superstardom in America*, New York: Simon & Schuster.

McMurtry, L. (1990), 'How the west was won or lost', *The New Republic*, 22 October 1990.

McNeill, W. (1982), 'The care and repair of public myth', *Foreign Affairs*, 61.

McVeigh, S. (1998), 'Interview with W. D. Ehrhart', unpublished.

Milford, C. (1972), *Bar-20*, T-Stacey.

Miller, A. (1984), *Timebends*, New York: Harper & Row.

Milner II, C. A., A. M. Butler and D. R. Lewis (eds) (1997), *Major Problems in the History of the American West*, Boston: Houghton Mifflin Company.

Milner, C. A., C. A. O'Conner and M. A. Sandweiss (1994), *The Oxford History of the American West*, Oxford: Oxford University Press.

Milton, J. R. (1980), *The Novel of the American West*, Lincoln: University of Nebraska Press.

Mitchell, L. C. (1996), *Westerns: Making the Man in Fiction and Film*, Chicago: University of Chicago Press.

Mulford, Clarence E. (1910), *Hopalong Cassidy*, New York: McClurg & Co.

Munby, J. (1999), *Public Enemies Public Heroes*, Chicago: University of Chicago Press.

Musser, C. (2002) 'Introducing cinema to the American Public: the Vitascope in the United States, 1896–7', in Gregory A. Waller, *Moviegoing in America*, Oxford: Blackwell.

Nadel, A. (1996), *Containment Culture*, Durham: Duke University Press.

Neustadt, R. E. (1990), *Presidential Power and the Modern Presidents: the Politics of Leadership from Roosevelt to Reagan*, New York: The Free Press.

Neve, B. (1992), *Film and Politics in America: a Social Tradition*, London: Routledge.

Nichols, B. (ed.) (1976), *Movies and Methods*, Berkeley: University of California Press.

Nichols, B. (ed.) (1985), *Movie and Methods, vol. II*, Berkeley: University of California Press.

Nixon, R. M. (1960), *The Challenges we Face*, New York: McGraw-Hill.

Nixon, R. M. (1962), *Six Crises*, New York: Doubleday & Company Inc.

Nixon, R. M. (1978), *RM: the Memoirs of Richard M. Nixon*, New York: Doubleday & Company Inc.

Nowell-Smith, G. (ed.) (1996), *The Oxford History of World Cinema*, Oxford: Oxford University Press.

Nuwer, H. (1973), 'An Interview with Jack Schaefer', *South Dakota Review*, Spring 1973.

O' Brien, D. (1996), *Clint Eastwood: Film-Maker*, London: Batsford.

O'Connor, M. A. (ed.) (2001), *Willa Cather: the Contemporary Reviews*, Cambridge: Cambridge University Press.

Padover, S. K. (1960), *The Genius of America: Men whose Ideas Shaped Our Civilization*, New York: McGraw-Hill.

Paul, S. (1976), *Repossessing & Renewing: Essays in the Green American Tradition*, Baton Rouge: Louisiana State University Press.

Pauly, T. H. (2005), *Zane Grey: His Life, His Adventures, His Women*, Urbana: University of Illinois Press.

Pratt, G. C. (1973), *Spellbound in the Darkness: A History of Silent Film*, New York: Little, Brown.

Prince, S. (1992), *Visions of Empire: Political Imagery in Contemporary American Film*, New York: Praeger.

Prince, S. (ed.) (1999), *Sam Peckinpah's The Wild Bunch*, Cambridge: Cambridge University Press.

Proulx, A. (2000), *Close Range: Wyoming Stories*, London: Fourth Estate.

Proulx, A. (2005), *Bad Dirt*, London: Harper Perennial.

Pusey, M. J. (1956), *Eisenhower the President*, New York: Macmillan.

Quinn, A. (1997), *The Rivals: William Gwin, David Broderick, and the Birth of California*, Lincoln: University of Nebraska Press.

Quinones, R. (1991), *The Changes of Cain: Violence and the Lost Brother in Cain and Abel Literature*, New Jersey: Princeton University Press.

Ray, R. B. (1985), *A Certain Tendency of the Hollywood Cinema, 1930–1980*, New Jersey: Princeton University Press.

Reagan, R. (1990), *Speaking My Mind: Selected Speeches*, London: Hutchinson.

Reed, I. (2000), *Yellow Back Radio Broke-Down*, Illinois: Dalkey Archive Press.

Reisner, M. (2001), *Cadillac Desert: the American West and its Disappearing Water*, London: Pimlico.

Remington, F. (1981), *Selected Writings*, New Jersey: Castle.

Rentschler, E. (1996), 'Germany: Nazism and after', in G. Nowell-Smith (ed.), *The Oxford History of World Cinema*, Oxford: Oxford University Press.

Riesman, D. (1970), *The Lonely Crowd: A Study of the Changing American Character*, New Haven and London: Yale University Press.

Roberts, R. and J. S. Olson (1995), *John Wayne: American*, Lincoln: University of Nebraska Press.

Robinson, F. G. (ed.) (1998), *The New Western History: the Territory Ahead*, Tucson: The University of Arizona Press.

Rogin, M. (1967), *The Intellectuals and McCarthy: The Radical Specter*, Cambridge, MA: MIT Press.

Rogin, M. (1987), *Ronald Reagan, the Movie and Other Episodes of Political Demonology*, Berkeley: University of California Press.

Rood, K. L. (2001), *Understanding Annie Proulx*, Columbia: University of South Carolina Press.

Roosevelt, T. (1899), *Ranch Life and the Hunting-Trail*, New York: The Century Co.

Roosevelt, T. (1902), *The Strenuous Life: Essays and Addresses*, London: Grant Richards.

Roosevelt, T. (1913), *An Autobiography*, London: Macmillan.

Roosevelt, T. (1995a), *The Winning of the West. Volume 1: From the Alleghanies to the Mississippi, 1769–1776*, Lincoln: University of Nebraska Press.

Roosevelt, T. (1995b), *The Winning of the West. Volume 2: From the Alleghanies to the Mississippi, 1777–1783*, Lincoln: University of Nebraska Press.

Roosevelt, T. (1995c), *The Winning of the West. Volume 3: The Founding of the Trans-Alleghany Commonwealths, 1784–1790*, Lincoln: University of Nebraska Press.

Roosevelt, T. (1995d), *The Winning of the West. Volume 4: Louisiana and the Northwest, 1791–1807*, Lincoln: University of Nebraska Press.

Roosevelt, T. (1998), *The Rough Riders*, Lincoln: University of Nebraska Press.

Roosevelt, T. (2004), *Hunting Trips of a Ranchman & The Wilderness Hunters*, New York: The Modern Library.

Roper, J. (1998), 'Richard Nixon's political hinterland: the shadows of JFK and Charles de Gaulle', *Presidential Studies Quarterly*, 28: 2.

Roper, J. (2000), *The American Presidents: Heroic Leadership from Kennedy to Clinton*, Edinburgh: Edinburgh University Press.

Rose, R. (1991), *The Postmodern President*, New Jersey: Chatham House.

Roseblatt, R. (1999), 'The age of Einstein', *Time*, 31 December 1999.

Rosenblum, S. and C. Antin (eds) (1968), *LBJ Lampooned: Cartoon Criticism of Lyndon B. Johnson*, New York: Cobble Hill Press.

Rothman, Hal K. (ed.) (1998), *Reopening the American West*, Arizona: University of Arizona Press.

Rotter, A. J. (ed.) (1999), *Light at the End of the Tunnel: a Vietnam War Anthology*, Wilmington: Scholarly Resources Inc.

Rovere, R. H. (1956), *Affairs of State, 1950–1956: the Eisenhower Years*, New York: Farrar Straus and Cudahy.

Russell, B. (1995), *A History of Western Philosophy*, London: Routledge.

Sandburg, C. (1954), *Abraham Lincoln: The Prairie Years and The War Years*, one vol. edn, New York: Harcourt Brace & Company.

Sarris, A. (1996), *The American Cinema: Directors and Directions 1929–1968*, New York: Da Capo.

Schaefer, J. (1932a), 'Decline of the West', *New Haven Journal Courier*, 1932.

Schaefer, J. (1932b), 'Lincoln', *New Haven Journal Courier*, 1932.

Schaefer, J. (1932c), 'Washington', *New Haven Journal Courier*, 1932.

Schaefer, J. (1960), *The Kean Land*, London: Andre Deutsch.

Schaefer, J. (1964), 'Biographically speaking', *La Gaceta*, II: 5, December.

Schaefer, J. (1979a), *First Blood*, London: Heinemann Educational Books.

Schaefer, J. (1979b), *Old Ramon*, London: Heinemann Educational Books.

Schaefer, J. (1981), *Monte Walsh*, Lincoln: University of Nebraska Press.

Schaefer, J. (1984), *Shane: The Critical Edition*, Lincoln: University of Nebraska Press.

Schatz, T. (1996), *The Genius of the System: Hollywood Film-making in the Studio Era*, London: Faber & Faber.

Schell, J. (1975), *The Time of Illusion*, New York: Alfred A. Knopf.

Schell, J. (2000), *The Real War: the Classic Reporting on the Vietnam War*, New York: Da Capo.

Schickel, R. (1996), *Clint Eastwood*, London: Jonathan Cape.

Schlesinger Jr, A. M. (1960), 'On heroic leadership and the dilemma of strong men and weak peoples', *Encounter*, 15: 6, December.

Schlesinger Jr, A. M. (1960), *Kennedy or Nixon: Does it Make Any Difference?*, New York: Macmillan.

Schlesinger Jr, A. M. (1965), *A Thousand Days: John F. Kennedy in the White House*, London: Andre Deutsch.

Schlesinger Jr, A. M. (1978), *Robert Kennedy and His Times*, New York: Ballentine.

Scott, B. B. (1994), *Hollywood Dreams and Biblical Stories*, Minneapolis: Fortress Press.

Scott, I. (2000), *American Politics in Hollywood Film*, Edinburgh: Edinburgh University Press.

Sevareid, E. (1959), *Candidates 1960*, New York: Basic Books Inc.

Seydor, P. (1999), *Peckinpah, the Western Films: a Reconsideration*, Urbana: University of Illinois Press.

Sheehan, N. (1990), *A Bright Shining Lie*, London: Picador.

Siegal, D. (1993), *A Siegal Film*, London: Faber & Faber.

Silberstein, S. (2002), *War of Words: Language, Politics and 9/11*, London: Routledge.

Slide, A. (ed.) (1996), *De Toth on De Toth: Putting the Drama in front of the Camera*, London: Faber & Faber.

Slotkin, R. (1992), *Gunfighter Nation: the Myth of the Frontier in Twentieth-Century America*, New York: HarperCollins.

Slotkin, R. (1994), *The Fatal Environment: the Myth of the Frontier in the Age of Industrialization, 1800–1890*, New York: HarperCollins.

Slotkin, R. (1996), *Regeneration through Violence: the Mythology of the American Frontier, 1600–1860*, New York: HarperCollins.

Smith, H. N. (2000), *Virgin Land: the American West as Symbol and Myth*, Cambridge, MA: Harvard University Press.

Smith, P. (1993), *Clint Eastwood: A Cultural Production*, Minneapolis: University of Minnesota Press.

Sorensen, T. (1965), *Kennedy*, London: Hodder & Stoughton.

Spoto, Donald (1978), *Stanley Kramer: Film Maker*, New York: Putnam.

Staig, L. and T. Williams (1975), *Italian Western: The Opera of Violence*, London: Lorrimer.

Taylor, J. R. (1983), *Strangers in Paradise: the Hollywood Émigrés, 1933–1950*, London: Faber & Faber.

TIME International Magazine, 7 October 1996, 148: 15.

Tompkins, J. (1993), *West of Everything: The Inner Life of Westerns*, Oxford: Oxford University Press.

Trachtenberg, A. (1982), *The Incorporation of America*, New York: Hill & Wang.

Tripp, E. (ed.) (1992), *Sagebrush and Spurs: Classic Western Short Stories*, London: Bellew.

Turner, F. J. (1996), *The Frontier in American History*, New York: Dover Publications.

Tuska, J. (1976), *The Filming of the West*, London: Hale.

Tuska, J. (ed.) (1995), *The Western Story: a Chronological Treasury*, Lincoln: University of Nebraska Press.

Twain, M. and C. D. Warner (2001), *The Gilded Age: A Tale of Today*, London: Penguin.

Twain, M. (1965), *Roughing It*, New York: Holt, Rinehart & Winston.

Utley, R. M. (1998), *Custer and the Great Controversy: the Origin and Development of a Legend*, Lincoln: University of Nebraska Press.

Utley, R. M. (2000), *Billy the Kid*, London: Bloomsbury.

Van Tillburg Clark, W. (1940), *The Ox Bow Incident*, New York: Random House.

Wallach, R. (2000), *Myth, Legend, Dust: Critical Responses to Cormac McCarthy*, Manchester: Manchester University Press.

Walsh, M. (2005), *The American West: Visions and Revisions*, Cambridge: Cambridge University Press.

Warshow, R. (1970), *The Immediate Experience: Movies, Comics, Theatre and Other Aspects of Popular Culture*, New York: Atheneum.

Webb, W. P. (1953), *The Great Frontier*, London: Secker & Warburg.

Weddle, D. (1994), *Sam Peckinpah: 'If They Move . . . Kill 'Em!'*, London: Faber & Faber.

Weston, J. (1988), *The Real American Cowboy*, New York: New Amsterdam Books.

White, R. (1993), *"It's Your Misfortune and None of My Own": a New History of the American West*, Norman: University of Oklahoma Press.

White, R. and P. N. Limerick (1994), *The Frontier in American Culture*, Berkeley: University of California Press.

White, T. H. (1962), *The Making of the President in 1960*, London: Jonathan Cape.

Whitfield, S. J. (1991), *The Culture of the Cold War*, Baltimore: Johns Hopkins University Press.

Whitman, N. and E. Spalding (1997), *Where Wagons Would Go*, Lincoln: University of Nebraska Press.

Wilkinson, R. (ed.) (1992), *American Social Character: Modern Interpretations*, New York: HarperCollins.

Wills, G. (1987), *Reagan's America: Innocents at Home*, New York: Doubleday & Company Inc.

Wills, G. (1997), *John Wayne: The Politics of Celebrity*, London: Faber & Faber.

Wister, O. (1930), *Theodore Roosevelt: The Story of a Friendship, 1880–1919*, London: Macmillan.

Wister, O. (1998), *The Virginian*, Oxford: Oxford University Press.

Wister, O. (1999), *Salvation Gap and Other Western Classics*, Lincoln: University of Nebraska Press.

Work, J. C. (ed.) (1984), *Shane: The Critical Edition*, Lincoln: University of Nebraska Press.

Work, J. C. (ed.) (1990), *Prose and Poetry of the American West*, Lincoln: University of Nebraska Press.

Work, J. C. (ed.) (1996), *Gunfight!: Thirteen Western Stories*, Lincoln: University of Nebraska Press.

Wright, W. (1977), *Sixguns and Society: a Structural Study of the Western*, Berkeley: University of California Press.

Wright, W. (2001), *The Wild West: The Mythical Cowboy and Social Theory*, London: Sage.

Zinneman, F. (1992), *An Autobiography*, London: Bloomsbury.

Zmijewsky, B. and L. Pfeiffer (1996), *The Films of Clint Eastwood*, New Jersey: Citadel Press.

Web References

Bush, G. W. (11 September 2001), 'Address to the Joint Session of Congress and the American People', *Official White House Home Page*, http://www.whitehouse.gov/new/releases/2001/09/print/20010920-8.html

Bush, G. W. (11 September 2001), 'Remarks by the President after two planes crashed into the World Trade Center', *White House Official Home Page*, http://www.whitehouse.gov/news/releases/2001/09/20010911.html

Bush, G. W. (12 September 2001), 'Statement about terrorist attacks', *Associated Press Home Page: US Response Home Page*, http://multimedia.belointeractive.com/attack/news/0912bushstatement.html

Bush, G. W. (17 September 2001), 'President Bush's remarks at the Pentagon: September 17', *Association Press: US Response Home Page*, http://multimedia.belointeractive.com/attack/response/0917bushtext.html

Bush, G. W. (20 September 2001), " 'You are either with us or you are with the terrorists. This is civilization's fight." Address to the Joint Session of Congress and the American People', *Official White House Home Page*, http://www.whitehouse.gov/new/releases/2001/09/print/20010920-8.html

Bush, G. W. (20 September 2001), 'Address to the Joint Session of Congress and the American People', *Official White House Home Page*, http://www.whitehouse.gov/new/releases/2001/09/print/20010920-8.html

Kennedy, J. F. *The Presidency in 1960*, www.cs.umb.edu/jfklibrary/j011460.htm

Moore, M. (1995) 'Midnight never came: the history of the Doomsday Clock', www.bullatomsci.org/clock.html

PNAC (September 2000), *Rebuilding America's Defenses: Strategy, Forces and Resources for a New Century*, www.newamericancentury.org/RebuildingAmericasDefenses.pdf

Watson, R. (2 October 2001), 'George W. Bush: Wartime President', *BBC News Home Page*, http://news.bbc.co.uk/1/hi/world/americas/1574277.stm

Index

Abbey, Edward, 151
Actors' Studio, the, 72
Adams, Herbert B., 24
Adams, Sherman, 106, 115
Afghanistan War, 215
Al Qaeda, 217–18
Alamo, The (1960), 218
Alamo, The (2004), 218, 219
Aldrich, Robert, 170, 177
Alliance Movement, 9–12
American Civil War, the (1861–5), 28–9,
    193
American Historical Association, 1
Anderson, Bronco Billy, 61–2, 63
Antiquities Act (1906), 19
Aronson, Max *see* Bronco Billy Anderson
Arriaga, Guillermo, 220
atomic threat, 79–81, 105, 115, 129–30,
    136
Autobiography (Roosevelt), 14, 15, 16

Bad Girls (1994), 202
Bailey, James, 36
Ballad of Cable Hogue, The (1970), 181
Ballad of Little Joe, The (1993), 202
Bar 20 (Mulford), 47
barbed wire, 5–6
Barber, James David, 107–8
Baudrillard, Jean, 213–14
Beat Generation, the, 111, 116–17
Beatles, The, 125
Beguiled, The (1971), 181
Ben Tre, village of, 190
Bend of the River (1952), 74
Benton, Thomas Hart, 19
Berger, Thomas, 151
Billington, Ray Allen, 21–2, 140
Bin Laden, Osama, viii, 216
Birth of a Nation (1915), 65–6
Blazing Saddles (1974), 181

*Blood Meridian: or the Evening Redness in
    the West* (McCarthy), 152–4
Bower, Bertha Muzzy, 46
Bradford, Richard, 151
Brand, Max, 39, 47, 48
Brennan, Walter, 167
Bride Comes to Yellow Sky, The (Crane), 42
Bright Shining Lie, A (Sheehan), 190
Bring Me the Head of Alfredo Garcia (1974),
    220
Brokeback Mountain (2005), 220
Broken Arrow (1950), 75
Bronco Billy's Redemption (1910), 62
Brookeman, Christopher, 110, 111, 112, 115
Browning, Robert, 40
Buffalo Bill *see* Cody, William F.
Buffalo Bill and Pony Bill Company, 36
Buffalo Bill, the King of the Border Men,
    Buntline, Ned, 30
Buffalo Bill's Wild West, 17, 27–8, 32–7,
    61, 66
Bulletin Clock, 80–1, 105
Bulletin of the Atomic Scientists, The, 80–1
Bumpo, Natty, 39
Buntline, Ned, 29–31, 39
Burke, Major John, 32–3
Bush, George W., vii–viii, 203, 215–18
Butch Cassidy and the Sundance Kid (1969),
    181

Caan, James, 167
Carter, Jimmy, 191
Castro, Fidel, 156, 157
Cat Ballou (1966), 181
Cather, Willa, 39, 48–9, 148
cattle drive, 5
Cawelti, John, 46
Census of 1890, 2, 22
Chandler, Raymond, 38, 73, 123
Chip of the Flying U (Bower), 46

Cimino, Michael, 193
Cinnecittà Studios, 169–70
Cleveland, Grover, 6, 8, 17
Clinton, Bill, viii, 202, 213
Close Range (Proulx), 220
Cody, William, F., 13, 26, 27–37, 39
Cody, Wyoming, 35–6
Cold War, the, viii, 50, 55–7, 71, 75, 76–8, 81–2, 85–8, 98, 103, 105, 109, 111, 115, 126, 129–30, 159, 162, 212, 213, 215, 216
Colonel W. F. Cody (Buffalo Bill) Historical Pictures Company, 36–7
color writing, 12
Communism, 76–8, 86, 104–5, 110, 111, 115, 116, 213
Comstock, William, 29
Congress of Rough Riders of the World, the, 33, 35
containment, 159
Contributions of the West to American Democracy (Turner), 24
Coogan's Bluff (1968), 181
Coolidge, Calvin, 128
Cooper, Gary, 69, 75, 98, 103, 123
Cooper, James Fennimore, 38, 39
Costner, Kevin, 218
counter-culture, 116–17
Covered Wagon, The (1923), 66–7
Cowboy Culture, (Dary), 5
cowboys, 5–7, 17, 33–4, 39, 42, 43–6, 58, 62–3
Crane, Stephen, 18, 42
Crazy Horse, 4
Cripple Creek Bar-room (1898), 61
Cuba, 14, 156–7, 162
Cuban Missile Crisis, the (1962), 163, 177
Cunningham, John M., 88–9, 99
Custer, George Armstrong, 4, 22, 31

Dallas (1950), 75
Daves, Delmer, 75
Dawes Severalty Act (1887), 4
Deadwood (TV series), 219
Destry Rides Again (Brand), 48
Didion, Joan, 166–7
dime fiction, 12, 29–31, 41
Dirty Harry (1971), 181, 197
Doctorow, E. L., 152
Dodge City (1939), 74
"Doomsday Clock," the see Bulletin Clock
Douglas, Kirk, 162
Dylan, Bob, 117

Eastwood, Clint, 155, 161, 169, 172, 173, 178, 179, 181–3, 184, 186, 189, 191, 192, 193–4, 197, 202, 204, 207–8, 209, 211–12
Edison, Thomas, 36, 59, 60, 61
Ehrhart, W. D., 188–9
Einstein, Albert, 78–9, 81
Eisenhower, Dwight, 87–8, 93–7, 98, 102, 103–4, 105, 106–11, 113–17, 126, 127–8, 129, 132, 135, 136, 138, 157, 159, 203
Eisner, Michael, 219
El Dorado (1966), 167
Essanay Company, 36
European artists and film makers, impact on Hollywood of, 70–1
Evans, Max, 151

Fiedler, Leslie, 38, 122
film noir, 72–5
Firefly (TV series), 219
Fisher, Vardis, 148
Fistful of Dollars, A (1964), 165, 168, 171–7, 179, 180, 181, 183, 185, 192, 195, 203, 206
Flynn, Errol, 74, 75
Flynn, Robert, 151
Fonda, Henry, 93, 162
Foote, Mary Hallock, 12
For a Few Dollars More (1965), 173, 177, 178
Ford, Gerald, 191
Ford, John, 61, 67, 68, 70, 75, 100, 157, 158, 159, 191, 194
Foreman, Carl, 97
Forest Reserves Act (1891), 18
French Connection, The (1971), 182
Frontier Thesis see Significance of the Frontier in American History, The
Frontiere, Dominic, 178–9
Frost, Robert, 138
Fukyama, Francis, 214

gangster movies, 69–70, 168
Garland, Hamlyn, 12, 42, 148
Geronimo, 27–8
Gift Outright, The (Frost), 138
Goldwater, Barry, 165
Good the Bad and the Ugly, The (1966), 173, 178
Grange movement, the, 9
Grant, Ulysses S., 130
Great Depression, the, 69, 140, 161, 168
"Great Die-Up," the (1886–7), 16

Great Train Robbery, The (1903), 60, 61, 194

Green Berets, The (1969), 167

Grey, Zane, 39, 47–8

Griffith, D. W., 65–6

Gulf War, 213–14

Gunfighter, The (1950), 77, 78, 81–7, 101, 104, 105, 113, 122, 156, 159, 175, 202–3

Guthrie Jr, A. B., 118, 119, 148

Hammett, Dashiell, 73, 172

Hancock, John Lee, 218

Hang 'em High (1967), 178–80

Hanna, Mark, 11, 18

Harding, Warren, 128

Harrison, Benjamin, 17

Hart, William S., 62–3, 66, 123

Harte, Bret, 12, 41, 42

Hat Creek, 31

Hathaway, Henry, 165, 166

Hawks, Howard, 99, 103, 167

Hay, John, 17

Heaven's Gate (1980), 193

Helen of Troy (1955), 170

Heritage of the Desert, The (Grey), 47

heroic leadership, 55–7, 81–2, 108–9, 111, 113–17, 122–3, 124–39, 203, 215–18

Hidalgo (2004), 218

High Noon (1952), 77, 78, 81, 82, 86–8, 89, 92–3, 97–105, 108, 110, 112–13, 117, 121, 122, 124, 138, 156, 159, 178, 182–3, 197, 202–3

High Plains Drifter (1973), 180–91, 192, 194, 195, 196, 203, 206, 211

Hinckley, John, 193, 197

Hofstadter, Richard, 148

Hollywood, 33, 48, 65, 69–73, 76, 97, 168–70

Home on the Range (2004), 218

Homestead Act (1862), 5

Homesteaders, 6

Hopalong Cassidy (Mulford), 47

House Un-American Activities Committee (HUAC), 111, 113, 203

Howard, Ron, 218

Hunting Trips of a Ranchman (Roosevelt), 16

Huntingdon, Samuel, 214

immigrants, 63–4, 66

Ince, Thomas H., 62–3

Inceville *see* Miller 101 Bison Ranch, the

Incorporation of America, The (Trachtenberg), 3, 5, 24–5

Indian wars, 20

Indians *see* Native Americans

Ingraham, Prentiss, 30

Iron Horse, The (1924), 67–8

Italian neo-realism, 72

James, Henry, 40

Jazz Singer, The (1927), 69

Jennings, Bryan William, 9, 11–12

Jesse James (1939), 70, 74, 85

Johnny Guitar (1954), 74

Johnson, Lyndon B., 163–4

Jones, Tommy Lee, 220

Jory, Victor, 164

Judson, Edward Z. C. *see* Buntline, Ned

Kael, Pauline, 122, 160, 162, 177

Kazan, Elia, 72

Kelly's Heroes (1970), 180–1

Kennan, George, 77, 213

Kennedy, John F., 57, 87–8, 110, 114–15, 122, 125–39, 140, 146, 155–6, 159, 161, 162, 163, 164, 165, 177, 216

assassination of, 155, 161–2, 163, 165, 180, 197, 203

Kennedy or Nixon: Does it Make Any Difference? (Schlesinger Jr), 126, 132–4

Kennedy, Robert, 163

Kent State University, shootings at, 146

Kinetoscope, 36, 59, 61

King, Henry, 68, 81, 105

Korean War, the, 106–7, 108, 111, 115, 117, 121, 136, 203

Koster and Bial Music Hall, the, 59–60, 61

Kramer, Stanley, 97–8

Kurosawa, Akira, 156, 172

Ladd, Alan, 123

Lancaster, Burt, 162

Leather Stocking Tales, The (Cooper), 38, 39

Lee, Ang, 220

Legacy of Conquest: the Unbroken Past of the American West, The (Limerick), 141

Leone, Sergio, 161, 165, 168–73, 177, 178, 183

Life of an American Fireman, The (1903), 61

Limerick, Patricia Nelson, 141–3, 146, 147–8

Lincoln, Abraham, 130–1, 132–3

Lindbergh, Charles, 69

Lindsay, Vachel, 64

Liszt, Franz, 40
Little Big Horn, battle of (June 1876), 4, 22, 31
Little Big Man (1970), 181
Little Rock, Kansas, 114
London, Jack, 12
Lone Star (1996), 220
Lonely Crowd, The (Reisman), 111–12
Lonesome Dove (TV series), 219
Lonesome Land (Bower), 46
Louisiana Land Purchase, the, 20
Lucas, George, 193
lynching, 45

McCarthy, Cormac, 152–4, 220
McCarthy, Senator Joseph, 97, 104–5, 111, 116, 136
McCarthyism, 98–9, 104–5, 111, 121, 203
McCrea, Joel, 160, 167
MacDonald, Ross, 38
McKinley, William, 9, 11–12, 17, 18
McLintlock! (1963), 165
McMurtry, Larry, 145
McTeague (Norris), 42
Mader, Fred G., 30
Magnificent Seven, The (1960), 156–7, 178, 186
Mailer, Norman, 108, 109, 110, 111, 114, 115, 115, 126, 135–9
Main-Traveled Roads (Garland), 42
Malpaso, 179
Man Called Horse, A (1970), 181
Man from Larame, The (1955), 74
Man Who Shot Liberty Valance, The (1962), 100, 157, 158–60
Manchester, William, 114
Manhattan Project, the, 79–80
Mann, Anthony, 74, 75, 92–3, 194
Manson, Charles, 187
"Mark of Cain," 100, 102–3, 136–7, 173, 174, 175, 184, 196, 206
Marshall plan, the, 169
Martin, Dean, 167
"Martyl," 80, 105
Marvin, Lee, 158
metal mining, 7–9
Miller 101 Bison Ranch, the, 62
Miller, Joaquin, 12
Mills, C. Wright, 112
Missing, The (2003), 218
Mitchum, Robert, 162, 167
Monroe Doctrine, the, 18
Monte Walsh (1970), 181

Morgan, J. P., 8
Morricone, Ennio, 173–4, 179
Motion Picture Patents Company Trust, the, 64–5
Mulford, Clarence Edward, 46–7
My Darling Clementine (1946), 74
My Lai, 181, 200

Naked and the Dead, The (Mailer), 110
Naked Spur, The (1953), 74
Nash, Gerald, 145–6
National Reclamation Act (1902), 19
National Socialism (Nazism), 70–1, 101, 110, 145
Native Americans, 2–5, 22, 27–8, 33–4, 36–7, 42, 75, 76–8, 86, 142, 144, 145, 148, 181, 217–18
Naval War of 1812, The (Roosevelt), 16
Nelson, Ralph, 179
Nelson, Ricky, 167
New Deal, the, 12
"New Frontier," the, 137–9, 140, 161, 163, 180
New Left, the, 145
New Western History, 140–6, 147–9, 152, 153, 154, 155
New Western History, the, viii, 12
Newlands Act (1902) *see* National Reclamation Act
nickelodeon, 60, 63–4
Nietzsche, Frederick, 100–1, 108
9/11, vii, viii, 215–20
Nixon, Richard, 93–7, 104, 125, 126, 127, 131–5, 159, 164, 183, 187, 188, 191
Norris, Frank, 12, 42
North, Major Frank, 29

O Pioneers! (Cather), 48–9
Octopus, The (Norris), 42
Once Upon a Time in the West (1966), 177
Open Range (2003), 218, 219
Outlaw Josey Wales, The (1976), 193
Outlaw, The (1943), 74
Ox-Bow Incident, The (1943), 70, 85, 178

Paint Your Wagon (1969), 181
Painted Angels (1998), 202
Pale Rider (1985), 191–202, 203, 204, 211
Panic of 1893, the, 7–9
Paramount Decrees, the (1948), 72
Pat Garrett and Billy the Kid (1973), 154
Pearl Harbor, 215
Peck, Gregory, 123

Peckinpah, Sam, 154, 160, 179, 220
Pentagon, vii
"People's Party" *see* Populist Party
Pinchot, Gifford, 18–19
Play Misty For Me (1971), 181
Poker at Dawson City (1898), 61
Pony Express, the, 28
Populist Party, 9–12
Porter, Edwin S, 60–1
Portis, Charles, 151
Posse (1993), 202
post-Cold War, 214–15, 219
post-modernity, 213–14
Power Elite, The (Mills), 112
Presidential Character: Predicting Performance in the White House, The (Barber), 107–8
presidential debates of 1960, 126, 134–5
presidential elections
   of 1896, 11–12
   of 1900, 18
   of 1952, 106–9
   of 1960, 125–39, 140
presidential inauguration of 1905, 27
presidential inauguration of 1960, 138
Presidential Papers, The (Mailer), 108
Prohibition, 69
Project for the Next American Century (PNAC), 214–15
Proulx, Annie, 220
Putnam, Carleton, 15

Quantrill, Col William C, 28
Quick and the Dead, The (1995), 202

railroads, 5, 8, 29, 42, 67–8, 79
Ranch Life and the Hunting Trail (Roosevelt), 16–17, 33, 44
Rawhide (TV series), 172
Reagan, Ronald, viii, 155, 191, 192–3, 197–8, 201, 202
   attempted assassination of, 193, 197–8, 203
Rebuilding America's Defences: Strategy, Forces, and Resources for a New Century (PNAC), 214–15
Reclamation Service, 19
Red Harvest (Hammett), 172
Red Legged Scouts, the, 28
Red River (1948), 74
Reed, Ishmael, 149–51
Reisman, David, 111–12, 114
relativism, 79

Remington, Frederick 13, 16, 40, 41
Revolution in Military Affairs (RMA), 214
Ride the High Country (1962), 160–1, 167
Riders of the Purple Sage (Grey), 47
Rio Bravo (1956), 92, 99, 100, 167
Rio Grande (1950), 74, 75
Rocky Mountain (1950), 75
Roosevelt Corollary, the, 18
Roosevelt, Franklin Delano, 79, 115, 161
Roosevelt, Theodore, 13–21, 25–6, 27, 32, 34, 35, 36, 40, 41, 44, 48, 57
Rossen, Robert, 113
Rough Riders, the, 17–18, 27, 35
Roughing It (Twain), 41–2
Rovere, Richard, 93, 96, 106

San Antonio (1945), 74
Sayles, John, 220
Schaefer, Jack, 39, 49–53, 88, 117, 118–25, 146–7, 148, 184, 194
Schlesinger, Jr, Arthur, 114, 126, 132–4, 161, 162, 163
Scorsese, Martin, 197
Scott, Randolph, 160
Scouts of the Prairie, The (Buntline), 30–1
Sells-Floto Circus, the, 36
Serenity (2005), 219
Sergeant Rutledge (1960), 157–8
Seventh Samurai (1954), 156
Shaft (1971), 182
Shane (1953), 57, 77, 82, 86, 87, 104, 117, 118–25, 155–6, 157, 159, 161, 162, 168, 171–2, 173, 174, 175, 176, 177, 180, 181, 183–202, 203, 204, 206, 207–8, 211, 219
Shane (Schaefer), 39, 49–57, 88, 104, 117, 118, 146–7, 184
Sheehan, Neil, 190
Sherman Anti-Trust Act (1890), 18
Sherman Silver Purchase Act (1890), 8
Shoshone Reclamation Act, the (1904), 36
Siegal, Don, 179
Significance of the Frontier in American History, The, 1–2, 13, 21–6, 77, 140–1, 202
silver, 7, 8, 9, 11–12
Sitting Bull, 4
Smith, Henry Nash, 29–30, 147
Soldier Blue (1970), 181
Sons of Katie Elder, The (1965), 165, 166–7
Sorensen, Theodore, 161, 162
Spaghetti Western, 161, 162, 165, 168–73, 177, 178, 179, 181, 183, 194

Spanish American War, the (1898), 14, 17–18, 35
Sputnik 1, 114, 115
Stagecoach (1939), 70, 74, 85, 166
Star Wars (1977), 193, 194
Stegner, Wallace, 147, 148
Stevens, George, 117, 118–21, 123, 183, 184, 192, 204
Stewart, James, 74, 75, 93, 100, 158, 162, 163
Strasberg, Lee, 72
Strode, Woody, 157, 158
Sturges, John, 156
Subtreasury Plan, the (1899), 10
Summit Springs, Battle of, 36
Superman Comes to the Supermarket (Mailer), 126, 135–9
Szilard, Dr. Leo, 79

Taxi Driver (1976), 197
Taylor, Buck, 34, 40
Teller, Henry, 11
Theodore Roosevelt: The Story of a Friendship, 1880–1919 (Wister), 41
Theory of Relativity, 78–9
Thomas Hart Benton (Roosevelt), 16, 19
Three Burials of Melquiades Estrada (2005), 220
Tidyman, Earnest, 181–2
time, 78–81, 86, 105, 122
Tin Star, The (1957), 92–3
Tin Star, The (Cunningham), 88–92, 104
Tombstone (1993), 202
"totalitarianism" (Mailer), 109–114, 116, 136–7
Truman, Harry S., 80, 106, 130, 136
Turner, Frederick Jackson, 1–2, 13–14, 20–6, 32, 34, 38, 48, 58, 64, 65, 77, 82, 140–1, 202
Twain, Mark, 12, 41–2
Two Mules for Sister Sara (1970), 181

Ulzana's Raid (1972), 181
Unforgiven (1992), 104, 169, 202–12, 213, 219
US Forest Service, the, 19

Van Cleef, Lee, 178
Van Tilburg Clark, Walter, 39, 70
Vaquero, 34
vaudeville houses, 60
Vera Cruz (1954), 177
Vichy regime, the, 72–3
"Vietnam syndrome," 201

Vietnam War, viii, 70, 117, 146, 147, 149, 151, 156, 164, 167, 173, 177, 180, 181, 183, 186, 187, 188–9, 190, 191, 192, 193, 197, 200, 201, 214
Virginian: a Horseman of the Plains, The (Wister), 16, 39–46, 47, 49, 51–2
Virginian, The (1929), 69

Wagon Master (1950), 75
Wallach, Eli, 156, 178
Walsh, Raoul, 170, 194
War Bonnet Creek, Battle of, 31–2
War on Terrorism, vii, viii, 215–18
War Wagon (1967), 167–8
Warlock (1959), 178
Warshow, Robert, 123
Waters, Frank, 148
Wayne, John, 63, 70, 74, 75, 99, 103, 155, 158, 161, 162, 163, 164–8, 178, 191, 218–19
Weaver, James B., 10
Welles, Orson, 170
Wellman, William, 70
Where Eagles Dare (1969), 180
White, Richard, 144, 146
White, Theodore H., 125–6
Wild Bunch, The (1969), 154, 181
"will to power," the 100–1, 108
Wilson, Woodrow, 129
Winning of Barbara Worth, The (1926), 68
Winning of the West, The (Roosevelt), 13, 16, 20–1, 25–6
Wise, Robert, 170
Wister, Owen, 13, 16, 39, 40–1, 47, 48, 49, 51–2, 69
World Columbian Exposition, Chicago (1893), 1, 22, 34, 59, 141
World Trade Center, vii
World War II, 70–1, 109, 115, 140, 148, 169, 171, 213
Worster, Daniel, 144, 146
Wounded Knee, massacre at, 37, 181
Wyatt Earp (1994), 202
Wyler, William, 170

"X" article (Kennan), 77

Yellow Back Radio Broke-Down (Reed), 149–51
Yellow Hair, 31–2, 36
Yellow Hand *see* Yellow Hair
Yojimbo (1961), 172

Zinneman, Fred, 88, 97–8, 99, 113, 170, 183